Islam

Faith and History

RELATED TITLES FROM ONEWORLD

Approaches to Islam in Religious Studies, edited by Richard C. Martin, ISBN 1–85168–268–6

The Crisis of Muslim History, Mahmoud M. Ayoub, ISBN 1–85168–326–7

Defenders of Reason in Islam, Richard C. Martin, Mark R. Woodward and Dwi S. Atmaja, ISBN 1–85168–147–7

Islam: A Short History, William Montgomery Watt, ISBN 1–85168–205–8

Islam: A Short Introduction – Signs, Symbols and Values, Abdulkader Tayob, ISBN 1–85168–192–2

Islam and the West, Norman Daniel, ISBN 1–85168–129–9

The Legacy of Arab–Islam in Africa, John Alembillah Azumah, ISBN 1–85168–273–2

The Mantle of the Prophet, Roy Mottahedeh, ISBN 1–85168–234–1

Muhammad: A Short Biography, Martin Forward, ISBN 1–85168–131–0

On Being a Muslim: Finding a Religious Path in the World Today, Farid Esack, ISBN 1–85168–146–9

The Qur'an: A Short Introduction, Farid Esack, ISBN 1–85168–231–7

Qur'an, Liberation and Pluralism, Farid Esack, ISBN 1–85168–121–3

Revival and Reform in Islam, Fazlur Rahman, edited and with an introduction by Ebrahim Moosa, ISBN 1–85168–204–X

Speaking in God's Name: Islamic Law, Authority and Women, Khaled Abou El Fadl, ISBN 1–85168–262–7

What Muslims Believe, John Bowker, ISBN 1–85168–169–8

Islam

Faith and History

Mahmoud M. Ayoub

ONEWORLD
OXFORD

"*Our Lord, Grant Us in Our Spouses and Our Offspring Comfort and Joy.*"
To Firas and Sumayya … my comfort and joy.

ربنا هب لنا من أزواجنا
و ذريتنا قرة أعين

ISLAM: FAITH AND HISTORY

Oneworld Publications
(Sales and editorial)
185 Banbury Road
Oxford OX2 7AR
England
www.oneworld-publications.com

A CIP record for this title is available
from the British Library.

ISBN 1–85168–348–8 (hb)
1–85168–350–X (pb)

Typeset by Jayvee, India
Cover design by Design Deluxe
Printed and bound in India by Thomson Press Ltd

Contents

Preface

The last hundred years of Muslim history have been full of surprises, challenges and transformative events. They began with the hope of a pan-Islamic state that would restore to Islam its original power and glory. But the First World War, the consequent demise of the Ottoman state on which pan-Islamic hopes rested, and the abolition of the caliphate by Mustafa Kemal Ataturk ten years later, threw the Muslim world into confusion and despair. This sad state was aggravated by the colonization of most Muslim nations by Western powers, a situation that persisted beyond the end of the Second World War and was responsible for most of the intractable problems that continue to bedevil many Muslim countries today.

While the two world wars devastated and left Europe too exhausted to continue its domination of the world of Islam, the period of colonization had already burdened Europe's former Muslim protectorates with insoluble problems in India, the Middle East and the Sudan, to name but a few examples. The West had reconstructed old countries, such as Syria, Arabia, and the Ottoman state, and created new ones, for instance some Gulf states, Pakistan, and a host of other Asian and African countries. At least officially, most, if not all of these countries adopted the Western nation-state model with its parliamentary democracy. This radical change, from a central Islamic state authority – be it that of a sultan or a figurehead caliph – to numerous nation states, fragmented the Muslim *ummah* into sometimes artificial and often mutually hostile states and forever altered the course of its history.

The Muslim nations reacted to Western incursions and influences in a variety of ways, both positive and negative. The creation of the Society of Muslim Brothers in Egypt in 1929, Jamāʿat-i Islami in India and later Indonesia, and the Arab League in 1945, as well as other such religious and nationalistic organizations, were attempts to redress some of the effects of this fragmentation and its economic, political, and military consequences. The most important reaction to the state of powerlessness and disunity which characterized the Muslim world in the second half of the twentieth century was the Iranian Islamic revolution, which sparked a number of smaller but highly significant uprisings. This revolution is a unique phenomenon in modern Muslim history in that it brought to power a religious establishment that had always been in moral opposition to the temporal authorities. It was a revolution, moreover, inspired not by any Western model, such as communism, socialism, or capitalism, but by Islam. Thus, in spite of its Shīʿī character, it in turn inspired the rise of a number of limited but effective revivalist movements in occupied Palestine, Egypt, Turkey, Algeria, Indonesia, and the Philippines.

Many Western and Muslim scholars have been trying to make sense of these events and developments and to place them in their proper historical perspectives. But events move so fast that many of these studies become outdated soon after, if not before, their appearance. The works of the late Fazlur Rahman and Seyyid Hossein Nasr are good examples of this laudable effort. However, the 1979 edition of Rahman's seminal book *Islam*, and final revision before his death in 1988, was made prior to the actual outbreak of the Islamic revolution in Iran. Likewise, while Dr. Nasr's latest introduction to Islam (2003) is clear and insightful, it is too brief and general to serve the need for a comprehensive book on the subject. Another scholar who deserves mention is Akbar Ahmad, whose sociological studies of Islam and contemporary Muslim society utilize post-modern theories and perspectives in examining many important issues. These are only a few examples of a large library of useful books that should be consulted. A good selection for further reading is presented at the end of this book.

In no way do I wish to minimize the importance of those excellent works of Western and non-Muslim Arab scholars that deal admirably with modern Muslim history, but I do feel that Muslims ought also to be engaged with their history and its problems and that the way in which they engage should reflect their special concern and commitments. This engagement, moreover, should give their works a special flavor and perspective. Of course, Muslim scholars must, and often do, strive for academic objectivity; still, they cannot divorce themselves from their faith and tradition. This should, however, make them even more critical than their sympathetic Western colleagues, whose appreciation for Islam and its civilization may make them more circumspect.

I have done my best in this book to balance my personal engagement in my faith and culture with objective academic integrity. I have also attempted to place the discussion of purely religious topics in their proper historical context. I begin in the prologue by presenting my personal religious experience as my own existential framework for the discussion of the faith and history of Islam.

The book is divided into eleven chapters. It begins with a discussion of the term *islām*, both lexically and conceptually. This is followed by a brief discussion of the origins and formative history of Islam, including the religious and social situation of pre-Islamic Arabia and the life and mission of the Prophet Muḥammad. The second chapter examines the prophetic career of Muḥammad, as well as the revelation and nature of the Qur'ān and its place in Muslim history and piety in the context of the general Islamic concept of prophethood and revelation.

These two chapters provide the necessary framework for the discussion of faith and action, including the "five pillars of Islam." The next three chapters present the formative period of Muslim history beginning with the death of the Prophet and the rise of the early caliphate, the age of the Umayyad and 'Abbāsid caliphs, and the spread of Islam into Asia, Africa, and Europe. Chapters six to nine deal with the religious sciences: the legal schools and sects, the mystical tradition, and the disciplines of theology and philosophy. These dimensions of Islam were first developed and nurtured within a rich Mediterranean culture under the Umayyads and later within an even richer cosmopolitan society under the 'Abbāsids. In chapter ten I examine the familial relations of men and women, as well as issues of gender in contemporary Muslim society. In the final chapter I discuss pre-modernist and modern Islamic ideologies and movements. The book concludes with an epilogue dealing with the Muslim *ummah* and the modern world. It also reflects on some of the issues raised in the prologue.

While I have included enough notes for the student who wishes to pursue the primary sources, they have been kept to a minimum so as not to burden the general reader. I have not created a bibliography of works cited as these are already fully referenced in the notes. I do hope that interested readers will avail themselves of the list of books for further reading.

Many have helped in one way or another in the making of this work. They all deserve my sincere thanks. I am infinitely grateful to my graduate assistant Roslan Abdul Rahim and his wife Rokiah Osman for their invaluable help in both the research and proofing of the manuscript. This book is in some respects a revision and expansion of my chapter on the Islamic tradition, which appeared in the first edition of volume one of *World Religions*, edited by my dear friend the late Willard Oxtoby (Toronto: Oxford University Press, 1996). I am grateful to Willard for his encouragement and to the Press for raising no objections to this publication. I am indebted to Temple University, particularly my colleagues and students, for the congenial atmosphere in which this book took shape. But my most sincere gratitude is to my friend and helper Rose Ftaya for her patient work in editing, correcting and proofing this work throughout its often difficult stages. Without her good efforts this book would have remained only an unfulfilled dream. Finally I wish to thank my friend Mr. Novin Doostdar and the staff at Oneworld Publications for their meticulous work in seeing this volume through to its publication.

Mahmoud Ayoub
Temple University
Philadelphia
Jumādā II 1425 / August 2004

A NOTE ON TRANSLITERATION

In this book I have followed the Library of Congress system for Arabic transliteration. I have kept the distinction between the *hamzah* and the *'ayn* and indicated the *alif* as well as the *alif maqṣūrah* (shorter *alif*) with the long vowel macron. This I did to distinguish the *alif* from the vowel *fatḥah*. I have always put an 'h' at the end of feminine Arabic nouns to indicate gender. Although Arabic does not have an upper case, I have capitalized proper nouns as well as the initial word of transliterated titles of major works, to act as a signpost for English readers.

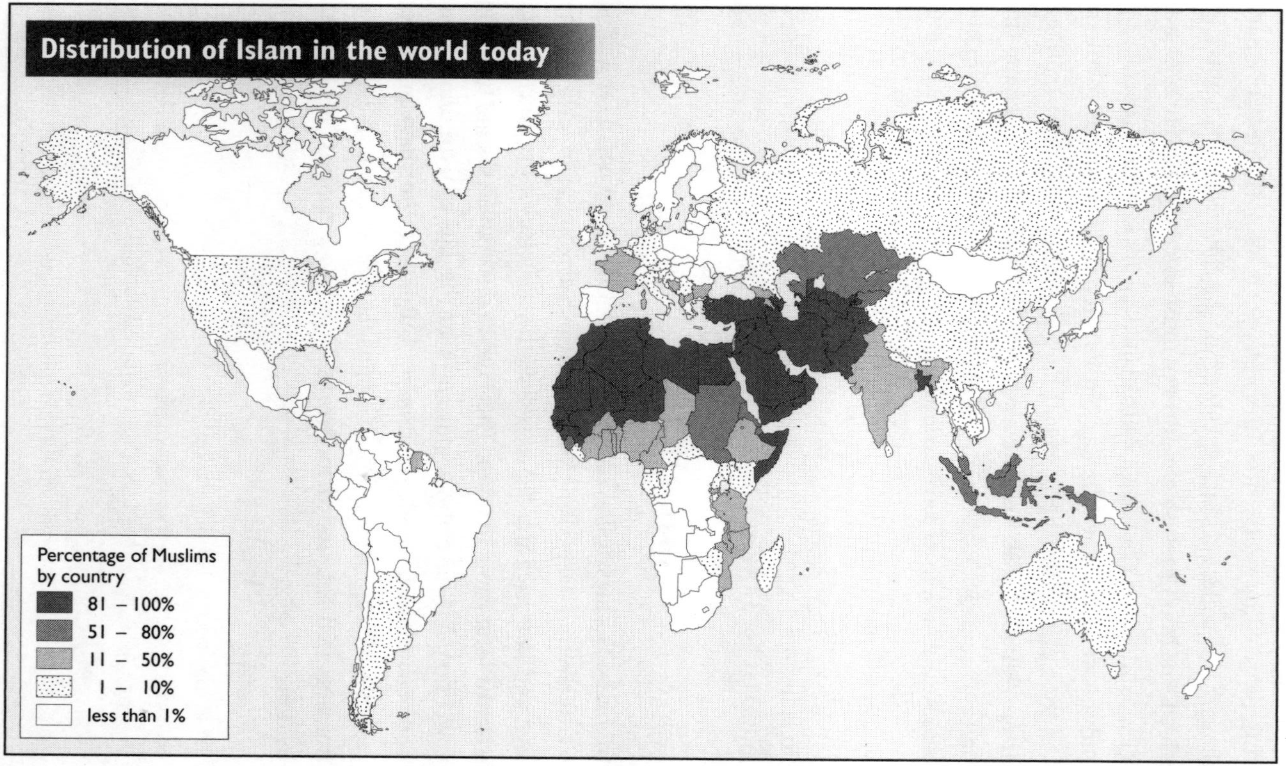
Distribution of Islam in the world today
Percentage of Muslims by country
81 – 100%
51 – 80%
11 – 50%
1 – 10%
less than 1%

Prologue
Islam: A Personal Faith?

With the worldwide ascendancy of science and reason following the Age of Enlightenment in the West, it has become increasingly out of fashion to be religious. Yet human religiousness, which is as old as humanity itself, refuses to go away. Thus religious men and women everywhere have sought to meet modern rationalist and materialist challenges to the innate human proclivity for faith and to the perennial human search for knowledge of, and contact with, ultimate reality in diverse ways. These ways have ranged from unyielding literalist fundamentalism to agnosticism, liberalism, and religious humanism.

Western Christian and Jewish communities have, at considerable risk to the integrity of their faith-identities, shown great flexibility in meeting these challenges and hence in making adjustments to the demands of the scientific, economic, social, political, and philosophical realities of the modern world. In contrast, Muslims have largely resisted making such adjustments and therefore have generally failed to meet the challenges of modern science and technology. An important reason for this failure is, in my view, the strong attachment of many educated and activist Muslims to the ideal of public religion and to the quest for the recovery of the past glory of *dār al-islām*, the sphere or abode of Islam, which is believed to be the proper framework of public religion.

As a traditional belief-system and worldview, Islam presents a credible and dynamic alternative to Western secularism and religious humanism. It is a worldview that categorically affirms that to have true faith in God is to accept total commitment to an all-inclusive way of life founded on an immutable divine revelation and actualized in a supremely authoritative prophetic model that, nonetheless, leaves wide scope for personal responsibility and self-expression. Although this Islamic belief and the worldview it fosters need not clash with modern Western values, it has contributed to an artificial but powerful conflict between traditional faith and secular modernity.

In recent years this conflict has led some scholars and thinkers in Europe and America to portray Islam as an inherently fundamentalist and intractable religion, and Muslims as dangerous extremists intent on subverting Western civilization and taking the world back to the age of medieval slavery and concubinage. This charge was made over a decade ago by a leading Western Islamicist who warned against Islam as an alternative to the progressive civilization of "Europe and her daughters,"[1] notably the United States and Canada. This view was then more broadly and systematically developed by Samuel Huntington under the rubric of the "clash of civilizations."[2]

The conflict between Islam and the West was further deepened by the events of September 11, 2001, which in effect placed all Muslims in the broad category of dangerous terrorists. Consequently, it has become virtually impossible for Muslims to publicly live their religious and cultural identity without fear of serious repercussions. This conflict has also obscured the profound continuity between the three Abrahamic faith-traditions and their universalist civilizations. It rendered interreligious dialogue, which has since the Second World War witnessed momentous progress, a futile and ultimately meaningless exercise. As a consequence, the age-old tensions among the three faith-communities continue to grow deeper and frighteningly more intense.

The tragic September 11 events and their equally tragic aftermath have raised more sharply than ever the question of whether Islam can be more than a personal faith, lived only in the privacy of one's home. For me, this is an existential question related to my own religious quest which culminated in the conviction that Islam, as indeed all living faiths, must guide both the private and public lives of its followers along the spiritual and moral straight path that leads to God and the Good. This conviction, moreover, has guided my own spiritual journey from Islam, the faith into which I was born, to fundamentalist Christianity and through Quakerism back to Islam. Let me demonstrate the reality for me of this conviction by briefly telling the story of my journey.

I was born in a small village in South Lebanon to a poor and uneducated but devout Muslim family. Before the age of one year I lost my sight, an event that determined the rest of my life and destiny.

Neither I nor my parents understood what it meant to be blind. As a child, I refused to accept the limitations imposed on me by my blindness and therefore tried to do all the things that my playmates did. As a result, I frequently injured myself by tumbling from the terraces of our village orchards and down staircases, falling off the roof of our village house, and plunging into my uncle's limestone pit, which was fortunately empty.

My parents had neither the time nor the education to help me understand my disability and cope with it. This was largely because they did not understand it themselves. My father was too busy toiling for a meager living for my mother, for me and my seven brothers and sisters, as well as for my mother's mother and niece – all of whom cooked, ate, and slept in one small room. My mother was busy taking care of us and fending off the gossip of other women in the neighborhood about her alleged neglect of a useless blind child.

In her effort to keep me off the streets, my mother tried all the schools in the Beirut slum to which we had moved after the shock of my blindness, but none would accept me. Finally she was led by a social worker to a Presbyterian British Lebanese missionary school for the blind. I was too young, not yet seven years old, to be admitted into a group of adult males. After much pleading, she succeeded in convincing the director of the school to let me in. She instructed me to say that I was seven years old and that I did not wet my bed. I proudly volunteered this piece of useful information several times to the director, his wife, and anyone who cared to listen.

The sole aim of the school was to teach its pupils the Bible, in Arabic and in English, and in any way possible. I recall how one day the director came to me offering to buy me a pair of shoes if I could learn, by heart, fifty verses of the Bible in two days. I learnt the verses in less than two days. Having been a bare-foot boy for most of my childhood and early adolescence, I was so excited that I dreamed of new shoes for many a night, but my dear director forgot to fulfill his promise. I was too afraid to remind him and eventually forgot the sacred verses.

I was not converted to Christianity, rather I lived it every day, devotionally and culturally, in my school life. More precisely, I grew up as a Christian at school and a Muslim at home. But as the years went by my Christian faith deepened, and with it my anxiety for the souls of my parents. My father and I had long discussions, during which I tried to convert him to Christianity, in order to save his soul. In desperation he threatened to disown me, but my mother with her simple faith always tried to temper his anger, as she was sure that I would eventually return to the faith of my birth.

In my zeal, I became a good witness to Christ and, if I may say so, many were moved by my testimonies. Finally I decided that my Presbyterian mentors were not zealous enough, thus I joined a Southern Baptist group and shouted plenty of "amens" and "hallelujahs."

After a long struggle to attain even a rudimentary level of formal secondary education, I received a scholarship from the well-known

Perkins school for the blind in Watertown, a suburb of Boston, Massachusetts, to be trained as a teacher of the blind. The problem was how to raise the necessary funds for the trip to America, which for me was a dreamland full of fun and excitement. Finally, the great philanthropic Lebanese First Lady, the late Mrs. Zalfa Chamoun, used her influence to get me a government travel grant and I was able to spend two years at Perkins.

The school principal agreed to let me use the first year of my stay to complete my high school education. I was, however, emphatically told by the school psychologist, "You are not college material. Be happy with what you have." I refused his verdict and instead tirelessly strove to realize my dream of becoming a well-educated person. Even then I dreamed of one day becoming a college or university professor.

Armed with a high school diploma, I returned to Lebanon and, after more struggle, was admitted to the American University of Beirut on an AID scholarship to study philosophy and education. Some local administrators opposed my admission on the grounds of my disability. In spite of them and thanks to the efforts of an American Quaker who was then dean of the College of Arts and Sciences, I was admitted and did very well, thus making it possible for other blind students to have the same opportunity.

As a student of philosophy, my purely emotional Christian religiosity no longer spoke to my spiritual condition. But, being by nature a religious person, even when unsure of my faith in God I never stopped being a seeker. I was attracted to the spirituality of the Quakers and thus joined the Beirut Friends Center and the Middle East Yearly Meeting. I subsequently joined the Philadelphia and later the Cambridge Yearly Meetings. I found much solace and peace in the silent worship of the Quakers, particularly in the principle of the presence of a divine spark in every human being.

It was in fact in America – first at the University of Pennsylvania, where I received a Master's degree in Religious Thought, and then at Harvard University, where I earned a Ph.D. in History of Religion – that

I discovered my Islamic roots. For this I am largely indebted to my esteemed mentor the late Wilfred Cantwell Smith. He guided me to an appreciation of Islam that made possible my becoming a committed and religiously pluralistic Muslim.

My Christian upbringing left an indelible mark on my moral and spiritual life and character. It has colored my Islamic faith, theology, and worldview. My Christian past and my present Islamic faith-commitment have convinced me that God is the absolute truth or ultimate reality, and that Islam, Christianity, and indeed all religions, are only ways to this transcendent Truth. They have taught me that personal faith cannot grow in isolation; rather, it must be nurtured in a faith-community – the Church or communion of faith for Christians, the *ummah muslimah* for Muslims.

Every religious obligation or act of worship in Islam has a personal and a public dimension, neither dimension can be truly fulfilled without the other. For instance, congregational prayers in the mosque are better than private prayers at home, yet private devotions are the nourishment of the spirit. Similarly, the fast of Ramaḍān is primarily a personal act of worship and yet it cannot be broken until one remits the "alms of breaking the fast" (*zakāt al-fiṭr*). Almsgiving (*zakāt*) is a public commitment to social welfare. And just as *zakāt* is the public dimension of the private act of worship, so the personal dimension of *zakāt* is *ṣadaqah*, or private free-will giving. The most public religious obligation of Muslims is the annual *ḥajj* to Makkah[3] in which hundreds of thousands of pious men and women participate; yet to be fully realized the *ḥajj* must be interiorized as a personal journey to God.

This brings me back to my original question of personal faith and its ultimate expression and validity. I believe that personal faith can live and grow only in a communal setting. This is as true of Christianity as it is of Islam. Christ's words of reproach, "I was hungry and you gave me no food, I was thirsty and you gave me no drink, I was a stranger and you did not welcome me, naked and you did not clothe me, sick and in prison and you did not visit me,"[4] are put by Islamic tradition in the mouth of God himself in a *ḥadīth qudsī* (divine utterance): On the day of judgment God will reproach Muslims who did not help alleviate the sufferings of others here on earth. He will accusingly say, "O, son of Adam, I was sick and you did not visit Me ... I asked you for food but you did not feed Me ... and I asked you for drink but you did not give Me drink."[5] The Prophet expressed this basic Islamic principle in the words: "All human creatures are God's own children and the most beloved of them to Him is he who is most beneficial to His children."[6]

The argument for private versus public religion has become a burning international and interreligious issue, especially after September 11. Many international Middle Eastern or Islamic philanthropic organizations have become suspect and thus are being severely curtailed or altogether closed down. Such pressures may in the end suffocate the humanistic spirit of Islam, without which it becomes a dead letter.

To conclude my story, I admit that many Christian and secular readers may ask why I returned to Islam after having found Christ, or after having discovered the values of democracy and human rights. My answer is that I see no contradiction between my faith in the one God, as a Muslim, and the values of equality, freedom, and the dignity of "all the children of Adam."[7] I regard my return to Islam not as a repudiation of Christianity, but as a deepening of my faith through the return to my cultural and spiritual roots. It is my personal quest to discover where the spiritual "abode of Islam" is for me. I wish this volume to be regarded as a modest attempt to reflect on this quest.

1

Origins and Early History

ISLAM: NAME AND CONCEPT

Islām is an Arabic word meaning submission, or surrender. The three-letter root, *s/l/m*, from which the word *islām* is derived also means peace (*salām*), soundness, and safety. *Islām* is therefore a person's total submission to the will of God, which gives him or her inner peace and soundness of nature in this life and safety from divine retribution in the life to come.

"Islam" is the name of the third and last of the monotheistic faiths that arose in the Middle East, coming after Judaism and Christianity. The name signifies the commitment of its adherents to live in total submission to God within a prescribed conduct as defined by the Qur'ān, the *sunnah* of the Prophet Muḥammad and the living tradition. A person who professes Islam is a Muslim. The earlier English rendering of this word as "Moslem" is erroneous and therefore seldom used. The Persian word "Musalman," derived from the Arabic word *muslim*, is used in Iran and the Indo-Pakistan subcontinent and was also adapted into the French language. The words "Muḥammadan" and "Muḥammadanism," which were sometimes used to mean "Muslim" and "Islam," are highly offensive to Muslims because they imply that Muslims worship the Prophet Muḥammad. They therefore should not be used.

A Muslim is either one who is born to a Muslim family and is thus a member of the Muslim community by birthright, or one who accepts Islam by repeating before two Muslim witnesses the *shahādah*, or profession of faith: "I bear witness that there is no god except God (*allāh*), and I bear witness that Muḥammad is the Messenger of God." Whether this public profession with the tongue is truly held in the person's heart is for God alone to judge. By simply making the *shahādah*, a man or woman becomes legally a Muslim with all the rights and responsibilities entailed by this new identity. No other ceremony is required.

The *shahādah* of the oneness of God and of the messengership of Muḥammad is not simply a formula for acquiring membership in the Muslim community. Rather, it is the affirmation of faith in the one God, creator and sustainer of all things, and of the centrality of prophethood. The following two texts, one from the Qur'ān and the other from *Nahj al-balāghah* (a collection of 'Alī's orations), give two important statements of divine oneness, which is the essence of the faith, or *islām*, of all creation.

From the Qur'ān, *sūrah* 27, *al-Naml* ("The Ants"), verses 59–64:

> Say: "Praise be to God and peace be upon His servants whom He has elected." Is God better or the things they associate with Him?
>
> For, who created the heavens and the earth and sent down for you from heaven water with which We cause to grow gardens of delight, whose trees you could not cause to grow? Is there any god beside God? Rather they are people who deviate [from the truth].
>
> Or, who made the earth a resting place and made through it rivers and made immovable mountains and placed between the two seas a barrier? Is there any god beside God? Rather most of them know not.

Or, who answers the call of him who is in distress when he calls upon Him and removes hardship, and makes you inheritors of the earth? Is there any god beside God? Little do you heed.
Or, who guides you through the dark places of land and sea? And who sends forth the winds bearing glad tidings [that is rain] ahead of His mercy? Is there any god beside God? Exalted be God over all the things they associate with Him.
Or, who originates creation then repeats it, and who provides for you sustenance from the heaven and the earth? Is there any god beside God? Say, "Bring forth your proof if you are truthful."

From Nahj al-balāghah:[8]

> Praise be to God whose praise cannot be encompassed by orators; nor could any reckoners enumerate His bounties. Diligent men can never truly render His due, which cannot be apprehended by men of vigorous intellects; nor could deep thought attain it. The beginning of true faith is knowledge of Him. The perfection of knowing Him is assent to Him. The perfection of assenting to Him is professing His oneness and the perfection of professing His oneness is sincere faith in Him. He originated the creation out of nothing, and alone made it what it is. He did not need to think out His creation, nor did He benefit from any previous experience, nor did He resort to any movement towards His purpose, nor did His creation cause Him any worry or concern.

The Qur'ān, the Islamic scripture, presents *islām* as the universal and primordial faith of all the prophets from Adam to Muḥammad and of all those who believe in God, the one sovereign Lord, creator and merciful Lord of all things. *Islām* is also God's eternal way for his creation. The heavens and earth – the sun, moon, and stars – follow a predetermined course, thus expressing their obedience, or *islām* to God. The Qur'ān states: "Then He turned to the heaven while it was yet smoke, and said to it and to the earth, 'Come [forth] voluntarily or by force,' they said, 'Rather we come fully obedient'" (Q. 41:11).

Inanimate things, animals, and plants, as well as the angels are *muslims* to God by nature or instinct. Only human *islām* is an *islām* of rational choice. Human beings may voluntarily accept or willfully reject faith but, on the day of judgment, they will face the consequences of their choices. Each will be rewarded for faith, or punished for the rejection of faith. The Qur'ān warns the first generation of Muslims, and also subsequent generations, "Be not like those who forgot God, and thus He made them forget their own selves" (Q. 59:19).

It was stated above that *islām* is believed by Muslims to be the universal faith of all those who affirm the oneness of God in total submission to his will. Beyond this, Muslims also believe that *islām* is the natural faith of all human beings. Thus the inner source of Islam is the natural inclination of every person towards faith and the inner capacity of each to know God. This original state of purity or innocence is called in the Qur'ān *fiṭrah*, the pattern "upon which God originated humankind; there is no altering of God's creation" (Q. 30:30). This innate *islām* is the "pure religion of Abraham" to which the Prophet Muḥammad came to call his people: "It is the religion of your father Abraham; he called you *muslims* aforetime" (Q. 22:78).

Abraham, the Qur'ān tells us, was guided from the idol worship of his people to the knowledge of God by his innate human capacity to know God. When he was still a youth, he deduced that since idols made of wood or stone could not hear the supplications of their worshipers, they could do them neither good nor harm. Searching for God, Abraham gazed one night at a brilliant star and believed it to be God; but the star set and he was disappointed. He then considered the full moon, on account of its splendor, but when the moon set Abraham said, "I love not those that set." He then gazed at the bright sun and said, "This is my lord, this is bigger!" When the sun too set Abraham exclaimed, "I turn my face [that is entire person] to Him who originated the heavens and the earth, a man of pure faith; and I am not one of the Associators [that is of other things or beings with God]"(Q. 6:77–79).

This and other Qur'anic accounts of Abraham's life and faith link him physically and spiritually to the Arab people and to Islam. Muḥammad (the Prophet of Islam) and the Arab people are said to be the direct physical descendants of Abraham, through his son Ishmael. Abraham's faith in the one God – long before the Torah and the Gospel were revealed – is described as the true *islām* which, according to the Qur'ān and Islamic tradition, provided the spiritual basis for the Islamic faith. These beliefs signify for Muslims the close theological and spiritual kinship of the Qur'ān and Islam with biblical history, and consequently with the Judaic and Christian religious traditions.

The following passage from the Qur'ān dramatically tells the story of Abraham breaking the idols of his people and affirming faith in the one God:

From *sūrah* 21, *al-Anbiyā'* ("The Prophets") verses 51–73:

We bestowed upon Abraham his rectitude aforetime and were well acquainted with him.
When he said to his father and his people, "What are these idols that you so fervently worship?"
They said, "We found our fathers worshiping them."
He said, "Both you and your fathers are in manifest error."
They said, "Have you come to us with the truth, or are you one of those who jest?"
He said, "Your Lord is indeed the Lord of the heavens and the earth, for He originated them; and to this I am one of those who bear witness.
By God, I shall confound your idols as soon as you turn your backs."
He thus utterly destroyed the idols except for the chief one, so that the people might turn to it [for petition].
They said, "Who did this to our gods? He is surely a wrongdoer."
Some said, "We heard a youth called Abraham speaking of them."
Others said, "Bring him here in the sight of the people, so that they may all witness."
They said, "Did you do this to our gods, O Abraham?"
He said, "No, it was their chief who did it. Question them – if they could speak."
The people then turned on one another, saying, "Indeed you are the wrongdoers!"
Then they all bowed their heads in humiliation, saying, "You know well [O Abraham], that these cannot speak."

[Abraham] said, "Would you still then worship instead of God a thing that can do neither good nor harm?
Fie on you and on what you worship instead of God; do you not reason?"
They said, "Burn him and stand up for your gods, if you would do anything."
We [God] said, "O fire, be coolness and peace for Abraham!"
They wished evil for him, but We turned them into utter losers.
And We delivered him and Lot to a land that We blessed for all beings.
We also granted him Isaac and Jacob as an added favor, and We made them both righteous.
We made them all leaders guiding others by Our command. We inspired them to do good deeds, perform regular worship, and give the obligatory alms; and they were true worshipers of Us alone.

ARABIA BEFORE ISLAM

For the most part, pre-Islamic Arab society had no well-developed religious ritual or belief systems. However, Jewish Arab and Christian Arab communities did exist in Arabia long before the advent of Islam; even in the absence of full-fledged communities the beliefs of Jews and Christians were not unknown. The city of Makkah, where Muḥammad was born, was a caravan station on the trade routes between Syria and the Mediterranean to the north and the Red Sea, Africa, and India to the south. It was therefore, like the rest of the Arabian peninsula, exposed to diverse cultural and religious influences. It was in fact permeated by Jewish and Christian moral and devotional ideas. In particular the desert monks, who preached and practiced holiness and healing, exercised a deep influence on many Arab seekers after a moral and spiritual life.

A group of Makkan Arabs known as *ḥanīfs* ("pious ones") accepted the ethical monotheism of Judaism and Christianity but did not join either of the two religious communities. The Makkans may have been put off by the discord and hostility between the two groups, as the Qur'ān reports: "The Jews say the Christians have nothing on which to stand and the Christians say the Jews have nothing on which to stand, yet they both recite the scriptures" (Q. 2:113). They may also have resisted Christian proselytization hoping for a scripture of their own (see Q. 35:42 and 6:157).

In any case, before Islam the Arabs had no well defined unifying religious cult. They worshiped many gods and goddesses, following time-honored custom without any particular feeling of devotion or moral commitment. They believed time to be synonymous with fate or death, which in the end would spare no one, and that therefore, while he could, a person should make the most of this life. Arab society thus combined a gloomy acceptance of a meaningless existence with an indulgence in hedonistic pleasures.

These sentiments were expressed in eloquent odes recounting deeds of chivalry and generosity, deploring fate, and praising the wise man who drowned his sorrows in the pleasures of wine, women, and sentimental verse, but who was sure to leave behind a good name for his tribe to boast of after him.

Before Islam the Arabs, like the ancient Hebrews, did not believe in an afterlife. As the Qur'ān reports, "They [the non-Muslim Arabs] say there is only this life of ours; we live and we die, and time alone will destroy us all" (Q. 45:24). They did believe, however, that the ghost of a slain man would linger and cry for vengeance until revenge was exacted from the killer himself, or from any man of similar status of his tribe. This belief, coupled with the virtues of manly prowess and tribal solidarity, often led to long and deadly feuds that decimated many tribes and forced others to migrate.

The Arabs shared the general Semitic idea of a sacred place (*ḥaram*) where no plant, no animal, no human, no living thing, could be harmed. The foremost *ḥaram* for Makkans, and most of the inhabitants of the Arabian peninsula, was the shrine of the Ka'bah and its environs. Even before Islam, the Arabs believed the Ka'bah to have been built by Abraham and his son Ishmael. They may have been aware of the tradition that Abraham brought the child Ishmael and his mother Hagar to settle in the valley of Makkah (see Q. 14:37). The Ka'bah is an ancient square building that in pre-Islamic times housed a large number of idols and images of gods and goddesses, perhaps even including a crudely painted image of Jesus and his virgin mother Mary.

Among the many deities that the Arabs worshiped in and around the Ka'bah were the god Hubal and the three goddesses Al-lāt, al-'Uzzā, and Manāt. Hubal was originally a moon god, and perhaps also a rain god, as *hubal* means "vapor." Al-lāt was perhaps a feminine form of Allah, whose name simply means the goddess. Manāt may have been a vague representation of the ancient goddess of love associated with the planet Venus. She was also associated with human fate and death. The three goddesses were believed to be the daughters of *Allāh*, the supreme God. Their worshipers believed that through them they could get closer to him (see Q. 39:3). The Qur'ān repudiates these goddesses, calling them mere "names which you [the Arabs] and your fathers named; God sent down no authority concerning them" (Q. 53:20–23).

Arabs from far and near journeyed to the Ka'bah especially during the pilgrimage season and the major market fair associated with it. This gave Makkah a special prestige and economic status in Arabia. Later, Islam purged the pilgrimage of its idolatrous elements and adopted it as one of the rites of worship. The sanctity of the Ka'bah was, moreover, greatly enhanced by making it the direction of prayer for Muslims everywhere.

While the Arabs professed *Allāh*, an Arabic word meaning "the God," to be the supreme deity, they did not worship him, nor did he play an active role in their lives. Arab society lived mainly by a system of social ideals and customs rather than religious values. As was the pilgrimage to Makkah, many of these were appropriated by Islam and molded into its comprehensive religious system.

Ideals such as manliness, hospitality, family honor, the neighborly protection of a defenseless person, and the keeping of one's covenant, were among the values that Islam adopted and transformed by giving them religious and moral meaning and purpose. Thus manliness was transformed into religious zeal, and hospitality into almsgiving and care for the poor, the orphan, and the wayfarer. Family honor was reconceptualized as moral chastity and respect and love between parents and children, and keeping one's covenant into a system of sociopolitical, religious, and economic relations amongst Muslims and between the Muslim community and other communities, notably Christians and Jews.

Islam repudiated but could not fully eradicate the custom of tribal or kinship solidarity (*'aṣabiyyah*),[9] which often took priority over the bond of religion. Although the Prophet Muḥammad attempted to refashion it into the ideal of a brotherhood of faith, tribal interests and inter-tribal conflicts dominated the social and political life of early Muslim society, as will be demonstrated later.

THE CITY OF MAKKAH

Makkan society consisted largely of one tribe, the Quraysh, which was divided into various clans. Before Islam, the men of the Quraysh had already established an efficient and just system for arbitration and for the payment of blood money to the kinsfolk of victims who suffered injury or death. Thus the community was able to avoid endless cycles of revenge and counter-revenge. They had built a town hall, called *dār al-nadwah*, where important meetings to settle these and other disputes were held. Nonetheless, bitter rivalries persisted. One in particular, between the two closely related houses of Umayyah and Hāshim, would be instrumental in determining the course of Muslim history. A primary cause of this rivalry was the guardianship of the Ka'bah, which remained with the house of Hāshim until the coming of Islam.

As Makkah lay in the arid and agriculturally poor valley of Najd, its people lived on trade and the revenues of the Ka'bah. The importance of these two sources of livelihood is vividly described in the following brief *sūrah* of the Qur'ān:

> This [the sparing of the Ka'bah is] for the sake of the pact of safety of the Quraysh,
> For the sake of their safety during the winter and summer journeys.
> Let them then worship the Lord of this House,
> Who provided them with food against hunger, and made them secure from fear (Q. 106).

The sparing of the Ka'bah becomes even more significant when taken with the event it heralds. According to Muslim tradition, the Negus, or king, of Abyssinia – an important Christian power at the time – built a rival shrine in southern Arabia to divert pilgrimage away from the Ka'bah. Having failed in this endeavor, in 570 or 571 he sent his general, Abraha, to destroy the sacred structure. The army was led by an elephant, an unusual sight in Makkah. After a short siege of the sacred shrine Abraha's army was decimated, perhaps by a smallpox epidemic, and the Ka'bah was miraculously spared. This momentous event is celebrated in another early *sūrah* of the Qur'ān:

> Have you not considered how your Lord dealt with the people of the elephant?
> Did He not turn their evil scheming to no avail?
> For He sent against them birds in great flocks,
> Which hurled at them stones of baked clay.
> And He thus made them as dry leaves chewed up (Q. 105).

It was during that year, the "year of the elephant," that Muḥammad, the Prophet of Islam, is believed to have been born.

MUḤAMMAD THE PROPHET: HIS LIFE AND MISSION (*c.* 570–632)

Muḥammad was the son of 'Abdallāh son of 'Abd al-Muṭṭalib son of Hāshim of the tribe of Quraysh. Before the child was born his father died while on a caravan journey. His mother, Āminah, daughter of Wahb, and also of the Quraysh, died a few years later. Muḥammad thus grew up an orphan, cared for first by his paternal grandfather ʻAbd al-Muṭṭalib and, after he too died while Muḥammad was still a youth, by his uncle Abū Ṭālib. Beyond these few details little is known about his early life.

In his youth, Muḥammad may have accompanied his uncle on one or more caravan journeys to Syria. His earliest biographer reports that during one such journey, Muḥammad met Baḥīrā, a Syrian monk. The monk invited the whole company for a meal and declared Muḥammad to be a prophet. He then told Muḥammad's uncle to take him back to Makkah and guard him well.[10]

Later Muḥammad worked as a merchant for a rich widow, Khadījah. Muḥammad is described in the early sources as a contemplative, honest, and mild-mannered young man, who was called *al-amīn* ("the faithful" or "trustworthy one") because of the confidence he inspired in his dealings with his fellow merchants. Although Khadījah may have been considerably older than him, he married her when he was around the age of twenty-five. The marriage freed him from financial cares and allowed him to turn his thoughts to higher things.

It is quite probable that Muḥammad belonged to the small circle of *ḥanīfs*, already mentioned. Certainly, tradition reports that Muḥammad loathed his people's idol worship and their immoral and foolish ways. Once a year, during the hot summer month of Ramaḍān, Muḥammad spent days in seclusion in a cave on Mount Ḥirā', a short distance from Makkah. It was during one of these retreats that he received the call to prophethood and the first revelation of the Qur'ān.

As Muḥammad sat one night in the solitude of his retreat, a superhuman being, later identified as Gabriel (Jibrīl in Arabic) appeared to him. Taking hold of him and pressing him so hard that he could not breathe, the angel commanded: "Recite [or, 'read']!" Muḥammad answered: "I cannot read." After repeating the command a second and third time, the angel continued:

> Recite in the name of your Lord who created,
> Created man from a blood clot.
> Recite, for your Lord is most magnanimous,
> Who taught by the pen;
> Taught man that which he knew not (Q. 96:1–5).

These five verses are generally believed to constitute the first of the revelations of the Qur'ān.

A terrified Muḥammad ran home and shivering with fear and apprehension begged the people of his household to cover him up. This experience so filled him with misgivings that he began to wander aimlessly among the Makkan hills, trying to understand the meaning of the encounter. Gabriel would not leave him be. Often, tradition reports, the angel would appear seated on a throne and filling the horizon, so that in whichever direction he looked Muḥammad could not but see him. The angel would proclaim, "O Muḥammad, I am Gabriel, and you are the Messenger of God." Khadījah always consoled and encouraged her young husband, insisting that what he saw was not an evil spirit.

Muḥammad's fear and confusion, and Khadījah's response, are connected to several Arab beliefs of the time. First, it was believed that poets were possessed by a demonic spirit of the *jinn*, which inspired them and made them mad (*majnūn*) while they recited their verses. In addition to this, the nearest parallel to the priest or prophet of the ancient religious civilizations of the Middle East was the *kāhin*, or soothsayer, who was often a poet. Such a man or woman spoke in rhymed and mysterious phrases that were meant to announce important events, answer perplexing questions, or evoke feelings of fear and wonderment in those who listened. Finally, the idea of a prophet, called in both Arabic and Hebrew *nabī*, was not unfamiliar to Muḥammad's people. In fact, tradition frequently asserts that the Arabs did expect a prophet of their own and that others before Muḥammad had falsely claimed to be prophets.

Muḥammad, an illiterate merchant, found himself reciting eloquent verses that named him "the Messenger of God." He could not know if this was demonic possession, madness, the poetry of second sight, false prophecy, or a true call to prophethood. Khadījah finally took him to her cousin, a Christian savant named Waraqah b. Nawfal. Waraqah confirmed Muḥammad in his mission, declaring him to be the Prophet sent by God with a sacred law like that of Moses.

The following three passages from the Qur'ān describe the beginnings of the revelation to the Prophet Muḥammad and his mystical vision of the angel of revelation, of Paradise, and of God.

Sūrah 73, *al-Muzzammil* ("The Enwrapped") verses 1–5:

O you who are enwrapped [in garments]!
Rise up [for prayer] the whole night – except for a small portion thereof
The half of it, or a little less
Or a little more – and chant the Qur'ān slowly and deliberately.
We shall surely lay upon you heavy speech.

Sūrah 74, *al-Muddaththir* ("The Enshrouded") verses 1–7:

O you who are shrouded [in a cloak],
Rise up and warn!
Your Lord magnify;
And your garments purify;
Shun all abomination;
And do not begrudge what you give and reckon it to be too much;
Before your Lord be steadfast!

Sūrah 53, *al-Najm* ("The Star") verses 1–18:

By the star when it plunges,
Your companion [Muḥammad] has not erred or strayed.
Nor does he speak out of caprice,
It is but a revelation revealed.
He was taught by one mighty in powers
Endued with strength. He [Gabriel] sat up straight
Being in the highest horizon.
Then he came near and was suspended,
Until he was at a distance of two bows or closer.[11]

Then He [God] revealed to His servant what He revealed.
His [Muḥammad's] heart did not believe what he saw,
Would you then dispute with him concerning what he saw?
He saw him [Gabriel] yet another time,
by the Lote-tree, of the outermost boundary –
By it is the garden of refuge –
While the Lote-tree was shrouded with that which covered it.
His sight did not swerve nor did it go wrong,
For he saw some of his Lord's greatest signs.

* * *

The message that Muḥammad the Prophet of *Allāh* preached in Makkah was a religion with practical moral and social consequences. He called the Makkans to worship God alone, through prayers and almsgiving. He admonished them to care for the orphan, to feed the hungry, to assist the oppressed and destitute, and to offer hospitality to the wayfarer. He warned them of an impending doom, on a day when the deeds of all humankind would be weighed in a just balance, to be rewarded or punished. The following two brief early Makkan *sūrahs* vividly depict this awesome day and its aftermath.

Sūrah 81, *al-Takwir* ("The Folding Up"), verses 1–14:

When the sun shall be folded up
When the stars shall be darkened
When the mountains shall be set in motion
When the ten-month pregnant camels shall be neglected
When the wild beasts shall be brought together
When the seas shall be set boiling
When souls shall be coupled
When the female infant buried alive shall be asked
For what sin she was killed
When the scrolls shall be spread out
When the heavens shall be stripped off
When the Fire shall be set blazing
And when Paradise shall be brought near
Then shall every soul know what it has stored up.

Sūrah 101, *al-Qāri'ah* ("The Smiter"):

The smiter!
What is the smiter?
Would that you knew what the smiter is.
On a day when men shall be like scattered moths,
And mountains shall be like fluffed tufts of wool.
As for him whose scales shall weigh heavy [that is with good deeds],
He shall be in a pleasing life.
But as for him whose scales shall weigh light,
His mother [i.e. abode] shall be the pit.
It is a fire hotly blazing.

For twelve years Muḥammad preached the new faith to his people, but with little success. The Makkans objected not so much to the abstract contents of the Prophet's message but to its practical demands and its consequences. Loyalty was a powerful value in their society and they did not wish to abandon the ways of their forebears. The Qur'ān reports them saying, "We found our fathers following a custom and we shall follow in their footsteps" (Q. 40:22). Most of all, they objected to the effect that a change in their social customs would have on the religious and economic status of the Ka'bah.

The first to accept the new faith was the Prophet's wife Khadījah. She was followed by his cousin and son-in-law 'Alī b. Abī Ṭālib, his slave Zayd b. Ḥārithah – whom he later freed and for a while adopted as his son – and his faithful companion Abū Bakr. Slowly, person by person, a small band of believers began to form. At first it consisted of slaves and the poor of society. Soon, however, the piety, moral uprightness, and egalitarianism that characterized the small group of Muslims began to attract men of substance and prestige. Two such would later become the second and third caliphs of Islam, 'Umar b. al-Khaṭṭāb and 'Uthmān b. 'Affān.

As the Muslim community grew in stature, those who had a vested interest in the continuation of established Makkan society began to vilify Muḥammad and his followers. The most vulnerable slaves and others who had no tribal protection were severely persecuted. Conditions became so difficult that the Prophet advised a group of them to migrate to Abyssinia, a Christian country, where they were well received.

Following the deaths of his uncle Abū Ṭālib and wife Khadījah within no more than two months of one another, Muḥammad too lost all support and protection. Among his bitterest enemies, one singled out in the Qur'ān for damnation (see *sūrah* 111), was his paternal uncle Abū Lahab, a powerful Makkan leader. The Prophet was forced to leave Makkah and go around to the neighboring tribes and towns, asking in vain for protection to preach his new faith.

In 622 Muḥammad finally found a new home. After long negotiations he was invited to arbitrate between two feuding tribes in the city of Yathrib, about 250 miles north of Makkah. In return, the tribes of Yathrib agreed to be united into a new Muslim community. The Prophet, his Companions, and his followers emigrated to Yathrib, thenceforth known as *madīnat al-nabī* ("City of the Prophet") or Madīnah (the "City"). And Muslims very early adopted the migration (*hijrah*) to Yathrib as the founding event of their history. It marks the official beginning of Islamic history and the beginning and focus of the Muslim calendar. Hence, within the Muslim world, events are dated from or after the *hijrah*: 622 C.E. becomes 1 A.H. (from the Latin for "year of the *hijrah*").[12] The Qur'ān honors the people of Madīnah by calling them *anṣār* ("Helpers" or "Supporters"), that is to say the first supporters and protectors of Islam and its Prophet.

Madinan society had a far more heterogeneous social structure than that of Makkah. It consisted largely of two hostile tribes, the Aws and the Khazraj, and a substantial Jewish community which often took advantage of the old tribal rivalries. All these tensions kept the city in a continuous state of civil strife. As the flow of Muslim immigrants from Makkah increased, a new social group was added to an already diverse society. The new immigrants, along with those who came with or shortly after the Prophet, were appropriately called *muhājirūn* ("Emmigrants"). The Emmigrants were predominantly members of the tribe of Quraysh and eventually they formed a closely knit and powerful group within the Muslim community.

Muḥammad sought to weld all these disparate elements into one social unit which, while he lived, he achieved with remarkable success. His first act was the promulgation of a brief constitutional document known as the constitution of Madīnah. The constitution stipulated that all the people of Madīnah would thenceforth be one Muslim commonwealth. It also recognized the Jews and granted them full religious freedom and equality with the Muslims, provided that they supported the state and did not enter into any conflicting alliance with the Quraysh of Makkah or any other tribe. Because of the close kinship of the Qur'ān's narratives and worldview with biblical prophetic history, the Prophet expected the Jews of Madīnah to recognize a continuity between Judaism and Islam and thus to be his natural allies.

Muḥammad adopted a number of Jewish practices, including the fast of *yaum kippur* (Yom Kippur, the "Day of Atonement"). It also seems that at first the Muslims followed Jewish custom and faced Jerusalem during their prayers. The Jews, however, rejected Muḥammad's claim that he was a prophet and the Qur'ān a sacred book. The tensions this created between the two communities are clearly reflected in the Qur'ān's treatment of the Jews. Increasingly, Islam began to distinguish itself from Judaism. Within two years of the Prophet's migration to Madīnah, the fast of Yom Kippur was dropped in favor of the fast of Ramaḍān, and the *qiblah*, or direction of prayers, was changed from Jerusalem to the Ka'bah in Makkah.

The Qur'ān presents an increasingly widening scope for Muḥammad's mission. At first he was only enjoined to warn his nearest kinsfolk. Then he was commanded to proclaim his message publicly; then "to warn the mother of towns [Makkah] and its environs" (Q. 6:92). Finally he was ordered to declare, "O humankind, I am God's Messenger to you all" (Q. 7:158). This no doubt reflects the Prophet's own growing consciousness of the potentially universal scope and significance of his new religion.

We have already seen that the Ka'bah, and hence the city of Makkah, was an integral part of the sacred history of Islam. If, therefore, Islam was to grow beyond the confines of its new home in Madīnah, Makkah had to be restored to its rightful place in the realized prophetic history of Abraham and Ishmael and their Arabian descendants, notably the Prophet Muḥammad whose mission was to call the Arabs back to the religion of their father Abraham. In short, without Makkah Islam would be incomplete, without the rest of Arabia it would remain powerless.

The Makkans, however, remained intransigent; they would not accept Islam. And so the Prophet resorted to the familiar strategies of economic and military pressure: Muslims intercepted and raided Makkan caravans on their way from Syria. The Makkans were forced to defend their trade routes. In 2/624 they sent out an army of about a thousand men which was met by a three-hundred man Muslim detachment at the well of Badr. Poorly equipped and far outnumbered but highly motivated, the Muslims inflicted a crushing defeat on the Makkans.

The Battle of Badr remains one of the most memorable events of Muslim history and is celebrated in the Qur'ān as a miraculous proof of the truth of Islam. The Qur'ān declares: "You [Muḥammad] did not shoot [the first arrow] when you shot it; rather God shot" (Q. 8:17), and "God supported you [Muslims] at Badr when you were in an abased state" (Q. 3:123).

The victory earned the fledgling Muslim state a great deal of prestige among the neighboring tribes and forced the Makkans to deal with Muḥammad on a basis of equality. The Makkans decided to avenge the humiliation of Badr and the following year they met the Muslims by Mount Uḥud, not far from Madīnah. At Uḥud the Prophet was badly injured and false reports that he had been killed quickly circulated. The Muslims were not only defeated but, because their defeat was largely due to their own negligence and lack of motivation, they were also demoralized.

Immediately following the defeat at Uḥud the Prophet decided to expel the Jews from Madīnah and its neighboring settlements. The reason given was that the Jews, by aiding the Makkans through economic alliances against the Muslim state, had breached their covenant and forfeited their right to protection. The deeper motive behind this drastic measure may have been, at least in part, to free the Muslim state of outside influences at this critical stage of its formative history.

The battle of Uḥud, however, was not decisive, as the men of the Quraysh did not pursue their victory further and the Muslims quickly recovered. The Muslims continued to grow in strength and stature and their occasional skirmishes against the caravans of the Quraysh did not cease. Finally, the Makkans decided to attack Madīnah.

Upon learning of their plan Salmān the Persian, a former slave who had accepted Islam and become one of the Prophet's most prominent Companions, suggested a way for the defense of Madīnah. On his advice, the Prophet had a trench dug around the exposed parts of the city, so as to prevent the Makkan cavalry from advancing. In 5/627 the men of the Quraysh along with a large coalition of other tribes besieged Madīnah in what came to be known as the "Battle of the Trench" or the "Battle of the Confederates." As the siege failed to achieve its aim, the attacking armies became discouraged and left.

The Battle of the Trench was a turning point in the Prophet's goal of Islamizing all of Arabia. Islam was quickly spreading throughout Arabia, including Makkah and beyond. Finally the Makkans were impelled to seek a truce with the Muslims. The truce of Ḥudaybiyah was concluded in 6/628, which allowed the Prophet to consolidate the nascent state's military and diplomatic gains.

Two years later, in 8/630, Muḥammad led a large army against Makkah, the Quraysh having breached the truce by killing a man of the tribe of Khuzāʿah, which was closely allied with the Muslims. There was, however, no fighting, no bloodshed, no vengeance. The Makkans capitulated and accepted Islam en masse; the Prophet granted safe passage to all in the city. Clearly powerless after the Prophet's victory over them, the Makkans asked him what he intended to do with them. He answered, "I will do with you what Joseph did with his brothers. Go, you are free." Then quoting Joseph's words to his brothers, he continued: "There is no blame on you today; God forgive you" (Q. 12:92). Such was his magnanimity that it touched even his bitterest enemies and helped in the healing of the wounds of years of conflict and bloodshed.

Muḥammad was primarily a prophet, not a conqueror. He did not wage this or any battle for the sake of building an empire; rather he sought to establish a faith and a faith-community. Whenever an individual or tribe accepted Islam, all hostilities ceased and the enemy became brothers in faith. Muḥammad regarded his victory over Makkah not as his own but as God's victory. The victory and its purpose are celebrated in the Qur'ān in the words not of a conqueror but of a thankful servant:

> When support from God comes, and victory,
> And you see men enter into the religion of God in throngs,
> Proclaim the praise of your Lord and seek His forgiveness, for He is truly relenting (Q. 110).

The Prophet did not remain in Makkah as might have been expected, but returned to Madīnah where he spent the last two years of his life. In the tenth year of the *hijrah*, a few months before his death, Muḥammad led the Muslims on his farewell pilgrimage to Makkah and its sacred shrine, the Ka'bah. He gave his farewell speech after this, the only *ḥajj* on which he led the Muslims.

From Muḥammad the Prophet's farewell pilgrimage speech we read:[13]

> O people, listen to my words, for I know not whether I will ever meet with you after this year in this place. O people, surely your blood and your wealth is as inviolable for you as this day and this month until you meet your Lord [the reference here is to the sacred month and the sacred days of the *ḥajj*]. You shall indeed meet your Lord and He will

> question you concerning your actions. O God, I have conveyed! Anyone of you who has a trust belonging to another person, let him return it to him. All usury is forbidden, and you will only have the capital of your wealth; you will do no wrong nor will you be wronged. O people, Satan has despaired of ever being worshiped in your land. Yet, he will be content with your obedience apart from being worshiped, even to the least of your acts; beware of him concerning your religion. O people, you have certain rights over your women, and they too have rights over you. Your right over them is that they will not allow any man to lie in your bed. It is incumbent upon them not to commit any act of lewdness. But if they do, then God has permitted you to desert their bed and beat them, but not severely. If they desist, they shall have their lodging and clothing in kindness. Be kind toward women, for they are your helpmates, having no power for themselves. You have taken them in marriage in accordance with God's right; and their chastity was made lawful for you in accordance with the words of God. I have left with you the Book of God and the *sunnah* of His Prophet. If you hold fast to them, you will never go astray. O people, listen to my words and understand them: you know that every Muslim is a brother to every other Muslim, and that all Muslims are brothers. It is not lawful for anyone to take from his brother except what he gives him willingly. Do not wrong yourselves. O God, have I conveyed?

With this the ritual of the *ḥajj* was officially instituted, and Islam was complete. The Qur'ān declares this in God's words: "Today I have perfected your religion for you, have bestowed fully My grace upon you and have accepted Islam as a religion for you" (Q. 5:3).

* * *

Muḥammad has always been known as *rasūl allāh* (the "Messenger of God"), not as a ruler or military leader, although he was all of these. He waged war and made peace and laid the foundations of an Islamic order. He established laws and social and religious institutions, which are still accepted as Islamic laws and institutions. Islam thus came to encompass all aspects of life. The community (*ummah*) he established was to be a religious community, an *ummah muslimah.* It was founded on the ideal of a balanced community, "a community of the middle way," as the Qur'ān states: "Thus have We made you [Muslims] a community of the middle way in order that you may be witnesses over all people, and that the Messenger may be a witness over you" (Q. 2:143).

Before Muḥammad died after a short illness in 632, he had firmly established Islam in Arabia and sent at least one expedition to Syria. After the conquest of Makkah, Arab tribal energies were turned outward, towards the Persian and Byzantine empires. By 711, within less than a century of the Prophet's death, the Muslims administered an empire stretching from the southern borders of France through North Africa and the Middle East into central Asia and India. But before I tell this story I shall discuss the concepts of prophethood and revelation, the history and place of the Qur'ān in Muslim piety, as well as the expression of this piety in the rites of worship. I shall later discuss the Qur'ān, the Prophet's life-example (*sunnah*) and Prophetic tradition (*ḥadīth*) as sources of Islamic law in chapter 7.

2

Prophethood, Revelation, and the Qur'ān

The three monotheistic religious traditions of the Middle East, Judaism, Christianity, and Islam, are firmly rooted in history: history begins with the creation of all things by God and will end with the Day of Judgment. On the stage of history, between its beginning and end, God and humankind act out the great drama of good and evil, of salvation and damnation, that will culminate in the final reward of everlasting bliss for the righteous and eternal punishment for the wicked.

Salvation is not the goal of the individual man or woman alone, but of the entire community. The drama of salvation, moreover, unfolds not in heaven, but here on earth. Its ultimate goal is "the coming of the kingdom of God," "the coming of the age of the Messiah," and the establishment of God's rule over all of human society, so that "God's word may be uppermost" on his earth. This goal, Muslims believe, is the sole purpose of the human quest for the good, expressed in the principle of *jihād*, "striving in the way of God." They also believe that God is immanent in history and guides humanity in its striving after him.

From the Islamic point of view the meeting between divine history and mundane history occurs in prophetic history. God's role in human history is not played by him directly through self-disclosure or incarnation in a divine human being, as Christians affirm of Jesus the Christ, but through his prophets and messengers who convey his will in revealed scriptures and seek to establish his sacred law in the lives of their communities.

PROPHETHOOD AND HISTORY

According to the Qur'ān as interpreted by Muslim tradition, God made a covenant with humankind even before humanity came into existence, when human beings were "in the realm of atoms." At the time of this primordial covenant, reports the Qur'ān, "Your Lord brought forth from the children of Adam, from their loins their progeny and made them witness over themselves saying, 'Am I not your Lord?' They said, 'Yes, we witness.' He said, 'Lest you say, on the Day of Resurrection we were unaware of this'" (Q. 7:172).

According to this covenant, revelation is incumbent upon God. God must send prophets and messengers to humankind to remind them of their obligation to the one and only sovereign Lord and to warn them against heedlessness and disobedience. The covenant, however, has two sides: "Lest you say ... we were unaware ..." Revelation is not only a source of salvation through faith in and obedience to God, it is also a criterion for judgment and damnation of those who knowingly disobey God and reject faith in him and his messengers. When a community willfully denies the prophet sent to it, it is destroyed and thus becomes an example for future generations. The Qur'ān warns the Arabs of Muḥammad's time: "We have destroyed [many] generations before you, when they committed wrongdoing. Their messengers came to them with elucidations, but they would not accept faith. Thus do We recompense sinful people" (Q. 10:13).

For Muslims, the history of prophecy begins with the father of humankind, Adam. He is the first man, the first prophet, and the first human sinner. He and Eve and their descendants were, as the Qur'ān clearly affirms, made for the earth and not for Paradise. Before he created Adam, God announced to the angels, "I am about to place a vicegerent on the earth" (Q. 2:30). Thinking themselves more worthy, the angels protested against God's choice of Adam, an insignificant creature, and his potentially wicked progeny as stewards of the earth. Then "God taught Adam all the names" (Q. 2:31), and with this revelation to his earthly creature God challenged the angels. When they could not name the objects that God displayed before them and Adam could, the angels confessed their ignorance: "We have no knowledge save what You have taught us. You alone are the All-knowing, the All-wise" (Q. 2:34).

In recognition of the high status of Adam the prophet, God ordered the protesting angels to reverently bow down before the man. Only Satan (also called in Arabic "Iblīs") arrogantly refused, declaring that he was better than Adam, was created of fire, and would not bow down before a creature of clay. Because of this sin of arrogant rebellion, Satan was expelled by God from the company of the angels. According to the Qur'ān and Islamic tradition Iblīs was originally of the *jinn*. He was placed in the company of the angels as a reward for his assiduous worship of God. By refusing to recognize Adam's special status in the creation, Iblīs committed the sin of arrogance and thus became the first sinner.

Until the Day of Resurrection, however, Iblīs has been given permission to tempt Adam and the weak among Adam's descendants into disobeying God.[14] He succeeded in his temptation of Adam and his spouse and they ate of the forbidden tree. Through his disobedience Adam sinned by violating the principle of submission (*islām*) to God, but after his sin of disobedience, Adam "received certain words from his Lord, and He turned towards him" (Q. 2:37). The sin of Adam and Eve was, according to the Qur'ān, theirs alone. They begged forgiveness of God and God forgave them. The words of revelation that Adam and his spouse received from God are their prayer for forgiveness: "Our Lord, we have wronged ourselves and, if You turn not towards us and have mercy upon us, we shall surely be among the losers" (Q. 7:23).

It may be inferred from this Qur'anic narrative that revelation is itself prayer and a source of salvation. In fact, after Adam and Eve – and by implication the rest of humankind – are expelled from the Garden, God promises salvation through revelation: "There shall come from Me to you [humankind] guidance, and whoever follows My guidance, no fear shall come upon them, nor will they grieve" (Q. 2:38).

Islamic tradition asserts that after Adam, God sent 124,000 prophets at different times and to every community. The Qur'ān declares: "There is not a nation but that a warner was sent to it" (Q. 35:24). The Qur'ān, however, mentions only twenty-five prophets and messengers by name, most of whom are well known biblical personages. Among them are Abraham, Moses, David, Solomon, Elijah, Jonah, John the Baptist, and Jesus. The Qur'ān also speaks of three Arabian prophets: Shu'ayb (possibly Jethro, Moses' father-in-law), Hūd, and Ṣāliḥ. They were sent to Midian and to the Arabian tribes of 'Ād and Thamūd respectively. Their communities, however, stubbornly rejected them and their messages and so were utterly destroyed by God in punishment. For Muslims, this is a warning, the other side of revelation: obedience to God's prophets and messengers brings salvation; disobedience to God's prophets and messengers brings damnation.

MESSENGERS OF GOD

Islamic tradition distinguishes between prophets and messengers. A prophet (*nabī*) is one who conveys God's message to his people. He warns them that if they are wicked they will suffer God's wrath; he promises them blessing and prosperity if they are righteous. The message conveyed is limited to a specific people and for a particular time. It does not therefore constitute a sacred law or a new religious dispensation. The Qur'ān offers several examples of such limited prophetic missions and their outcomes. We have seen, for instance, the punishment that the people of Midian and the tribes of 'Ād and Thamūd suffered when they defied their prophets. On the other hand, the people to whom the prophet Jonah was sent by God heeded his call, repented of their evil ways, and lived in prosperity and happiness.[15]

A prophet sent by God to a specific community and bringing a new and universally binding sacred law (*sharī'ah*) is a messenger (*rasūl*). Moses and Muḥammad are the best examples of such apostolic missions. This is because each not only brought a new and universal religious dispensation, but each also founded an actual community wherein God's law was to be implemented. In other words, Moses and Muḥammad fulfilled the social and political, as well as the religious demands of their missions.

Although Moses was given the Torah on Mount Sinai for the ancient Hebrews, the Torah was binding on all those who knew it, Hebrews and others, till the coming of the subsequent revelation, the gospel (*injīl*) of Jesus. Thenceforth the Torah remained binding, but only as modified by the scripture that God revealed to Jesus. In the Qur'ān Jesus, addressing his fellow Jews, declares, "I shall confirm the Torah that was before me, and will make lawful for you some of the things that were before unlawful for you" (Q.3:50).

In the schema of prophets and messengers, not every prophet is a messenger, but every messenger is a prophet. Among the prophets, five are called *ulū al-'azm* (Q. 46:35), "prophets of power" or "firm resolve." They are Noah, Abraham, Moses, Jesus, and Muḥammad; all of them are messengers. For Muslims, their special significance lies in the fact that they all received revelations from God that, whether extant now or not, contained laws or precepts that were important landmarks in the long and progressive process of divine revelation and hence of human religious development.

According to the Qur'ān, Noah was sent to an obstinate people. For nine hundred and fifty years he called to them in vain, beseeching them to turn to God (see Q. 29:14; 11:25–49). The people mocked him and rejected his message until God finally sent the flood that destroyed them and Noah became the father of the second humanity. Noah is said to have received dietary and marriage laws that constitute the first *sharī'ah*, or sacred law. The Noachic laws reported in Muslim tradition closely correspond to the Noachic covenants in Jewish tradition.

It has already been observed that the primary mission of all the prophets is to be warners to their people of the moral and religious obligation to serve and worship God alone, without associating any partners with him. Thus the primary mission of Abraham was to convert his people from idol-worship to the worship of God alone. Had his people accepted his message, there would have been no reason for Abraham to migrate to a new land. The covenant that God made with Abraham is similar to the covenant made with all the prophets before and after him. The Qur'ān states:

> Remember when God made a covenant with the prophets saying, "Whereas I have given you the Book and wisdom, then an apostle shall come to you confirming that which is with you, you will have faith in him and assist him" (Q. 3:81).

The prophets who followed Abraham were largely his descendants through his two sons Ishmael and Isaac.

Muslim tradition presents Muḥammad in many ways as "a prophet like Moses," and Moses occupies more space in the Qur'ān than any other prophet, including Muḥammad; he is mentioned over two hundred times. As we have seen, Muḥammad grew up as an orphan. A parallel can be made with Moses who, although not an orphan, grew up as if an orphan, away from his parents' home. Moses' mission began as did that of Muḥammad, in solitude with God in the wilderness. The scripture revealed to him, the Torah, is for Muslims second in importance to the Qur'ān and most like it in content and purpose.

Moses was sent as a messenger of God not only to his own people, but also to Pharaoh and his people. Pharaoh, however, persisted in his sin of the association (*shirk*) of other beings, notably himself, with God. An early Makkan *sūrah* gives the following account of the call of Moses and the nature of his mission.

From *Sūrah* 79, *al-Nāzi'āt* ("The Extractors"), verses 15–25:

> Has the account of Moses reached you [Muḥammad]?
> The time when his Lord called out to him in the hallowed valley
> Ṭuwā:
> "Go to Pharaoh, for he has waxed arrogant!
> Say to him, 'Have you the desire to purify yourself
> And that I guide you to your Lord and that you shall fear [Him]?' "
> Even though he [Moses] showed him the great sign,
> Still he gave [it] the lie and rebelled.
> He [Pharaoh] then turned away in haste;
> And gathering [his people], he cried out
> And proclaimed, "I am your lord most high!"
> But God seized him with the torment of both the next world and this.

The Qur'ān (Q. 10:79) describes Pharaoh assembling his magicians in order to counter God's miracles wrought at Moses' hands. It goes on to relate that the magicians were themselves converted and died as martyrs for their faith. This is an important point as Muslims believe that God never leaves his prophets without followers, for that would mean that wicked men could thwart his holy and inscrutable will. Besides the believing magicians, the Qur'ān speaks of the man of faith of the people of Pharaoh (*mu'min āl Fir'awn*), but without naming him. Muslim tradition also asserts that Pharaoh's wife accepted faith in God and died a martyr.[16]

Here again, had Pharaoh and his people accepted faith in God, there would have been no reason for the children of Israel to leave Egypt. In fact Egypt would have been a "Madīnah" for the prophet Moses. It was Pharaoh's rejection of faith in God and his prophet that necessitated the exodus of the Israelites from Egypt and led to his perdition (see

Q. 79:25, quoted above). His declaration of faith in "the God of the children of Israel" at the point of death by drowning was too late to save him. Since at that point, however, he professed faith in God, which can be interpreted as an act of repentance, both the Qu'rān and subsequent tradition suggest at one and the same time that Pharaoh perished and that he was spared (see Q. 10:90–92).

Muslims believe that every major prophet was supported by evidentiary miracles in his claim to be a prophet sent by God. Moreover, part of the proof is that these miracles are always suited to the prophet's mission as well as to the condition of his people. The miracles of Moses, for instance, can be interpreted as affirming God's power and wisdom against the magic and might of the Egyptians.

Jesus is presented in the Qur'ān as a miracle in himself. His virgin birth,[17] healing of the sick, feeding of the hungry, and raising of the dead were life-giving miracles. Muslims see these miracles as affirmations of God's creative and life-giving power, against the denial of the resurrection and life to come by many Jews and non-Jews of Jesus' time. Furthermore, the miracles were performed at a time when Greek medicine, science, and philosophy were putting into question the sovereignty, power, and wisdom of God as the sole creator and Lord of the universe. The miracles of Jesus therefore served to assert the power of God over human science and wisdom.

The Qur'ān portrays Jesus as a messenger of God to the children of Israel, one who brought the message: "God is surely my Lord and your Lord. Worship Him, therefore; this is the straight way" (Q. 3:51). Jesus is for Muslims, and particularly the mystics among them, an example of a world-renouncing ascetic. He had no home or possessions, "his mount was his two feet and his servant his two hands." He was a wandering prophet of stern piety, but deep compassion for the poor, suffering, and oppressed.[18]

The Qu'rān presents the births of both Jesus and his mother as miraculous events, setting them apart from all other prophets and righteous men and women. The narrative of the birth of Mary has no parallel in the Gospels. It parallels the apocryphal Protevangelion of James. The birth of Jesus in contrast resembles in many ways the account of Luke's Gospel; like it, it is not a pure narrative but a celebratory account.

Mary's birth and early life are recounted in *Sūrah* 3, *al-'Imrān* ("The Family of 'Imrān"), verses 35–37:

> Remember when the wife of 'Imrān said, "My Lord, I have vowed to You that which is in my womb, a pure dedication. Accept it from me! You are the All-hearing, the All-knowing."
>
> When she gave birth to her she said, "Lord, I have delivered her, a female" – yet God knows best what she delivered – "and the male is not as the female. I have called her Mary, and I seek refuge in You for her and her progeny from the accursed Satan."
>
> Thus her Lord received her with a gracious acceptance and nurtured her into gracious maturity. He placed her in Zechariah's custody. Whenever Zechariah went into her prayer chamber, he found her well provisioned. He said, "Mary, whence comes this to you?" "From God," she said, "God surely provides whomsoever He wills without reckoning."

The birth of Jesus is related in *Sūrah* 19, *Maryam,* ("Mary"), verses 16–33:

> Mention in the Book, Mary when she withdrew from her people into an easterly place.
>
> She placed a curtain between her and them. Then We sent to her Our spirit who appeared to her as a well-proportioned man.
>
> She said, "I seek refuge in the All-merciful from you, if you have fear [of Allah]."
>
> He said, "I am the messenger of your Lord to grant you a pure male child."
>
> She said, "How could I have a child when no man has touched me nor have I been an unchaste woman?"
>
> He said, "Thus says your Lord, 'It is easy for Me for We shall make him a sign for human kind and a mercy from Us. This is a matter already decreed.'"
>
> She conceived him and withdrew with him into a far place.

> Her child-labor brought her to the trunk of a palm tree. She said, "Would that I had died before this and were something forgotten!"
> He [either Jesus or the angel] called out from beneath her saying, "Be not grieved for your Lord has placed beneath you a running stream.
> Shake the trunk of the palm tree towards you and it shall drop for you ripened dates ready to be picked.
> Eat and drink and be of good cheer; and when you see any human being say, 'I have vowed a fast for the All-merciful. I shall not speak today to any human being.'"
> She then brought him [Jesus] to her people in her arms. They said, "O Mary, you have done something disgraceful.
> O sister of Aaron, your father was not a wicked man nor was your mother an unchaste woman."
> She pointed to him but they said, "How can we speak to a child in the cradle?"
> He declared, "I am surely the servant of God; He gave me the Book and made me a prophet.
> He made me blessed wherever I am and enjoined upon me prayers and almsgiving so long as I live.
> He likewise enjoined kindness upon me towards my mother and did not make me a tyrannical wretch.
> Peace be upon me the day I was born, the day I shall die, and the day I will be raised up alive."

While the Qur'ān categorically denies Jesus' divinity and divine sonship (see Q. 5:116; 19:34–35; and 5:17 and 72), it presents him as a great prophet. His role extends far beyond his earthly existence as a prophet, into sacred history. Jesus, the Qur'ān insists, did not die but was lifted up by God to heaven (Q. 4:157–158). He will return at the end of time as "a sign of the knowledge of the Hour [that is the Day of Resurrection]" (Q. 43:61). He will kill the anti-Christ (*al-dajjāl*, "the deceiver") and establish true Islam on earth.

We have already noted that human history, according to the Qur'ān and Islamic tradition, is prophetic history. We have also noted that each prophet within this history must, in accordance with God's covenant with all prophets, prepare the ground for and support the prophet to come after him. Thus, in the Qur'ān Jesus announces the coming of Muḥammad saying: "O children of Israel, I am the messenger of God to you, confirming the Torah that was before me, and announcing a messenger who shall come after me whose name is Aḥmad" (Q. 61:6).

Muḥammad is presented in Muslim tradition as "the Prophet of the end of time." He is "the seal of the prophets," and the sacred book he received directly from God, the Qur'ān, is the final revelation. His way or life-example (*sunnah*) provides for Muslims the prophetic model that will guide history till its final consummation in the day of judgment. Likewise, the Qur'ān is believed by Muslims to be God's final revelation for humanity, confirming and supplanting all previous revelations (see Q. 5:48).

Although the Qur'ān attributes no miracles (aside from itself) to Muḥammad, later tradition ascribed to him a large number of other miracles, often exceeding those of other prophets. These miracles continue to inspire the pious with greater love for their Prophet. It is the Qur'ān, however, that is accepted as Muḥammad's enduring miracle.

THE QUR'ĀN: ITS HISTORY, TEACHINGS, AND ROLE IN THE COMMUNITY

Revelation was given to the Prophet Muḥammad over a period of twenty-two years. Both the Qur'ān and tradition assert that the angel Gabriel repeatedly appeared to the Prophet, often in human guise, and transmitted the words that came to constitute the verses and *sūrahs* ("chapters") of the Qur'ān. During the moment of revelation the Prophet would fall into a heightened state of consciousness, the effects of which were visibly manifest in his physical appearance and behavior. It is said that at times he sensed in his ears sounds like the ringing of a bell. These sounds were then apprehended by him as direct revelations from God, which he then conveyed to the people in human words.[19]

The first revelation to Muḥammad, as we have seen, was a command to "recite" or "read" (*iqra'*). The term *qur'ān* is derived from the same tri-lateral root, *q / r / a*, meaning "to read" or "to recite." The Qur'ān is therefore a sacred book meant to be recited or chanted aloud, not silently perused or read. The "reading" of it demands an oral recitation that imitates its actual revelation to Muḥammad.

As revelations came to the Prophet, he immediately dictated them to one of a group of men known as "the scribes of revelation." He did this because he was, according to the Qur'ān and Muslim tradition, an unlettered (*ummī*) prophet, that is he could neither read nor write. This fact constitutes for Muslims an incontrovertible proof of the truth that the words that Muḥammad conveyed to his people were not his own, but were revealed to him by God. It is also understood to mean that his mind was not contaminated by human wisdom. Rather it was a pure receptacle for the divine word in the same way that Mary's virginity means for Christians that her body was a pure vessel fit to receive Christ, the Word of God.

In fact there is an interesting parallel between Christ and the Qur'ān. Christ is, for Christians, the incarnate Word of God. For Muslims, the Qur'ān is an earthly exemplar of the eternal word of God. While the Qur'ān is, like Christ, the eternal divine word, it does not play a role in the creation of the world. It is the eternal word of God preserved for moral and spiritual guidance. It is an eternal book: "This surely is a glorious Qur'ān, preserved in a well-guarded Tablet" (Q. 85:21–22).

In size, the Qur'ān is nearly that of the New Testament. It consists of 114 *sūrah*s, or "chapters," of varying length. The shortest, *sūrah* 108, consists of three brief verses, while the longest, *sūrah* 2, contains 286 long verses. The Qur'ān was revealed, literally "sent down," to Muḥammad in separate portions varying in length and content from one or a few verses dealing with one or several unrelated themes or ideas, to coherent and fairly lengthy *sūrah*s. The history of the process of revelation is closely related to the history of Muḥammad's mission and the creation of the first Muslim community.

Muḥammad began his prophetic mission within the framework of the Qur'ān. For twelve years in Makkah he recited the Qur'ān and, through it, preached faith in the one God, *Allāh*, warning his recalcitrant people of an impending divine chastisement which awaited them unless they mended their immoral and callous ways.

The *sūrah*s revealed during this period are known as the Makkan revelations. These *sūrah*s can be further categorized into the early, middle, and late Makkan *sūrah*s. The early Makkan *sūrah*s are generally brief admonitions couched in terse and powerful verses. The later ones, in contrast, are didactic narratives or illustrative tales of earlier prophets and their communities. Through stories, parables, and exhortations, the Qur'ān aims at creating a society united by faith, "an *ummah* enjoining good conduct and dissuading from evil and indecent behavior" (Q. 3:110).

This aim became even more intensely focused in Madīnah where the Prophet was no longer the powerless preacher of Makkah, but a law-giver and head of the new Islamic commonwealth. The *sūrah*s revealed in Madīnah are fewer in number but longer than those revealed in Makkah. They consist largely of lengthy discourses on the moral, social, and political affairs of the community, legal pronouncements, and polemical arguments against religious and political opponents of the Muslim state and its faith. The change of idiom, however, did not constitute a break in the Prophet's mission, nor did it affect the essential message of the Qur'ān.

In Madīnah the Qur'ān becomes intimately tied to the life of the community. Verses are often revealed in answer to questions or special circumstances touching the daily realities of the people. Theological and social issues regarding the "People of the Book," Jews and Christians, are hotly argued and relations between the Muslim community and members of these two communities are regulated. Other laws concerning marriage and divorce, child rearing, and inheritance are promulgated. Likewise, laws governing cases of retaliation and compensation for injury or death are instituted as a substitute for the pre-Islamic custom of vendetta. Laws pertaining to retribution for theft and highway robbery, adultery, and false witness, unfounded accusation of a chaste man or woman of indecent conduct, and other offenses are legislated.

In short, the Qur'ān is not only the primary source of moral and religious guidance for the Muslim community, it is also its legal, political, and social constitution. It may therefore be argued that while the Christian Church produced its canon of scripture as part of its tradition and witness, the Qur'ān produced the Muslim community and shaped its tradition and history.

As a heavenly book, the Qur'ān is believed by Muslims to be immutable, preserved by God in the "mother of the Book," or source of all revelation. But as an earthly book or *muṣḥaf*, "preserved between the two covers," the Qur'ān has not only shaped Muslim history – it has been shaped by it.

When the Prophet died in 632, ten years after he migrated from Makkah to Madīnah, the Qur'ān was scattered in fragments and in partial private collections written on stones, bones, palm leaves, and skin parchments. Private collections varied in length, form, and content. Minor, but often significant variations in the reading of certain words or phrases existed as well. These variant readings persisted and finally became identified with specific Qur'ān readers of the first and later generations of Muslim scholars. As Islam spread beyond Arabia, major disagreements in reading and actual grammatical mistakes by reciters led to a call for an official collection to be used throughout the Islamic domains.

This task may have been initiated by Abū Bakr, the first caliph or successor to the Prophet as head of the Muslim community. Abū Bakr is said to have been motivated by the deaths of many Qur'ān reciters in the wars of apostasy (to be discussed in chapter 4 below). The reasoning is that although the Qur'ān had been preserved in books it had, from the beginning, been primarily kept in "the breasts of men [and women]" known as Qur'ān reciters. The death of a large number of oral transmitters of the Qur'ān could have resulted in the loss or grave distortion of the sacred text.

The process of producing an official and universally recognized codex (*muṣḥaf*) of the Qur'ān was completed under the aegis of the third caliph 'Uthmān b. 'Affān (r. 24–35/644–656), within twenty years of the Prophet's death. Tradition asserts that while the verses of each individual *sūrah* were arranged by the Prophet at Gabriel's instruction, the order of the *sūrah*s as it has come down to us was fixed by the committee appointed by 'Uthmān to compile the official *muṣḥaf*, or recension of the Qur'ān.

Except for *sūrah*s 8 and 9, the 114 *sūrah*s of the *muṣḥaf* are separated from one another by the invocation, "In the name of God, the All-merciful, the Compassionate" (*bism-illāh al-raḥmān al-raḥīm*). Since that time, the Qur'ān has remained unaltered except for some orthographic adjustments having to do with vocalization and some minor reordering of certain verses. This process culminated in the Royal Egyptian edition, produced in the 1930s, which remains the most widely accepted edition of the Qur'ān.

In outward form and structure, the Qur'ān does not present a unified and coherent narrative with beginning, middle, and end. Rather, it reflects the gradual, often circumstantial and long process of its revelation. Furthermore, the Qur'ān served as a practical moral and legislative guide for the Prophet and his nascent community. It is neither a story with a well-defined and developed plot, nor is it a well-argued philosophical or theological treatise. Behind this apparent disunity and incoherence, however, there is a clearly discernible unity of message, purpose, and worldview. It is a book of moral and spiritual guidance.

The Qur'ān urges Muslims to ponder its verses in order to discern its divine authorship and inner unity (See Q. 4:82, 47:24, and 38:29). The community has therefore dedicated some of its best minds to the task of understanding and interpreting the Qur'ān. The result has been a long and rich history of exegetical literature which began in the second/eighth century and continues to the present.

By the fourth/tenth century, Qur'ān interpretation (*tafsīr*) was developed into a science with a number of ancillary fields of study. These include the grammatical and general linguistic structure of the Qur'ān, the meaning or purport of its metaphors and parables, and the historical and hagiographic contexts of its stories. The term *tafsīr* means "unveiling," or elucidating the meaning of a text. The primary sources for the sciences of *tafsīr* are the Qur'ān itself, Prophetic tradition, and the opinions of the Prophet's Companions and their successors.

Most important for Muslims has always been the need to understand and live by the precepts, commands, and prohibitions of the Qur'ān, but these have not always been self-evident. For instance, it was observed above that the arrangement of the *sūrah*s of the Qur'ān was fixed by its original compilers. They generally placed the longest *sūrah*s first, after the opening (*al-fātiḥah*) *sūrah*, and the shortest *sūrah*s last. This meant that the earliest *sūrah*s (the shortest) came at the end, and this made it impossible to determine with certainty the chronology of the Qur'ān. Yet it is important for jurists to place the various revelations in their historical context in order to determine whether a particular ruling is abrogated by a later ruling, or itself abrogates an earlier one. It is also important for historians to precisely relate certain revelations to the appropriate events in the Prophet's career in Makkah and Madīnah. The Qur'anic science developed for this purpose is known as knowledge of the occasions of revelation (*asbāb al-nuzūl*) of the *sūrah*s and verses of the sacred text.

Qur'ān interpretation, like the Qur'ān and the Prophetic tradition, is an orally transmitted legacy. In fact, at least ideally, interpretation of the Qur'ān should always be based on Prophetic tradition or the opinions of the Companions. In reality, however, every legal or theological school, religious trend, or political movement in Muslim history sought to find in the Qur'ān its primary support and justification. The result has been a wide exegetical diversity reflecting the historical development of the Islamic tradition, its sects and legal schools, mystical and philosophical movements, as well as its hagiography and popular piety.

Despite the multiplicity of interpretations, the Qur'ān's centrality as the locus of interpretation has united Muslims and given their lives meaning. I have already touched on the Qur'anic worldview in my discussion of the Islamic view of human history and God's role in it. Since I shall return to this important subject frequently in the course of this presentation, it will be useful to now examine a few of the many major themes of the Qur'ān. And it is appropriate that I begin this brief discussion with the Qur'anic concept of God. This will then help to further elucidate the Qur'anic view of creation and its purpose and humankind's special place in it.

The Qur'ān presents its view of God not in any clearly formulated theological statement or creed, but rather in direct and unambiguous declarations of faith in the one and only God, creator and sovereign Lord over all his creation. The following brief *sūrah* known as "Sincere Faith" (*ikhlāṣ*) or "Divine Oneness" (*tawḥīd*) is regarded by Muslims as the clearest expression of their faith:

> Say: God, He is One (*aḥad*).
> God is the eternal refuge (*ṣamad*).
> He neither begets, nor was He begotten.
> Nor is there any one equal to Him (Q. 112).

The first verse of the *sūrah* declares God's absolute transcendence in the word "*aḥad*" which means "one," not only in number but also in uniqueness. This idea is again affirmed in the final verse: "Nor is there any one (*aḥad*) equal to Him." Here too the word *aḥad* is used to express God's absolute uniqueness and transcendence over his creation.

The second verse proclaims God's power, mercy, and providence in the word *ṣamad*, which literally means "solid," the opposite of hollow. The meaning is that God is as dependable as a hard and immovable rock. He is the only source of strength, help, and mercy. He is the only true object of trust, the one to whom the people of faith must turn for support in times of adversity and misfortune.

Finally, the *sūrah* affirms God's eternity and immutability in the statement "He neither begets, nor was He begotten." Birth implies composition, decay, and death and it also implies multiplicity. For Muslims, God is above any such creaturely phenomena. Islamic tradition insists that God is the merciful creator and sustainer of all things. It rejects the concept of God as father to any one of his creatures on the grounds that such an idea violates the principle of his absolute uniqueness, transcendence, and sovereignty.

Muslims believe that God, in his essence, is unknowable, inconceivable. He is above all categories of time and space, form and number, or any other material or temporal attributions. Yet he can be known through his attributes, called in the Qur'ān "God's most beautiful names." These divine attributes are manifested in the creation, in power and mercy, life and knowledge, might and wisdom. The Qur'ān declares:

> He is God other than whom there is no god, Knower of the unknown and the visible, He is the All-merciful, the Compassionate.
> He is God other than whom there is no god, the King, the Holy One, the Peace, the Faithful, the Guardian, the Majestic, the Compeller, the Lofty One (Q. 59:22–23).

As do Judaism and Christianity, Islam affirms that God is a moral and jealous god who abhors sin and wickedness and tolerates no other gods beside him. The purpose of all things in creation is to manifest his glory, power, and wisdom. While the rest of creation proclaims God's praise by its very nature, human beings and the *jinn*, as rational creatures, must actively choose worship and show faith through action.[20] The ultimate end of human existence is to worship God in righteousness, gratitude, and obedience. God says in the Qur'ān, "I have not created the *jinn* and humankind except that they should worship me" (Q. 51:56).

Human worship is, according to the Qur'ān, both personal and communal. It is expressed in ritual, moral, and social obligations that must be fulfilled by each individual alone and by the community as a whole. Consequently not only each individual but also the community is collectively responsible before God and therefore is rewarded or punished for its good or evil conduct, either in this world or in the hereafter. The Qur'ān conceives of all orders of creation as communities similar to those of humankind: "There is not a beast in the earth, nor a bird that flies with its two wings, but that they are communities like you" (Q. 6:38). Therefore, not only human beings, but animals too will be assembled on the Day of Resurrection for the final judgment.[21]

In anticipation of the Day of Resurrection, the Qur'ān calls humanity to righteousness. Righteousness, as described in the Qur'ān, consists in faith, good works, and worship. These three elements are so closely interrelated that no one of them can be truly fulfilled without the others. A fourth and equally important element that appertains to the individual person of faith is the inner intention behind an act of worship or a righteous deed. The Qur'ān broadly defines righteousness first as faith in God, his angels, Books, prophets, and the last day; second, as the giving of one's wealth, however cherished it may be, to the orphans and the needy, and for the ransoming of slaves or war captives. Righteousness also means being patient and steadfast in times of misfortune and hardship and in times of war. And finally, righteousness requires that one be honest in fulfilling one's covenant with others.[22]

All these concepts, the oneness of God and his attributes, the importance of worship, the meaning of righteousness – the message of the Qur'ān – all these and other major themes of the sacred text have united Muslims in a community of faith. In itself the Qur'ān also binds Muslims to each other and to God.

The Qur'ān presents itself, and is regarded by Muslims, as an inimitable miracle of speech. It is Muḥammad's chief miracle and in its own words challenges the Arab masters of eloquence and poetic genius, as well as all of humankind and the *jinn*, to invent ten, or even one like its *sūrahs* (Q. 2:23–24; 10:38; 11:13). Although other miracles were attributed to the Prophet by later hagiography, the Qur'ān is held to be his supreme and everlasting miracle.

The language of the Qur'ān came to set the standard for Arabic literary expression and has permeated all other Islamic languages with its powerful and eloquent words and phrases. The words of the Qur'ān are recited in a child's ear at birth for blessing. They are recited to bless and seal a marriage contract or a business deal, to celebrate a successful venture, or to express sorrow and solace in times of misfortune. Through the art of calligraphy, the words of the Qur'ān have become the focus of Islamic art and are used to decorate Muslim homes, mosques, and public buildings.

The Qur'ān is ever present in the community through its recitation, daily and on most special public occasions, on radio and television throughout the Muslim world. Qur'ān recitation, which was developed into an independent art, exercises a hypnotic power over its listeners. There are basically two styles of Qur'ān recitation. The first is *tartīl*, which is a slow and measured chant. It is generally used by beginners and those who wish to learn a simple style of recitation. The second is *tajwīd*, which literally means "to make something beautiful." It is an embellished style wherein the skill, knowledge, and virtuosity of the reciter are displayed. Qur'ān reciters often achieve great fame and occupy a place of honor in Muslim society.

For private devotional recitation, the Qur'ān is divided into thirty parts of equal length to be recited over a month, particularly during the fasting month of Ramaḍān. The completion of a full recitation of the Qur'ān by a child is an occasion of great celebration for the entire family and an act of merit and blessing for everyone.

Tradition asserts that a person's station in Paradise will be determined by the number of verses of the Qur'ān he or she memorizes in this life. On the Day of Judgment, the Qur'ān will intercede with God on behalf of those who recite it and live by its precepts in this world and will condemn those who neglect it. The Qur'ān is described in the

Prophetic tradition as a rope or link between heaven and earth, between God and the pious. With its words they pray to God and its recitation accompanies them to their final resting-place.

The Qur'ān has been a vital and unifying force in an otherwise diverse religious and cultural tradition. It is the primary source of Islamic faith and morality, law and piety. "It is indeed a noble Qur'ān in a treasured Book. None but the pure shall touch it" (Q. 56:78–79).

3

Faith and Worship

The primary mission of the Prophet Muḥammad was to preach faith in the one God. His political career and the state he founded were not meant to create an empire, but to establish a socio-political framework within which Islam as a religious system of faith and worship could be freely practiced and propagated. This system rests on faith in, and worship of, the one God, *Allāh.*

Allāh is not the name of any particular deity, but the Arabic name for God, "the Lord of all beings" (Q. 1:2), who demands faith and worship from all his rational creatures. Moreover, the name *Allāh* for God is used by Arabic-speaking Muslims, Christians, and Jews, and was also used by the pagan Arabs before Islam. It is misleading therefore to use the word "Allāh" to speak of God in any language other than Arabic.

It was observed earlier that although the Arabs before Islam recognized *Allāh* as the supreme creator God, he was not worshiped; nor did knowledge of him make any moral or spiritual difference in their lives. This long period of pre-Islamic Arab history is called by the Qur'ān and

Muslim tradition "the age of *jāhilīyah*" ("foolishness" or "ignorance"). *Jāhilīyah* is here meant to designate not only a state of ignorance or lack of knowledge (*'ilm*), but also a lack of moral consciousness, magnanimity, or prudence (*ḥilm*).[23] Thus Islam, as the alternative to *jāhilīyah*, stresses the equality of knowledge and righteous action as the two essential components of true faith.

The Qur'ān, particularly in the Madinan revelations, frequently addresses the Muslims with the words "O you who have accepted faith and perform good deeds." The Arabic word *imān* means faith, trust, and a personal sense of well-being and safety in God's providential care, mercy, and justice. On this level of inner personal commitment, *imān* is synonymous with *islām* ("submission") as the total surrender of human will and destiny to the will of God.

This personal faith must, according to the Qur'ān and Prophetic tradition, be manifested in individual and social goodness, moral conduct, and civic responsibility. It is an ongoing process of personal and social reform. The demand to translate inner faith into concrete social responsibility is clearly expressed in the Qur'anic injunction that Muslims "enjoin good and decent conduct and dissuade from evil and indecent behavior" (see Q. 3:104, 110, 114; 9:71, 112; and 31:17).

The opposite of *imān* is *kufr*, or rejection of faith. Faith is to know the truth and assent to it in the heart, profess it with the tongue, and manifest it in concrete acts of charity and almsgiving. *Kufr*, on the other hand, is to know the truth but willfully deny or obscure it by acts of rebellion against the law of God, which is believed by Muslims to be revealed in the Qur'ān and promulgated by the Prophet. The word *kufr* in fact literally means to "cover up," "deny," or "obscure."

Between the "people of faith" (*mu'minūn*) and the "rejecters of faith" (*kāfirūn*) stand, in the view of the Qur'ān, the hypocrites (*munāfiqūn*) who waver between faith and rejection of faith and thus create sedition and discord in the community. During the Prophet's rule in Madīnah, the hypocrites were, as described in the Qur'ān, people motivated purely by narrow self-interest and thus lacking the commitment of faith which often called for the sacrifice of wealth and life in the cause of Islam and its emerging community. The Qur'ān represents the hypocrites as those who say one thing but in their hearts hold its opposite (see Q. 2:8–15 and 61:3).

The Qur'ān makes a further important distinction between Islam and faith. Islam is a religious and legal institution that governs the daily affairs of the community. Faith, on the other hand, is an inner conviction that governs a person's relationship with God in worship and his or her moral relations with others. Islam is a religious, social, and legal identity that signifies membership in the worldwide Muslim *ummah*, with all the rights and responsibilities this membership entails; faith is a personal commitment to a way of life and worship whose sincerity or insincerity God alone can judge.

This distinction is sharply drawn with regard to the nomadic Arabs who are reported in the Qur'ān to have said "We have accepted faith (*imān*)." The Prophet is commanded to say to them, "Do not say 'we have accepted faith'; rather say 'we have accepted Islam,' for faith has not yet entered your hearts" (Q. 49:14). This was a harsh judgment of the nomadic Arabs as too fickle to accept the discipline of the new ethical religious system – they accepted Islam but without accepting the responsibilities of faith. This lack of true commitment to their faith made them, from the Qur'anic point of view, hypocrites, not people of faith.

FAITH AND ACTION

Faith and Islam converge in worship of God and service to others. An important and widely accepted Prophetic tradition defines *imān* as faith in God, his angels, his books and prophets, and the last day (see Q. 2:177, 285). "Islam" is to declare or bear witness that there is no god except God and that Muḥammad is the Messenger of God; to establish regular worship; to pay the *zakāt* (obligatory alms); to observe the fast of Ramaḍān; and to perform the *ḥajj* (pilgrimage to Makkah).[24]

In other Prophetic traditions, Islam, as a fully integrated way of life, is defined as acts of worship (*'ibādāt*) and human relations or transactions (*mu'āmalāt*). Thus transactions, such as buying and selling, establishing any agreement or pact with others, as well as family, social and international relations, should be legislated and conducted in accordance with the moral dictates of faith. Faith as a comprehensive framework of worship and moral conduct is implicit in a response that the Prophet is said to have given to the question "What is faith?": "Faith," he said, "is seventy odd branches, the highest of which is to say 'There is no god except God' and the lowest to remove a harmful object from the road."[25]

Above Islam and *imān* stands *iḥsān* ("doing good"). On the level of human interrelations, *iḥsān* is a concrete manifestation of both *islām* and *imān*. On the level of the personal relationship of the man or woman of faith with God, *iḥsān* constitutes the highest form of worship. In the course of defining Islam and *imān*, a well-attested Prophetic tradition states that "*iḥsān* is to worship God as though you see Him, for if you do not see Him, He sees you."[26]

From the preceding discussion it should be clear that not every Muslim is a man or woman of faith (*mu'min*), but every person of faith is a *muslim*. Furthermore, a Muslim who believes in all the principles of Islam may not necessarily be a righteous person, a doer of good (*muḥsin*), but a truly good and righteous person is both a *muslim* and a true person of faith.

It may be further concluded that neither Islam as a social and legal identity, nor *imān* as an underlying faith commitment can exist without the framework of personal and communal worship. This is because worship is the devotional and social context within which the daily life of a Muslim moves. It is to this aspect of ritualistic practice that we must now turn.

THE FIVE PILLARS OF ISLAM

It has been rightly observed by Western as well as Muslim scholars that Islam is more concerned with practice than with dogma and seeks orthopraxy over orthodoxy. In our discussion of the Qur'ān we noted that the purpose of all rational creatures – the angels, the *jinn*, and humankind – is to worship God and serve him. Thus acts of worship (*'ibādāt*) are obligatory duties (*farā'iḍ*) incumbent on all Muslims. The regular performance of these obligations in sincere faith and obedience to God assures the pious of salvation and the bliss of Paradise on the Day of Resurrection; neglect of them is an act of rebellion against God and therefore leads to eternal perdition.

According to a well-attested Prophetic tradition, Islam is built on five pillars.[27] The five pillars are the fundamental principles or foundations of Islamic faith and worship. All except the first are both personal and communal enactments of worship. Without them, Islam, as an all-embracing religious, social, political, and economic system, cannot stand.

The first of the five pillars is the *shahādah*: "I bear witness that there is no god except God, and I bear witness that Muḥammad is the messenger (*rasūl*) of God." The *shahādah* is not a creed, a philosophical argument, or even a statement of faith. It is simply a testimony or witness to what the Qur'ān asserts to be a primordial fact: "God bears witness that there is no god but He, as do the angels and those who are possessed of knowledge" (Q. 3:18). This means that knowledge of God's oneness is true knowledge; it is true *islām*, the antithesis of *jāhilīyah.*

The *shahādah* consists of two declarations. The first, affirming the oneness of God, expresses the universal and primordial state of faith (*fiṭrah*) in which every child is born. The Prophet is said to have declared: "Every child is born in this original state of faith (*fiṭrah*); then his parents turn him into a Jew, Christian or Zoroastrian, and if they are Muslims, into a Muslim."[28]

It seems that initially only this first declaration was required of non-Muslims for admittance into the Muslim *ummah*. Belief in the oneness of God was assumed to be a given for the People of the Book (Jews, Christians, and others) and was the pre-condition for their being granted the legal status of protected peoples. This conclusion is supported by another widely accepted tradition in which the Prophet says:

> I have been commanded to wage war against people until they say "There is no god except God." When they say this, they protect from me their lives and their possessions, except what is required of them [as the *zakāt* alms], and their final reckoning is with God.[29]

The second declaration of the *shahādah*, affirming the apostleship of Muḥammad, signifies a person's acceptance of the truth of Muḥammad's claim to prophethood and, hence, the truth of his message. It is the assertion of one's Islamic identity and one's commitment to live by the law (*sharī'ah*), which Muḥammad is believed by Muslims to have brought from God. Thus, while the first declaration of the *shahādah* is meant to unite all those who believe in God in the affirmation of his oneness and the repudiation of all other gods, the second is meant to unite all those who accept Islam by the affirmation of their commitment to live by its institutions.

The second pillar of Islam is the ritual of obligatory prayers (*ṣalāt*), which every rational Muslim must regularly observe. The *ṣalāt* prayers are distinguished from other devotional acts, such as meditations and personal supplicatory prayers. For, while the latter are voluntary devotions and may be offered at any time, the former must be performed five times in a day and night – at dawn, noon, mid-afternoon, sunset, and after dark.

The *ṣalāt* prayers must always be preceded by ritual washing: either a partial washing, *wuḍū'*, or a washing of the entire body, *ghusl*. *Wuḍū'*, meaning "to make pure" or "radiant," involves washing the face, rinsing the mouth and nostrils, washing the hands and forearms to the elbows, passing one's wet hands over the head, and wiping the feet for

Shi'ites, or alternatively washing the feet up to the ankles for Sunnis. If water is unavailable or too scarce, clean sand or earth may be used. This is called *tayammum. Ghusl* is used to remove major impurities, such as those caused by sexual relations, menstruation, or direct contact with either blood or a dead corpse.

Fulfilling the obligation of *ṣalāt* is a personal act of worship performed within a communal ritual of worship. Thus five times a day, on radio and television, from loudspeakers and from high minarets, a *mu'adhdhin* chants the call to prayer (*adhān*):

> God is most great. I bear witness that there is no god except God, and I bear witness that Muḥammad is the Messenger of God. Hasten [all of you Muslims] to the prayers! Hasten to success! [Shi'ite Muslims insert the phrase: Hasten to the best action!] God is most great. There is no god except God.

In a melodious voice, repeating each phrase at least two times for greater effect and emphasis, he invites the faithful to pray together in a mosque behind a prayer leader (*imām*), or at home in solitude. But whether praying alone or in congregation, a Muslim is always conscious of countless other men and women engaged in the same act of worship.

The *ṣalāt* prayers are actually a combination of prayer recitation and prayer through formalized movement. As the words of prayer are uttered, worshipers complete a cycle of standing, bowing, standing, prostration, kneeling, prostration, and standing again. Each of these cycles or units of spoken and enacted prayer is called a *rak'ah.* The dawn *ṣalāt* consists of two cycles, the noon and mid-afternoon of four each, the sunset prayer of three, and the night prayers of four.

The ritual of *ṣalāt* begins with the proclamation of consecration (*takbīrat al-iḥrām*) "God is most great" (*allāhu akbar*). Just as ritual washing before prayers has an effective inner aspect, physical purity symbolizing an interior state of inner purity, the proclamation of consecration outwardly announces a person's faith-commitment while signifying a total inner separation from the world: a standing before God, as though in the balance for the last judgment.

The obligatory words recited during each *rak'ah* of the *ṣalāt* are largely liturgical and mostly consist of passages of the Qur'ān. Apart from some moments of contemplation and personal supplication, and during every *sajda*, if wanted, the prayers are fixed and are repeated in every *ṣalāt* worship. Most prominent is the Qur'ān's opening *sūrah*, *al-fātiḥah* ("The Opening"), a prayer whose function is similar in some ways to the "Lord's Prayer" for Christians. It reads:

> In the name of God, the All-merciful, the Compassionate,
> Praise be to God, Lord of all beings,
> The All-merciful, the Compassionate;
> King [or master] of the Day of Judgment.
> You alone do we worship, and to you alone do we turn for help.
> Guide us to the straight way,
> The way of those upon whom You have bestowed Your grace,
> Not those who have incurred wrath, nor those who have gone astray.

"The Opening" is recited in every *rak'ah*, and therefore at least seventeen times in a day and night.

Unlike Judaism and Christianity, Islam has no sabbath or day of rest. For Muslims Friday is, as its Arabic name *jumu'ah* ("day of assembly") implies, the day of gathering for congregational prayers. The Qur'ān enjoins upon all Muslims: "O you who have faith, when the call to prayer is made on Friday [at noon], hasten to the remembrance of God and leave off all manner of trade. But when the prayer is accomplished, disperse in the land and seek God's bounty" (Q. 62:9–10). The Friday congregational prayers consist of two short sermons that substitute for the first two *rak'ahs* of the noon prayer, followed by the remaining two *rak'ahs*. Friday sermons usually deal with religious, moral, and political issues. They have often served as platforms for launching social, political, and military activities and movements. This is particularly so in today's troubled Muslim world.

The Islamic place of worship is called *masjid*, "place of prostration in prayer," or *jāmiʿ*, which literally means "the gatherer." The English "mosque" is a distortion of the word *masjid.* Friday prayers, as well as all other congregational prayers, are usually performed in a mosque, or any place temporarily designated for that purpose.

Other traditional congregational prayers are those performed on the first days of the two major festivals, *ʿīd al-fiṭr* and *ʿīd al-aḍḥā*, which begin at the end of Ramaḍān and of the *ḥajj* respectively. Where possible, these prayers are held in the open, so as to allow for the largest possible number of participants. In many countries the Prophet's birthday is another occasion for Muslims to come together to prayer in the mosque and to listen to Qur'ān recitations and religious and political speeches extolling the Prophet and calling upon the Muslim community and its leaders to emulate his example.

The *ṣalāt* prayers are obligatory for all Muslims, insofar as they are able to perform them. On a journey or in a state of fear in battle, the noon, mid-afternoon, and night *ṣalāt* may be shortened from four to two *rakʿahs*. If a person is sick and unable to perform all the genuflections and prostrations of the prayers, they may pray in any position, sitting or lying down. During menstruation women are exempt from prayers until they are cleansed. Children below the age of reason and persons suffering from mental illness, senility, or dementia are likewise excused.

Among the rituals of Islam, the *ṣalāt* prayers were the first to be instituted. During the Prophet's Makkan period, and until the second year of the *hijrah*, Muslims prayed facing the holy city of Jerusalem. Then the Prophet was ordered by God to change the direction of prayer (*qiblah*) to the "sacred House," that is, the Kaʿbah of Makkah (see Q. 2:142–150). Since that time, Muslims throughout the world have faced Makkah in prayer.

We noted earlier the close relationship between worship of God and service to the poor and needy. The Qur'ān itself frequently couples the observance of regular worship with almsgiving (see Q. 2:43; 5:55; and

9:71). This relationship is realized in the third pillar of Islam, namely the paying of *zakāt* (obligatory alms).

The *zakāt* is an obligatory welfare tax, to be paid annually by all adult Muslims on all surplus earnings. The tax is set at two and a half percent of the value of all wealth accumulated during the year above a certain minimum. This includes savings earned through trade, any other gain – be it financial or in livestock, agricultural produce, or revenues from real estate – and all other revenues.

The root meaning of the word "*zakāt*" is "to become purified" or "be increased." Hence, by offering the *zakāt* Muslims purify themselves from greed and attachment to material possessions, while the wealth spent assures the giver of blessing and increase in this world and rich rewards in the next. In the meantime, the poor and the needy and the community in general all benefit.

During the early centuries of Islam, when the community was cohesively controlled by a central authority, the *zakāt* revenues were kept in a central treasury and disbursed for public, educational, and civic projects, for care of the orphaned and the needy, and for the ransoming of Muslim war captives. Now that the Muslim world is divided into so many independent nation states, most of which have adopted some form of modern Western taxation, the giving of *zakāt* has become a largely voluntary act that some fulfill through donations to private organizations and others ignore.

The fourth pillar of Islam is the fast of Ramaḍān. Fasting is recognized in the Qur'ān as a universal form of worship prescribed for all previous peoples. The Prophet is believed to have observed a variety of voluntary fasts in Makkah and these are still honored by many pious Muslims. Chief among these are the weekly Monday and Thursday fasts, as well as a monthly three day fast. In Madīnah, the Prophet saw the Jewish community observing the fast of Yom Kippur and enjoined it upon the Muslims. In the second year of the *hijrah*, and after the Battle of Badr which took place in the month of Ramaḍān of that year, the fast of Ramaḍān was instituted.

While prayers and almsgiving are frequently dictated by the Qur'ān, fasting during the month of Ramaḍān is decreed in a single passage, which reads in part:

> O you who have faith, fasting is ordained for you as it was ordained for those before you, that you may fear God ...
>
> Ramaḍān is the month in which the Qur'ān was sent down as a guidance to humankind, a manifestation of guidance and the criterion. Therefore whosoever among you witnesses the moon, let him fast [the month], but whosoever is sick or on a journey, an equal number of other days (Q. 2:183, 185).

Here Ramaḍān is accorded the honor of being the month in which the revelation of the Qur'ān took place. This may simply be a reference to the beginning of the revelation of the Qur'ān to Muḥammad on Mount Ḥirā. Tradition, however, goes far beyond the simple interpretation to insist that not only the Qur'ān, but other scriptures – the Torah, Psalms (*zabūr*), and the Gospel (*injīl*) – were also revealed in the month of Ramaḍān. No doubt, the victory of Badr added greatly to the prestige and holiness of this month. Associating the revelations given to other traditions with Ramaḍān has the effect of further enhancing the month and suggesting the triumph of Islam in a larger sense.

Ramaḍān is a month-long daily fast that starts at the break of each dawn and lasts until sunset. It is a complete abstention from food, drink, smoking, and sexual relations. Each day the fast is broken as the sun sets, by the call to prayer and by the sound of a cannon, in large cities. Before the break of true dawn the next morning a light meal is consumed. The Qur'ān declares, "Eat and drink until the white thread becomes distinct for you from the black thread of dawn" (Q. 2:187), after which the fast is resumed till sunset.

Before Islam, Arabs observed a lunar calendar wherein the year consisted of 354 days, in contrast with the 365-day solar year. A month was added every three years to keep festivals and sacred months in their proper seasons. The Qur'ān abolished the intercalary month and thus the fast of Ramaḍān and all other religious festivals rotate through the year.

When Ramaḍān occurs during the long summer days fasting can be a real hardship, particularly in the hot countries of Asia and Africa. In any case, all work activities are sharply curtailed during Ramaḍān. Those who have the means often fast and sleep most of the day and eat, drink, and engage in religious and social activities at night. This reversal of day and night is disapproved of because no one, neither rich nor poor, should escape the hardship of the fast.

Ramaḍān ends with a joyous three-day festival called *'īd al-fiṭr* (lit: "feast of the breaking of the fast"). Everyone is involved. Children often receive special gifts and wear new brightly colored clothes for the occasion. People exchange gifts and visits of goodwill and friendship. In some countries, the graves of loved ones are visited and there special sweets are distributed to the poor.

But before celebration, even before a person may eat the first breakfast after the long fast, the head of each family must give special alms for breaking the fast, called *zakāt al-fiṭr* (lit: "alms of the breaking of the fast"), on behalf of every member of the household. Thus the fast of Ramaḍān becomes not a mere ritual, but a concrete expression of concern for those who are in need.

In the course of elaborating the rules of fasting (*ṣiyām*) of Ramaḍān, the Qur'ān declares: "God desires ease for you, not hardship" (Q. 2:185). Hence, if they can afford it, those who cannot fast for reasons of chronic illness or old age must feed a poor person for every fast-day missed. Those who are sick, travelers, children, and pregnant, nursing, or menstruating women are exempted from the fast until they are able to make up the missed days.

Religious obligations are meant to discipline Muslims and to test their commitment to fulfilling the demands of their faith. This is why prayers or fasts missed for legitimate reasons must be made up later. The sincerity and determination of a person in their effort to obey God's law will determine their state in the life to come. Since, unlike Christianity, Islam has no outside agency of redemption, the only means by which a person can earn salvation is to live a life of sincere faith and righteous action and to hope in God's mercy.

The Qur'ān asserts, "God will not charge a soul except to its capacity" (Q. 2:286). Therefore, any divinely ordained obligation is and must be within the capacity of the person so obligated; otherwise God would be in the position of having commanded an individual to do something that he knows they cannot do. This would be an act of wrongdoing on God's part, which is impossible. The principle is clearly articulated in the Qur'ān with regard to *ṣalāt* and *zakāt* and again with regard to the *ḥajj*: "God has made pilgrimage to the House [i.e. the Ka'bah] a duty for humankind, those who can make their way to it" (Q. 3:97).

The *ḥajj* is the fifth pillar of Islam and the most public and popular of its rites of worship. According to the Qur'ān, after Abraham and his son Ishmael were ordered to build it, he instituted the pilgrimage to the Ka'bah, again at God's command (see Q. 22:26–29; 2:125–127). Although tradition carries the *ḥajj* ritual back into Islamic sacred history, to Abraham and even to Adam, it is certain that the *ḥajj* is an ancient rite that was observed by the Arabs long before Islam. Islam modified and reinterpreted this rite so as to fit into the Islamic monotheistic faith and model of prophetic history. Thus, most of its ritualistic elements symbolically reenact the experiences of Abraham, whom the Qur'ān declares to be the father of prophets and the first true Muslim.

The obligatory pilgrimage, the undertaking of which is incumbent on every Muslim at least once in his or her life, occurs during the official pilgrimage season and is a ritual enacted in four main parts: consecration (*iḥrām*); circumambulation (*ṭawāf*) of the Ka'bah; standing on 'Arafāt; and finally, the sacrificial offering on the day of sacrifice (*'īd al-aḍḥā*), after which pilgrims are released from consecration.

Before the gathering pilgrims reach the sacred precincts of Makkah, they exchange their regular clothes for two pieces of white linen, symbolic of the shrouds in which they will be wrapped for burial. With this act, they enter the state of consecration (*iḥrām*). They approach Makkah with the solemn proclamation:

> Here we come in answer to Your call, O God, here we come! Here we come, for You have no partner, here we come! Indeed, all praise, dominion and grace belong to You alone, here we come!

Once in Makkah, the pilgrims begin with the ritual of circumambulation (*ṭawāf*) of the Ka'bah and the running between the two hills of al-Ṣafā and al-Marwā. Hagar, Abraham's handmaiden and mother of his son Ishmael, is said to have thus run between these two hills in search of water for her dying child. After her seventh circuit, water gushed out at the child's feet and Hagar contained it with sand. This, according to Islamic tradition, is the ancient well of Zamzam, meaning "the contained water." The water of Zamzam is regarded by Muslims as sacred and pilgrims frequently take bottles of it to give as blessed gifts to family and friends.

Pilgrims often reach Makkah a day or two before the actual *ḥajj* ritual. In this case they enter into the state of consecration and usually perform the lesser pilgrimage (*'umrah*) first, which consists of the circumambulation and running rituals. The *ḥajj* proper begins on the eighth of Dhū al-Ḥijjah, the twelfth month of the Islamic calendar. It begins with the throngs of pilgrims setting out from Makkah for 'Arafāt, a plain located about thirteen miles east of the city. In accordance with the Prophet's practice (*sunnah*), most pilgrims spend the night at Mina, while others press on to 'Arafāt.

'Arafāt is a large plain on which stands the Mount of Mercy (*jabal al-raḥmah*), the goal of every pilgrim. As the sun passes the noon meridian on the ninth of Dhū al-Ḥijjah, pilgrims gather for the standing (*wuqūf*) on 'Arafāt. This is the central rite of the *ḥajj*. Men and women stand in solemn prayer and supplication until sunset, as though standing for judgment before God on the last day.

This rite also links the present moment backward in sacred history, to the time when Adam and Eve stood on the plain of 'Arafāt after their expulsion from Paradise. In fact popular piety derives the name "'Arafāt," meaning to "know" or "recognize," from the reunion of Adam and Eve on that spot where they "recognized" each other. It also recalls the time when, according to Muslim tradition, Abraham and his son Ishmael made the first *ḥajj* and prayed on the Mount of Mercy. It evokes the occasion of Muḥammad's only *ḥajj*, when he stood on 'Arafāt and gave his farewell oration affirming the brotherhood of all Muslims. Tradition also reports that on 'Arafāt the last verse of the Qur'ān was revealed: "Today have I perfected your religion for you, bestowed fully my grace upon you and accepted Islam as a religion for you" (Q. 5:3).

At sundown, the somber scene of prayer and supplication abruptly changes as the pilgrims pour forth from 'Arafāt to Muzdalifah. This sacred spot is located a few miles on the road back to Makkah. Here the pilgrims combine the sunset and evening prayers and gather pebbles for the ritual lapidation (stoning) at Minā the next day. The pouring forth (*ifāḍah*) from 'Arafāt to Muzdalifah, where pilgrims are enjoined "to remember God at the sacred monument (*al-mash'ar al-ḥarām*)" (Q. 2:198), is an ancient pre-Islamic rite to which Islam gave a special significance.

The tenth of Dhū al-Ḥijjah, the first of the four days of the Festival of Sacrifice (*'īd al-aḍḥā*), begins at Minā. Here the last of the pilgrimage rites are completed. Tradition has it that on his way from 'Arafāt to Minā, Abraham was commanded by God to sacrifice to God that which was dearest to him, his son Ishmael. Satan whispered to him three times tempting him to disobey God's command. Abraham's response was to hurl stones at Satan to drive him away. At that spot, called al-'Aqabah (meaning the "hard" or "steep road"), a brick pillar was erected to represent Satan. In emulation of Abraham, pilgrims gather early in the morning and each flings seven stones at the pillar. Two other pillars in Minā, representing the three temptations, are also stoned.

Following the ritual of stoning, the pilgrims offer a blood sacrifice, a lamb, goat, or camel, to symbolize the paradisal victim with which God ransomed Abraham's son (Q. 27:107). After this, the pilgrims end the state of consecration by ritually clipping a minimum of three hairs from their heads, or shaving their heads completely. The *ḥajj* ends with a farewell circumambulation of the Ka'bah and those who have not done so, or who wish to offer an additional *'umrah*, also complete the rites of the lesser *ḥajj* (*'umrah*).

Often pilgrims spend the four days of the festival of sacrifice in and around Makkah. They then visit the Prophet's tomb in Madīnah, as well as other sites associated with important events and personalities of early Islam. When possible, pilgrims visit Jerusalem, Islam's third holy city. Shi'ite Muslims visit the graves of the Imāms (descendants of the Prophet through his daughter Fāṭimah and cousin 'Alī b. Abī Ṭālib) in Madīnah, Iraq, and Iran.

The *ḥajj* experience marks a new stage in the life of a Muslim. Tradition asserts that a person returns from a sincerely performed *ḥajj* free from all sins, as on the day when they were born. Furthermore, pilgrims are henceforth marked out, as it were, with the title "*ḥājj*" before their names.

* * *

The five pillars of Islam are not mere obligations whose efficacy and meaning depend on mechanical observance and superficial understanding. Rather, they are to be interiorized and observed as expressions of personal faith and piety. Thus each of the five pillars has an outer and public obligatory dimension and an inner and private voluntary dimension. It is the combination of the public and private dimensions of each of the five pillars that makes them, together, the foundations upon which Islam as a religious system of faith and social responsibility, worship and piety rests.

Outwardly, uttering the *shahādah* legally safeguards a person's rights as a member of the Muslim community. Inwardly, however, it is meaningless unless it becomes a true expression of personal faith (*imān*) and righteous living (*iḥsān*). Without this inner dimension of the *shahādah*, Islam loses its meaning as a faith-tradition.

The inner dimension of the obligatory five daily prayers is the extra-devotional prayers called *nawāfil*. These devotional prayers are offered by pious Muslims in the quiet of the night or after obligatory prayers, as a way for the individual woman and man of faith to draw near to God.

The inner devotional aspect of *zakāt* is voluntary almsgiving (*ṣadaqah*). The Qur'ān calls *ṣadaqah* a loan given to God, which he will repay in manifold measure on the Day of Resurrection (Q. 57:11). Although charity must begin at home, that is with one's nearest blood relatives, *ṣadaqah* is not bound by any considerations of race, color, or creed. It must be given to the needy and the destitute, the orphan, the beggar, and the wayfarer, whoever they are. Even *zakāt*, when offered willingly for God's good pleasure, becomes *ṣadaqah*, an expression of a person's true righteousness.

The following brief *sūrah* links faith to action by linking the validity of prayer to the helping of others:

> Have you considered him who gives the lie to the [day of] Recompense!
> Such is he who repulses the orphan,
> And who does not urge the feeding of the needy.
> Woe to them who pray
> But who are negligent in their prayers;
> Those who make a show,
> And withhold assistance (Q. 107, *al-Mā'ūn* "Assistance").

The fast of Ramaḍān becomes a true act of worship when a person shares God's bounty with those who have no food with which to break their fast. True fasting is not only giving up the pleasures of food and drink, it is also abstaining from slander or any idle talk, as well as turning one's heart and mind to God in devotional prayers and meditations.

The voluntary aspect of the *ḥajj* obligation is the lesser *ḥajj* (*'umrah*), which may be performed at any time as an act of personal devotion. The *ḥajj* is regarded by Muslims as a form of resurrection or rebirth. This adds an inner intense and long-lasting devotional aspect to the ritual. It becomes imperative for a *ḥajjī* to strive to maintain the purity and freedom from attachment to material and vain pleasures attained through the experience of pilgrimage.

To sum up, Islam is a religion of continuous personal and societal reform through disciplined worship. The five pillars of Islam involve individual and communal obligations meant to provide the proper context for social, religious and, above all, spiritual reform. This process of disciplined reform is called *jihād*, "striving" or "struggling." The greatest *jihād* is the struggle of every person against the evil of their own carnal soul. However, depending on social and political circumstances, *jihād* can become an obligation as well as a process.

Jihād may be regarded as a sixth fundamental obligation (*farīḍah*) incumbent on every Muslim when social and religious reform is gravely hampered or the community's integrity threatened. In a situation where the entire Muslim *ummah* is in danger, *jihād* becomes an absolute obligation (*farḍ 'ayn*). Otherwise it is a limited obligation (*farḍ kifāyah*), incumbent upon those who are directly involved. These rules apply to armed struggle, or the *jihād* of the sword. This, and the struggle to reform society and rectify its social, moral, and political ills, is called *jihād fī sabīl allāh* ("struggle in the way of God").

Another and closely related form of *jihād* is *jihād bi-al-qur'ān*, that is *jihād* by means of the Qur'ān. The Prophet is commanded, "Do not obey the rejecters of faith but wage a great *jihād* against them by means of it [the Qur'ān]" (Q. 25:52). This form of *jihād* is as imperative today as it was in the time of the Prophet.

Yet the greatest and most fundamental striving is the *jihād* of the spirit, which was called by the Prophet "the greater *jihād*." It is *jihād fi-allāh*, "struggle in God." As God declares in the Qur'ān: "As for those who strive in Us, We shall guide them to Our ways" (Q. 29:69). These are the ways of peace, to which God shall "guide those who seek His good pleasure" (Q. 5:16).

The goal of true *jihād* is to attain a perfect harmony between *islām* (submission), *imān* (faith), and *iḥsān* (righteous living). "It is to worship God as though you see him." The well-known Gabriel *ḥadīth* puts an elaborate definition of Islam, *imān*, and *iḥsān* in the mouth of the angel Gabriel:

> While sitting with the Messenger of God one day, a man appeared before us with pure white clothes and exceedingly black hair. No signs of travel could be seen on him nor did any one of us know who he was. He sat so close to the Prophet that their knees touched ... He then said, "O Muḥammad, tell me what Islam is." The Prophet answered, "Islam is that you testify that there is no god except God and that Muḥammad is the messenger of God, that you establish regular prayers, offer the *zakāt*, fast the month of Ramaḍān and make the *ḥajj* pilgrimage if you can make your way thither. The man said, "You speak the truth ..." He then said, "Tell me what *imān* is." He [Muḥammad] answered, "It is to have faith in God, His angels, His books, His messengers and the last day, and to believe in divine decree, be it good or evil ..." The man then said, "Tell me what *iḥsān* is." The Prophet answered, "It is to worship God as though you see Him, and if you do not see Him, He sees you."[30]

4

The Formative Period of Muslim History

Within less than a century of the Prophet's death, the Muslim community came to administer the largest dominion the world had ever known. Having set forth the religious framework within which Islam developed as a world religion and world power, we should now examine some of the principal events and developments that preceded and led to this unique phenomenon in history.

The Prophet established the first Islamic commonwealth in Madīnah and fixed the ideal for any future Islamic state. It was a model that could never be fully emulated. Madīnah was a truly theocratic state headed by a prophet who was believed to rule in accordance with the dictates of an ongoing revelation of divine scripture, the Qur'ān. But the Prophet was described in the Qur'ān as the "seal of the prophets," understood to mean the last prophet: after Muḥammad no further revelation could be expected. No future leader would be seen to have access to the immediacy of divine direction and the authority it granted. This limitation might have been circumvented had the

Prophet left a comprehensive legal or political system, but he did not. What he did leave were the broad sources for a sacred law, in the Qur'ān and in his own life-example (*sunnah*).

Before he died, the Prophet Muḥammad laid the social and religious foundations for an Islamic commonwealth in Arabia. The fact that he sent a military force on an unsuccessful foray into Syrian Byzantine territory and then, shortly before his death, ordered another much larger expedition, indicates that he did hope for wider expansion. He did not, however, leave a political system capable of supporting a world-empire; nor did he either clearly designate a leader to succeed him or specify guidelines for choosing one.

The authority of the Prophet Muḥammad in Madīnah depended not only on his personal charisma and political wisdom, but also, and to a far greater extent, on his prophetic office. Furthermore, these two spheres of authority were never separated. Rather, his political and social power derived from his prophetic authority. For Muslims therefore, obedience to the Prophet was and remains tantamount to obedience to God.

Obedience to the Prophet is an essential component of the faith-commitment of Muslims. The Qur'ān categorically asserts: "No, by your Lord, they will not have faith until they accept you as judge in whatever conflict may arise among them, find no blame in what you decide and submit absolutely" (Q. 4:65). Muslims, the Qur'ān further enjoins, should refer all matters of dispute to God and to the Messenger (see Q. 4:59). In short, the exalted status and concomitant authority of the Prophet in the community is best indicated by the *shahādah*, which couples his name with God's name: "I bear witness that there is no god except God, and I bear witness that Muḥammad is the Messenger of God."

The Prophet appears to have never abused his authority. Rather, the Qur'ān counseled him to consult with the Muslims on social, political, and military matters; then, however, he was to resolutely act on his own decision, but without being rough or hard-hearted (see Q. 3:159). It may be concluded from all this that Muḥammad's role, even as a political leader and social arbiter, was so unique that it could be assumed by no other man.

The Qur'ān admonishes Muslims to obey God and to obey the Messenger and those who possess authority or command (*amr*) among them. From the trilateral root *a / m / r* is derived the word *amīr*, meaning "chief" or "commander." Hence the chief or elder of a tribe, or the head of a raiding expedition, is an *amīr*. This admonition therefore may have referred to heads of military expeditions, or to respected elders of the community. No other type of authority existed in the Arabian peninsula at that time. Who exactly was meant by "those who possess authority" became an urgent question upon the death of Muḥammad.

THE CRISIS OF AUTHORITY AND THE CALIPHATE (632–661)

The death of the Prophet, after a short illness in June 632, precipitated a major crisis that eventually led to a permanent ideological rift in the Islamic community. Most probably the Prophet died without clearly appointing a successor. Given his unique status and all-inclusive power, no one could in reality fulfill that role; but the community could not remain leaderless, nor did it lack for men desirous of taking leadership. In the absence of any direction from the Prophet as to how to decide from amongst themselves, the question of who held the right to leadership, and on what basis, became paramount. As will be seen, the various Muslim sects and schools that arose soon after the death of the Prophet based their theological and political claims on interpretations of the legitimacy, scope, and nature of post-Prophetic authority in the community.

That this issue was of crucial importance for the disparate tribes of Madinan society may be seen in the urgency and decisiveness with which it was treated. While the Prophet lay dead and unburied, a group of the Helpers (*anṣār*) of Madīnah met to elect a leader. Hearing of the meeting, three of the Immigrants (*muhājirūn*) and early Makkan Companions of the Prophet, Abū Bakr, 'Umar b. al-Khaṭṭāb, and Abū 'Ubaydah b. al-Jarrāḥ, all men of high status in the community, rushed to the scene. The men of Madīnah were divided along old tribal lines and could not agree among themselves on a candidate. From the other side, 'Umar argued for the priority of the Immigrants and particularly for the right of the Quraysh, the tribe of Muḥammad, to succeed the Prophet in leadership. In the ensuing commotion he offered his hand to Abū Bakr as a pledge of allegiance and others quickly followed suit. Thus Abū Bakr became the first "successor (*khalīfah*) of the Messenger of God."

The Muslims were a collection of tribes unified into a new kind of religious and social entity under Muḥammad. When he died, the fragility of the new alliance was revealed in the events surrounding the election of Abū Bakr. Abū Bakr was not elected in accordance with the principle of consultation (*shūrah*) clearly enunciated in the Qur'ān (see Q. 42:38). Nor was he chosen by a representative tribal council, which customarily chose the *shaykh* or *sayyid* (chief) of the tribe. Rather the election of Abū Bakr, from the beginning, illustrated a number of deep divisions in the community: among the Helpers (*anṣār*) of the Madinan tribes themselves; between the Helpers and the Makkan Immigrants (*muhājirūn*); and among the Immigrants themselves, with the Hāshimites (Muḥammad's particular clan) on one side, and other clans of the Quraysh on the other.

The notables of the Quraysh outside the clan of Hāshim favored Abū Bakr because he was one of them, and a highly respected Companion and father-in-law of the Prophet. The Hāshimites, being the nearest relatives of Muḥammad, expected that one of them would be chosen, specifically 'Alī Ibn Abī Ṭālib, the cousin and son-in-law of the Prophet and the first to accept Islam after Khadījah the Prophet's wife. At the time of the death of the Prophet, 'Alī was about thirty years old. It was therefore argued that he was too young for such an awesome office. Still 'Alī, with most of the men of Hāshim and many of the men of the Anṣār, remained opposed to Abū Bakr's election. In the interest of Muslim unity, however, everyone finally gave the pledge of allegiance to Abū Bakr.

Abū Bakr's rule was brief (632–634) but highly significant for the survival of Islam and the Muslim community. He had to consolidate his own authority over the community's social and religious organization and also to fight several pretenders to the prophetic office after Muḥammad's death. Most important among these was Musaylimah of the rival tribe of Banū Ḥanīfah of the district of Yamāmah, whom Muslims call "Musaylimah the liar." Moreover, a number of the nomadic tribes around Madīnah, objecting to Abū Bakr's appointment and considering their pact with the Muslim community to have ended with the death of its leader, refused to pay the *zakāt.* Sensing the danger in such fragmentation of the community, Abū Bakr insisted, "By God, were they now to withhold from me even the hobbling-cord of a camel that they had previously given as *zakāt* to the Messenger of God, I would fight them over it." And fight them he did.

These wars, known as the wars of apostasy (*riddah*), occupied most of Abū Bakr's two and a half year reign. Even though they initially threatened the very existence of the community, in the long run these wars helped lay firm foundations for an Islamic state in an otherwise semi-nomadic Arabian peninsula. They also trained and disciplined the highly motivated army which would eventually burst out of Arabia. The resulting vast conquests changed the course of world history, spread Islam far beyond its original home, brought rich revenues into the Muslim treasury, and turned the energies of the disaffected tribes of Makkah and Madīnah, at least for a while, away from their inter-tribal squabbles.

Abū Bakr's rule also marks the first steps towards the creation of a new governmental form, the caliphate. The caliphate as an institution has no clear basis in the Qur'ān. The few references to the caliphate or individual caliphs in Prophetic tradition are depictions of later conditions and views, projected back to the Prophet and his immediate Companions. The Qur'ān uses the term *khalīfah* in two related senses. The first is "steward" or "vicegerent," and is generally applied to Adam and his descendants (see Q. 2:30). The second signifies a ruler or judge. King David, who according to Islam was a prophet, is addressed in the Qur'ān: "O David, We have made you a *khalīfah* in the earth; judge justly therefore among the people" (Q. 26:38).

In both cases, a *khalīfah* is one who represents or acts on behalf of another. Hence, the stewardship (*khilāfah*) of Adam and the authority of David are both exercised on behalf of God. Inasmuch as Muḥammad also acted on behalf of God in the community, his political and administrative authority is believed to have been bestowed upon him by God. Therefore, whoever assumed his authority after him would, at least in theory, inherit his prerogative. For this reason Abū Bakr was called the successor or representative of the Messenger of God (*khalīfat rasūl allāh*). Abū Bakr's successor, 'Umar b. al-Khaṭṭāb, was at first called the "successor of the successor of the Messenger of God."

The institution of the caliphate, however, was devised by the elders of the Muslim community. It was essentially modeled on the function of a tribal *shaykh* or chief. A tribal chief had no special status or authority over the tribe. Rather he was a first among equals. His authority was therefore of a moral and advisory nature. But because of the conjunction of tribal and caliphal authority, the caliphal institution had, from the beginning, immense and concrete authority. And this authority had both religious and temporal dimensions. As a successor of the Prophet, and later as the representative of God (*khalīfat allāh*) on earth,[31] a caliph was a religious leader. As a chief or administrative head of the community, a caliph was an *amīr* or commander of the Muslims in times of war and peace.

Perhaps conscious of the temporal dimension of his office, 'Umar is said to have adopted the title "Commander of the Faithful" (*amīr al-mu'minīn*) instead of the more cumbersome "successor of the successor of the Messenger of God." This title was henceforth assumed by all caliphs as well as by revolutionary leaders claiming caliphal authority. Nevertheless, the caliph continued to function as the chief religious leader (*imām*) of the community. Where he could not actually lead the prayers, he was represented by his appointed deputy or governor, who functioned as a prayer leader on his behalf.

Before his death, Abū Bakr appointed as his successor 'Umar b. al-Khaṭṭāb, who had stood by him throughout his brief reign. 'Umar ruled for ten years, 634–644. He was the first actual administrator of an ever-expanding Muslim state. In order to handle foreign correspondence and treaties and efficiently distribute vast revenues in gifts and stipends to a rapidly growing Muslim population and army, 'Umar instituted state registers and adopted the *hijrī* dating of Islamic history. Thereafter, the first year of the Prophet's migration (*hijrah*) to Madīnah became year A.H. 1 (622 C.E.).

During 'Umar's reign Syria, Palestine (including Jerusalem), Egypt, modern day Iraq, and Persia were conquered and incorporated into the Islamic state. Soon all these provinces became important centers of Islamic learning and culture.

While leading the morning prayers at the Prophet's mosque in Madīnah, 'Umar was fatally stabbed by a disgruntled Persian slave. Before he died, he appointed a consultative committee of six men to elect a new caliph from among themselves. The two candidates who emerged were 'Alī b. Abī Ṭālib, who had already been passed over twice, and 'Uthmān b. 'Affān, a rich scion of the influential Umayyad clan of the Quraysh. After much wrangling 'Uthmān was chosen over 'Alī. This decision ushered in an era of political strife and religious dissension in an increasingly troubled Muslim state.

'Uthmān ruled for twelve years (644–656). He was a pious and generous man, a close Companion of the Prophet and twice his son-in-law. 'Uthmān was, however, too prone to favoring his own Umayyad relatives. As he grew older and weaker, he virtually became a malleable tool in their hands, one that they freely manipulated to their own advantage.

'Uthmān's nepotism and frequent abuse of authority violated basic Islamic principles of justice and fairness as well as Arab custom. They led to the first major sedition (*fitnah*) in the Muslim community.

'Uthmān's governor of Egypt was a close relative against whom the people brought sharp complaints, demanding his resignation. 'Uthmān was unable to deal decisively with this grave conflict and soon matters were completely out of hand. 'Uthmān, the caliph of the Muslims, was besieged in his home in Madīnah for over forty days by an angry mob of both Egyptian and local insurgents; finally, some men broke into the house and killed him. His blood-stained shirt was carried to Damascus, the capital of the province of Syria. There the governor Mu'āwīyah b. Abī Sufyān, an Umayyad relative of 'Uthmān, used it to agitate the people into demanding that revenge be exacted for 'Uthmān's blood. Mu'āwīyah accused the Prophet's Companions, particularly 'Alī, of being accomplices in the murder of the caliph, as they had failed to protect him from the mob brutality.

Fearing that things might deteriorate even further, the men of Madīnah unanimously acclaimed 'Alī as the fourth caliph (r. 656–661). Mu'āwīya, however, continued with even greater zeal to demand that 'Alī, as caliph, punish the murderers of 'Uthmān. 'Alī refused to accept this demand as a condition for the legitimacy of his authority. This led to the division of the Muslims into two camps, the party (*shī'ah*) of 'Alī and the partisans of 'Uthmān.

At the same time, two well-regarded Companions and notables of the Quraysh, Ṭalḥah and al-Zubayr, also opposed 'Alī's rise to power. They persuaded 'Āishah, the Prophet's young widow who herself held an old grudge against 'Ali, to join them in leading a revolt against him. Near Baṣrah in southern Iraq, 'Alī's forces met those of Ṭalḥah and Zubayr in the first bloody battle of Muslims against brother Muslims. The battle raged around 'Āishah's camel, hence it was called the Battle of the Camel. 'Alī's opponents were defeated, Ṭalḥah and Zubayr were both killed and 'Āishah was sternly reprimanded and returned to Madīnah.

Following these serious developments 'Alī moved the capital, perhaps temporarily, from Madīnah to Kūfah, an important garrison town on the edge of the desert in southern Iraq. This move was no doubt motivated by the fact that 'Alī had strong support in that region of Iraq. It was in fact in Kūfah that the Shī'ah, or party of 'Alī, began to develop as a distinct political and religious movement within the Muslim *ummah*.

'Alī was a man of high ideals. He rejected the compromises and diplomatic maneuvers that an intricate political office, as the caliphate had become, demanded. He was therefore intent on removing 'Uthmān's favored relatives from office and appointing in their stead men whom he considered to be morally upright. In the name of an authentic Islam, he called for the resignation of all his predecessor's appointees. Mu'āwīyah, who had been appointed by 'Umar as governor of Syria many years earlier and confirmed in his position by 'Uthmān, and who ruled as a traditional monarch over a highly urbanized and loyal population, refused to abdicate.

Leading a large but undisciplined force, 'Alī met Mu'āwīyah and his well-disciplined army at Ṣiffīn, between Iraq and Syria, in 657. After skirmishes and negotiations had dragged on for several months, a decisive battle was fought. Faced with certain defeat, Mu'āwīyah was advised by his friend and collaborator 'Amr b. al-'Āṣ, another well-known Companion, to have his men lift up leaves of the Qur'ān on the tips of their spears and call on God to judge between the two parties. 'Alī was convinced that this was simply a ploy by Mu'āwīyah to avoid defeat and so refused to end the fight.

A large group in his camp, however, insisted on stopping the bloodshed and negotiating peace. 'Alī finally yielded and two men, 'Amr b. al-'Āṣ (representing Mu'āwīyah) and a venerable and peaceful Companion Abū Mūsā al-Ash'arī (representing 'Alī), were appointed as arbiters and given a year to consult with the people and come up with a binding solution.

While 'Amr was a staunch supporter of Mu'āwīyah, Abū Mūsā had no such commitment to 'Alī and may have, in fact, preferred to see a new caliph elected by the Muslims. Thus the arbitration on which a large number of 'Alī's supporters had insisted failed. Abū Mūsā and 'Amr agreed to remove both 'Alī and Mu'āwīyah from office and let the Muslims elect a new caliph. However, after Abū Mūsā had in fact annulled 'Alī's caliphate, 'Amr revoked the agreement and affirmed Mu'āwīyah's claim to the leadership of the *ummah*.

Those of 'Alī's men who had insisted on arbitration realized their mistake and considered his acceptance of human arbitration as an act of unbelief (*kufr*). Their slogan was, "No judgment but God's judgment." They argued that both they and 'Alī had committed a grave sin: they, by insisting that he accept arbitration; he by conceding to them. They demanded that 'Alī repent as they had done and join with them in their fight against their common enemy, Mu'āwīyah. 'Alī would not accept the charge of unbelief and the men left his camp and turned against him and everyone who opposed their view. They were thus called *khawārij* (Kharijites), meaning "seceders" or "dissenters."

Based on the argument for Abū Bakr's election and the growing religious, social, and political significance of the caliphate, a Prophetic tradition asserting that the imams (i.e. caliphs) should be of the Quraysh gained wide circulation. The Kharijites opposed this dictum on the grounds of the equality of all believers. They thus argued that anyone who was a pious Muslim was fit for the caliphate, even if he was "an Abyssinian slave with a mutilated nose." They further argued that any Muslim who committed a grave sin was an unbeliever whose blood could be legally shed and whose property, wives and children were lawful war booty for Muslims.

The Kharijites did not present a plan for the reform of the civil and religious system of Muslim rule, but a radical alternative that could never be implemented. Their anarchical and highly individualistic ideology was in the end rejected by all Muslims, including the moderate wing of their own movement.

While they accepted the two elders, Abū Bakr and 'Umar, as legitimate and righteous caliphs, the Kharijites regarded 'Uthmān and 'Alī as infidels and repudiated their caliphates. They likewise declared Muʿāwīyah and his collaborator ʿAmr b. al-ʿĀṣ to be unbelievers. Having thus condemned Muslim society and all its institutions, they took to pillaging and indiscriminately killing anyone who disagreed with them, in the name of what they considered to be true Islam. The Kharijites were also, however, pious men who spent long night hours in prayer and recitation of the Qur'ān and who strictly adhered to the precepts and obligations of the faith.

After repeated attempts to convince the Kharijites to return to the fold, ʿAlī finally inflicted a crushing defeat on them in the famous battle of al-Nahrawān. This only increased their determination and their quest for martyrdom. They called themselves *shurāt*, meaning "those who sell their lives to God." This they did in answer to the Qur'anic challenge that the people of faith exchange their lives for Paradise and God's good pleasure (see Q. 9:111 and 2:86).

After their defeat at Nahrawān, the Kharijites became an underground movement. They vowed to kill ʿAlī, Muʿāwīyah, and ʿAmr b. al-ʿĀṣ on the same day. The two men who were charged with killing ʿAmr and Muʿāwīyah failed and were themselves executed. As ʿAlī stood to lead the morning prayers on the nineteenth of Ramaḍān 40 (27 January 661), a Kharijite assassin dealt him a fatal blow on the head with a poisoned sword. Two days later ʿAlī died.

ʿAlī's supporters proclaimed his older son Ḥasan as caliph after him. Realizing his own weakness and Muʿāwīyah's strength, Ḥasan wisely chose to end the bloodshed and concluded a peace agreement with Muʿāwīyah. Thus Muʿāwīyah became the founder of the Umayyad dynasty, which ruled a vast Islamic empire for nearly a century.

5

The Age of the Caliphs

THE UMAYYAD CALIPHATE (661–750)

Mu‘āwīyah (r. 661–680) was a shrewd diplomat who quickly established peace and prosperity and managed to maintain them throughout most of his twenty-year-long reign. He moved the capital to Damascus, where it remained till the end of Umayyad rule. The shift of the center of power, first from Madīnah with its simple semi-nomadic Arab society to Kūfah with its heterogeneous and volatile populace, then from there to one of the oldest cities of the Middle East, greatly altered both the ideal and reality of the caliphate. It is said that many years earlier ‘Umar, who lived a simple and even austere life in Madīnah, had reproached Mu‘āwīyah, his then governor of Syria, as he observed the latter's great pomp and ceremony: "Is this a Persian imperial state, O Mu‘āwīyah?" Mu‘āwīyah justified his lifestyle on the grounds that were he to live in Damascus as did ‘Umar in Madīnah, no one would respect his authority.

Before his death, Mu'āwīyah appointed his son Yazīd as his successor. For many in the Muslim community, this was a shocking act. Although precedent existed for the appointment by tribal leaders of a successor on the basis of tribal kinship (Abū Bakr upon Muḥammad's death), for the appointment of his successor by a dying caliph (Abū Bakr of 'Umar), and even for the expectation that a son would be appointed to the caliphate by tribal acclamation on his father's death (Ḥasan after 'Alī), no leader had ever designated his own son as heir to his caliphal authority. In fact, 'Umar had expressly avoided such a procedure. Underlying the reluctance to dynastic inheritance was a sense, common to both Arab and Islamic tradition, that leadership/caliphate was not a possession but a bestowal. Mu'āwīyah's designation of his son Yazīd constituted a total break with these traditions and initiated a practice of patrilineal caliphal succession.

Yazīd (r. 680–683) succeeded his father in 680. The manner of his succession, and the recent memory of Mu'āwīyah's hostility to the sons of 'Alī and their followers, antagonized many of the notables of the holy cities of Makkah and Madīnah and strengthened opposition to the new caliph. From the start, Yazīd's brief reign was beset with grave problems. The most serious opposition to his appointment came from Ḥusayn b. 'Alī, Ḥasan's younger brother.

In contrast to the pragmatic Ḥasan, Ḥusayn was a man of uncompromising idealism. Ḥasan died during Mu'āwīyah's reign, poisoned, many believe, at Mu'āwīyah's instigation. Ḥusayn immediately began to prepare the grounds for a revolt against Umayyad authority. Finally in 680, following Mu'āwīyah's death, Ḥusayn led a small band of seventy-odd fighters to Kūfah, from whence he was to lead a general uprising against Yazīd.

Ḥusayn was intercepted by a large army dispatched against him by Yazīd's governor of Kūfah. Ḥusayn, with his women and children and a few supporters, was halted at Karbalā', a spot on the banks of the Euphrates river near Kūfah. On the morning of the tenth of Muḥarram, the first month of the Muslim year, 61/680, a brief battle between

Ḥusayn's followers and Yazīd's army ensued; it resulted in the massacre of Ḥusayn, his adult male relatives, and his supporters. The heads of Ḥusayn and his fellow martyrs were impaled on spikes and paraded aloft as his women and only surviving son, ʿAlī, known as Zayn al-ʿAbidīn ("the most excellent of all worshipers"), were carried captive, first to Kūfah and from there to Yazīd in Damascus.

The tragedy of Karbalā' has had far-reaching ramifications for Muslim faith, thought, and history. It imparted an ethos of suffering and martyrdom that contrasted sharply with what was otherwise the success story of early Islam. It inspired a rich devotional literature and provided the theme and context for numerous popular passion plays in Persian, Arabic, and other Islamic languages. While these developments became characteristic of Shīʿī faith and piety, the tragedy of Karbalā' has had a deep influence on Sunni piety as well.

Ḥusayn's tragic death earned him the epithet "prince of martyrs." His martyrdom drew, for Muslims, a clear distinction between the ideal of the Islamic polity and what was henceforth considered to be irreligious monarchical rule. Furthermore, it directly undermined the Umayyad caliphate and in the end brought about its demise.

The day of ʿĀshūrā', as the tenth of Muḥarram came to be known, continues to be commemorated throughout the Muslim world as a day of sorrow and reflection. During Umayyad rule, some tried to make it a day of merriment, as remains the case in Morocco. For most Muslims, however, it is a day of blessing and mystery, but above all of suffering and martyrdom. It is particularly observed by the Shīʿī community as a day of mourning, expressed in solemn processions, public readings or enactments of the story of Ḥusayn's martyrdom, liturgical pilgrimages to the sacred spot of Karbalā', and other devotional acts.

The tenth of Muḥarram, with its ethos of suffering and martyrdom, has come to express Shīʿī hopes and frustrations, messianic expectations, and a highly eschatological view of history. It has instilled in Shiʿite Muslims an attitude of quietist resignation in the face of injustice and wrongdoing, as well as a revolutionary spirit that does not tolerate tyranny and oppression. Both attitudes arise from a messianic expectation of a new just and holy order, and a revolution that will forever end what Shiʿites take to be the oppression perpetrated by illegitimate authority. The Islamic revolution of Iran, which began in fact on that day in 1962 and culminated in the fall of the Shah and the establishment of the Islamic Republic in 1979, is the latest manifestation of this spirit.

The immediate consequence of Ḥusayn's death was civil strife, lasting for over a decade and only put down by cruel repression. In the meantime, this instability allowed another Umayyad line, the Marwanids, to gain power. The Marwanids ruled for nearly three quarters of a century, generally with an iron hand. In spite of its cultural, military, and administrative achievements, Umayyad rule had little support, particularly among non-Arab Muslims.

Another phenomenon of the religious and political aftermath of the death of Ḥusayn was the rise of the first extremist Shiʿite sects. Most, if not all, were manifestations of political and economic unrest expressed in short-lived religious movements. They subsisted on the belief in the messianic phenomenon of denying the death of a leader, declaring him to be in occultation, and awaiting his imminent messianic return.

Most of these sects looked to a descendant of the Prophet Muḥammad, through his daughter Fāṭimah and cousin and son-in-law ʿAlī, for guidance and ultimate salvation. In time, not only the descendants of ʿAlī but in general descendants of Hāshim, father of the Prophet's ancestral clan, began to gain an aura of sanctity. They thus were able to assume leadership of a powerful opposition to Umayyad rule. It was among these Shiʿite movements that an effective revolution, which finally toppled the Umayyad dynasty, was organized.

The ʿAbbāsid revolution was so called after the descendants of al-ʿAbbās, the Prophet's uncle. It was largely organized by a Persian man called Abū Muslim in the province of Khurāsān, in northeast Iran. The slogan of this revolution was "we accept anyone of the family of Muḥammad." First in secret, then publicly, ʿAbbāsid men assumed leadership of the revolution and turned it decisively in their favor.

In 132/750, this remarkable religious movement achieved its purpose and the ʿAbbāsid dynasty came to power. Having become weak and ineffectual, the Umayyads were quickly vanquished, rounded up, and virtually massacred. One prince escaped and, after wandering as a fugitive for nearly four years, reached the Iberian peninsula of southern Spain. There he established a new and independent Umayyad emirate (later caliphate) which developed its own glittering culture.

In spite of the many problems that beset Umayyad rule from its beginning, theirs was an epoch of remarkable cultural, administrative, and military achievements. The Dome of the Rock in Jerusalem and the Umayyad mosque in Damascus are two of its great enduring monuments. These and other famous mosques became places of pilgrimage, second in importance to the sanctuaries of Makkah and Madīnah. It was also during this period that Qur'anic orthography was standardized.

ʿAbd al-Malik b. Marwān (r. 685–705), the caliph under whose auspices this cultural flowering reached a high point, changed the state administration from that of the conquered peoples, Greeks and Persians, into a strictly Arab administration. His Arabic coins set the standards not only for Muslim domains, but for other states as well. Even the legal, religious, and other sciences which flourished under the ʿAbbāsids had their beginnings during the Umayyad period.

The small Muslim community established in Madīnah by Muḥammad and his followers had traveled a great distance. This can, perhaps, be best appreciated through a comparison: It is reported that ʿUmar, the second caliph, remarked, on hearing the suggestion for a fleet of war ships, "I will not go to any spot that I cannot reach on my camel." In contrast, Muʿāwīyah built the first Muslim fleet and launched a program of sea warfare. This venture led to wider conquests and soon rendered the Mediterranean an Islamic lake at the service of Muslim traders and military expeditions. In 711 Umayyad armies sailed east to India and west to southern Spain. Sea-faring Arab traders, sailing from the ports of Arabia, carried Islam to Africa, China, and Southeast Asia.

THE ʿABBĀSID CALIPHATE (750–1258)

The Umayyad caliphate was an Arab state, both culturally and administratively. The Muslim conquerors who settled in Syria came from the Arabian Peninsula, including South Arabia. They found themselves amid other more sophisticated and cosmopolitan Arab tribes. The Arabs of Syria, who were largely Christians, had had long contact with Byzantium and Persia. Their poets, like the famous al-Akhṭal (*c.* 640–710), graced the Umayyad court; their administrators, like St. John of Damascus (*c.* 675–749), helped run an efficient state machinery.

The ʿAbbāsid revolution, in contrast, was conceived and developed in Iraq and Persia. It was therefore natural for the new regime to move its capital to that region. Al-Manṣūr (r. 754–775), the second caliph and real founder of the ʿAbbāsid state, built a new capital on the site of a small village in southern Iraq, Baghdad, by which name the capital came to be known. He observed with marked satisfaction that God had turned all previous rulers away from this site, preserving it for him.

Al-Manṣūr planned Baghdad, which he called *madīnat al-salām* ("the city of peace"), as the center of an international empire. Sitting as it did between Syria to the west, Arabia to the south, and Persia to the east, the new capital's location was ideal for his purpose. Baghdad did indeed live up to its expectations and was for centuries the administrative, cultural, and trade center of the ʿAbbāsid empire.

Because the ʿAbbāsids came to power on the strength of a religious ideology, they adopted messianic and highly eschatological names. Thus, the first of their caliphs was called al-Saffāḥ ("the bloodletter"), the second al-Manṣūr ("the victorious"), and the third al-Mahdī ("the rightly guided messianic ruler").

Under Hārūn al-Rashīd (r. 786–809) and his son al-Ma'mūn (r. 813–833) the ʿAbbāsid state reached its zenith as a world empire.

Hārūn al-Rashīd was immortalized in the stories of the Arabian Nights as a legendary patron of culture who surrounded himself with poets and musicians, singing girls and drinking companions. All this, of course, was a far cry from the austere life of Madīnah. The high culture of the 'Abbāsid court contrasted just as sharply with the rudimentary culture of the European court of the Holy Roman Emperor Charlemagne (r. 768–814), al-Rashīd's contemporary.

Although the 'Abbāsids rose to power on the tide of Shī'ī sympathy, they soon allied themselves with the majority Sunni establishment and ruthlessly repressed Shi'ite movements. Early in the caliphate of al-Manṣūr, 'Abd Allāh b. al-Ḥasan (a great grandson of Ḥasan, the son of 'Alī ibn Abī Ṭālib) and his two sons Muḥammad, known as al-Mahdī, and Ibrahīm, known as al-Nafs al-Zakīyah ("the pure soul") led an uprising against 'Abbāsid rule. The revolt was mercilessly put down, Muḥammad and Ibrahīm were killed, and their father and a large number of his 'Alid supporters languished in prison until they died. This repressive policy was followed by most of al-Manṣūr's successors.

The 'Abbāsids, however, did not abandon the religious character of their claim to caliphal authority; rather, they endeavored to distance themselves from the very revolution that had brought them to power. They thus patronized the well-known jurists and other religious scholars of their times. For example, it was for al-Manṣūr that Mālik b. Anas, the founder of the Mālikī legal school, wrote his important book *al-Muwaṭṭa'*, which is a primary source of prophetic *ḥadīth* and legal tradition. Furthermore, al-Rashīd appointed the well-known scholar of the Ḥanafī legal school, Abū Yūsuf, as chief judge. Only al-Ma'mūn among early 'Abbāsid caliphs clearly showed Shi'ite sympathies. Not long after him, however, al-Mutawakkil (r. 847–861) reversed this trend and turned vehemently anti-Shi'ite.

Within half a century of 'Abbāsid rule, the state began to show clear signs of disintegration. State defense and administration were gradually taken over by foreign army generals and state ministers, reducing the caliph to a mere figurehead with little or no authority.

Al-Manṣūr anticipated this danger and therefore eliminated potential rivals, including Abū Muslim – in spite of his loyalty to the ʿAbbāsid cause. Likewise, Hārūn al-Rashīd eliminated the powerful Barmecide family, in spite of the long and loyal service they had rendered to the ʿAbbāsid court.

The real danger, however, came not so much from state administrators but from foreign war lords. By the time of al-Muʿtaṣim (r. 833–842), al-Ma'mūn's successor, Baghdad had fallen under the control of the Turkish soldiers who were initially brought in to defend the caliph and his capital. Al-Muʿtaṣim had to flee Baghdad to a safer garrison city, Samarra', which he had built for that purpose.

The political conflicts, which ended in the fracturing of the ʿAbbāsid empire into numerous warring dynasties, were a direct outcome of the state's cosmopolitan character. Yet it was this character that encouraged the development of a universal and rich Islamic civilization through the interaction and synthesis of many cultures and religious ideas. Using Arabic as the common language of religion, science, philosophy, and literature, Muslim, Jewish, Eastern Christian, and Mandaean scholars developed a civilization that could never have been conceived in the confines of Arabia, or even in the entire Arab east.

The framework for this impressive synthesis was itself based on the science and philosophy of ancient Greece. Interest in Greek philosophy and science may have begun early in the Umayyad period. It culminated in the first official institution of higher learning, the Bayt al-Ḥikmah ("the House of Wisdom"), which was built in Baghdad by al-Ma'mūn. In this great academy, al-Ma'mūn gathered a number of scholars who translated the works of Plato and Aristotle and their commentators into Arabic, either directly from the Greek or from Syriac translations. These translations constituted the primary sources for Islamic philosophy, theology, and science.

As the central authority of the ʿAbbāsid state weakened and finally disappeared altogether, other cultural centers arose to rival Baghdad. It was in the new centers in Persia, Central Asia, North Africa, and Spain that the humanistic and religious sciences flourished. Hence, most of the noted historians, Qur'ān exegetes, *ḥadīth* traditionists, philosophers, and even Arabic grammarians were non-Arabs, yet they all wrote their most important works in Arabic. By the tenth century, however, Persian poetry and prose literature began to develop. This set the precedent for other Islamic languages, which in due course developed their own rich literary traditions.

In spite of its collapse as a central power, the 'Abbāsid caliphate was generally accepted as a legitimate institution by the Sunni majority on the basis of the 'Abbāsid claim to Prophetic family relations through descent from the Prophet's uncle, al-'Abbās. Shi'ite Muslims, however, recognized only the Prophet's descendants through 'Alī and Fāṭimah as *ahl al-bayt* ("People of the House," or "people of the Prophet's household"), and therefore only them as legitimate holders of authority in the Muslim community. 'Alid claims to authority continued to have a powerful appeal among Arabs and non-Arabs alike.

Around the middle of the tenth century the Buyids, a Persian dynasty, came to rule large areas of the 'Abbāsid domains, including Baghdad. The Buyids were Shi'ite sympathizers and thus patronized Shī'ī learning; their century-long rule is known as the "Shi'ite century." It was during the Buyid period (945–1055) that Shī'ī *ḥadīth* tradition, theology, and jurisprudence were developed.

After a period of revolutionary ferment in North Africa, the Isma'īlī Shi'ite Imām al-Mu'izz li-Dīn Allāh ("he who brings honor to God's religion"; r. 953–975) sent his armies to occupy Egypt in 969. This was generally assumed to be the first step of occupying the rest of the Islamic world, of which the dynasty of al-Mu'izz considered itself the rightful rulers. Two years later al-Mu'izz moved with his court permanently to the newly built Cairo. The dynasty of which he was the third caliph was known as the Fatimid caliphate, so called after Fāṭimah, the Prophet's daughter. From Cairo, which al-Mu'izz built as the capital of his realm, the Fatimids ruled Egypt and parts of Syria for over two centuries. Their authority rested on a powerful missionary organization that operated throughout the Muslim world. On more than one occasion, the Fatimids of Egypt threatened the 'Abbāsid caliphate of Baghdad.

In 912, 'Abd al-Raḥmān III (r. 912–961), the Umayyad ruler of Muslim Spain, had also proclaimed himself caliph. The Umayyads of Spain were effectively independent since 'Abd al-Raḥmān I had established himself in Andalus in 756, six years after the fall of Umayyads of Syria. But they had refrained from assuming the caliphal title out of respect for the notion of the *ummah*'s unity under one caliph. 'Abd al-Raḥmān III's decision to reverse this longstanding principle was prompted by the Fāṭimid's own assumption of the caliphal title in 909. The Umayyads, with their newly assumed title, held on to their turbulent and diminishing domain in southern Spain. Thus the caliphal office, which was meant to manage the affairs of the entire Muslim *ummah*, was occupied by three competing claimants. Among these, the 'Abbāsid caliphs were by far the weakest. They in fact became ceremonial figures used to legitimize the illegit-imate rules of sultans who seated and unseated them at will.

In this state of fragmentation and disunity, the Muslim dominion could not withstand the onslaught of a powerful common enemy. The Mongols of the steppes of inner Asia advanced upon the Muslim domains of Central Asia, Persia, and the Middle East like wild fire, leaving death and devastation in their wake. In 1258 the Mongol general Hulagu sacked Baghdad and killed the last 'Abbāsid caliph. Like most Asian conquerors of the Muslim world, the Mongols eventually became Muslims and in turn left their mark on Islamic civilization.

With the fall of Baghdad as a center of Islamic spiritual and material culture, a new era of Muslim history began. Henceforth, it was not the state or the military but traders, religious scholars, and Sufi masters who assumed the work of preserving and spreading Islam as a faith and civilization throughout Asia and Africa. These new domains produced their own religio-cultural centers. And although the caliphate ceased to exist as a reality, it has remained the ideal of Islamic rule; one that many Muslims still long to recover.

6

The Spread of Islam

Like Christianity, Islam is a universalist and therefore a missionary religion. Muslims believe that their message of faith in the one God, his angels, and all his prophets and scriptures, and in the principles of divine reward and retribution on the day of judgment is intended for all of humankind. Furthermore, they believe that Islam, as a social, political, and economic system based on these principles, can be fully implemented only in a sovereign community that transcends the limitations of cultural and linguistic barriers and geographic borders. The vast domain of this community has been legally designated as *dār al-islām*, meaning the "house" or "abode of Islam." The rest of the world is primarily divided into either the sphere of peace or truce (*ṣulḥ*), or the sphere of war (*ḥarb*), depending on the relationship of the Muslims to any particular area of the world. Yet the whole world is regarded by Muslims as potentially the house of Islam.

Islam grew and spread not simply as a collection of beliefs and rituals, but as a political and military power and a religious legal system.

To be sure, these orbits have often complemented and completed one another, but they have often also acted separately and even in conflict with one another. In general, it may be observed that most of what Islam achieved through conquest and military might was soon lost. What it achieved through the preaching and living examples of teachers, pious Sufi mystics, and traders has remained a vital part of the Muslim *ummah*, as will be amply demonstrated below.

ISLAM IN NORTH AFRICA AND SPAIN

After the consolidation of what came to be the heartland of Islam – Syria, Egypt, and Persia – Muslim forces conquered North Africa in the second half of the seventh century. Before Islam, North Africa was first an important Roman province, and then an equally important home of Latin Christianity. With its indigenous Berber and Phoenician, Roman, and Byzantine populations, North Africa was an area of rich cultural and religious diversity. It has always maintained a distinct religious and cultural identity, reflecting its ancient heritage.

Soon after its conquest, North Africa's Berber aristocracy were adopted into the Arab tribes and assumed the names of their conquerors. Thus the famous young general Ṭāriq b. Zīyād, who crossed the Atlantic straits into southern Spain in 711, was an Arabized Berber. Gibraltar, the small rock settlement on which his forces first landed, still bears his name, Jabal Ṭāriq ("Ṭāriq's mountain"). The complete integration of North Africa into Arab Islam, however, was a slow and often turbulent process lasting nearly four centuries.

With the shift of the capital from Damascus to Baghdad under the 'Abbāsids, the main orientation of the Islamic empire naturally became more Persian than Arab, more Asian than Mediterranean. On the other hand, the Arab/Mediterranean center of Islamic culture shifted from Syria to Qayrawān, the chief urban center of North Africa, and to Cordoba, Spain, Islam's Western capital, which rivaled Baghdad and Cairo in its cultural splendor. North African mystics, scholars, and philosophers played a pivotal role in the rise of these centers to prominence.

North African society under Islam was as diverse as it had been in Roman and Christian times. There were Shiʿites, or at least ʿAlid sympathizers, making it possible for the Fatimids to launch their successful missionary and military ventures. There were also Kharijites whose moderate Ibāḍī legal school is still represented among some Berber tribes.

The most lasting and creative expression of this diversity was the development of the Sufi orders and sub-orders known as *zāwiyahs*. Members of such orders, like the *murābiṭūn* (Almoravids) founded one of the dynasties that ruled Islamic Spain after the demise of the Umayyad caliphate. Originally the term *Murābiṭūn* referred to fighters who kept watch over the borders of the Muslim state. As many such fighters were pious Sufis, a *murābiṭ* ("Marabout") became a legendary figure, a saint venerated by the pious who visit his tomb for miraculous healing and other favors. Almoravid *zāwiyah* piety continues to influence North African Islam till the present.

More recently, in the North African struggle for independence from colonial rule, religious scholars and particularly Sufi masters have played a crucial role. They helped preserve the religious and cultural identity of their people and mobilized them to resist Italian and French colonization in Libya and Algeria. In spite of the deep influence of French language and secular culture, North African popular piety still reflects its classical heritage.

Before the appearance of Arab conquerors on the Iberian peninsula in 711, Spain was torn by civil strife. The Jews, who had for centuries lived in Spain, were often subjected to harsh restrictions by rulers newly converted to Latin Christianity. (Before the sixth century Spain professed Aryan Christianity, which had been introduced to them by the Gothic conquerors of the Roman empire.) The Jews aided the invading Arabs, seeing them as liberators.

With amazing rapidity, Umayyad forces conquered the land of Andalusia, or *al-Andalus* as the Arabs called southern Spain, and laid the foundations for the unique and fabulous Hispano-Arab culture. Arab men intermarried with local women, thus creating a mixed but harmonious society. The resulting culture was Arab in language and expression and Arabo-Hispanic in spirit. Muslims, Christians, and Jews lived together in mutual tolerance for centuries before fanatical Muslim and Christian forces stifled one of the most creative experiments in inter-faith living in human history.

The nine hundred year-long history (711–1609) of Arab Spain witnessed the usual symbiotic creativity as well as the tensions and conflicts that beset any multi-religious, multicultural society ruled by a minority regime. It also witnessed the great achievements and the ultimate failure of Islamic faith and civilization, not only in the Iberian peninsula but in other European centers such as Sicily and Portugal.

The Muslims of Spain adopted the conservative Mālikī legal school, introduced from North Africa where it prevails to this day. In spite of its religious conservatism, however, Arab Spain produced some of Islam's greatest jurists, mystics, and philosophers, such as the jurist, littérateur, and heresiographer Ibn Ḥazm (d. 1064), the mystics Muḥyī al-Dīn Ibn 'Arabī (d. 1240) and Ibn Masarrah (d. 931) and his mystical-philosophical school, and the great philosophers Ibn Ṭufayl (d. 1185) and Ibn Rushd (Averroës, d. 1198), among others.

Arabo-Hispanic mysticism and philosophy reflected their Islamo-Christian-Judeo environment. Christian Andalusian society was made up of three classes: the adopted (*muwallad*) converts who accepted both Islam and the Arabic language; the Arabized (*mozarrab*) who accepted the Arabic language and culture, but not Islam; and those who remained Latin in both religion and culture. Cluniac and Benedictine monks, who worked tirelessly to preserve Latin Christianity and culture in Spain, had at times to resort to extreme measures to counter the appeal of the Arabic language and culture among their co-religionists.

At the same time, Jews enjoyed a golden age of general prosperity and creative energy in the fields of philosophy, science, and mysticism.

Jewish scholars, court physicians, and administrators occupied high state offices and served as political and cultural liaisons between Islamic Spain and the rest of Europe.

The Umayyad caliphate, which ended in 1031, was followed by a period of competing petty dynasties known collectively as the "Party Kings." These were followed by two conservative Moroccan dynasties: the *al-Murābiṭūn* (Almoravids), 1056–1147, and the *al-Muwaḥḥidūn*, "the believers in the one God" known (in Spanish) as the Almohads, 1130–1269. The latter was a messianic movement that, by its nature and ideology, could not tolerate the multi-religious society of Umayyad Spain. The Almohads' repressive policies towards non-Muslims, and even towards Muslims who did not share their ideology, hastened the Christian reconquest of Spain, which had already begun during the Umayyad period.

By 1492, when King Ferdinand of Aragon and Queen Isabella of Castile were united in marriage, thus unifying most of Spain under one Catholic crown, only the city of Granada remained in Muslim hands. When the Nasrids, the last Muslim dynasty to exercise power in Spain, surrendered Granada in that year, the final vestige of Islamic political power disappeared from the Iberian peninsula. Also in 1492, the Jews were expelled from Spain, and those who remained suffered extreme persecution under the Inquisition instituted by the Catholic Church and enforced by the state authorities. Although the Muslims were not officially expelled until 1609, they too were subject to the Inquisition. For a while they practiced their religion secretly, but in the end Islam was ruthlessly obliterated from Spanish society and culture.

Under Islam, Spain was the cultural center of Europe. Students came from as far away as Scotland to study Islamic theology, philosophy, and science in the schools of Cordoba, Toledo, and other centers of higher learning. The European Renaissance was conceived in these centers, and the great universities in which it was nurtured were inspired by their Arabo-Hispanic counterparts.

Although the Muslims were stopped from advancing into France and the rest of western Europe in 732 by Charles Martel in the Battle of Poitiers, and although their armies were driven from the Iberian peninsula by the forces of Christian Spain, their scientific and cultural achievements succeeded where their military might failed. Arab learning did indeed penetrate deeply into western Europe and contributed directly to the rise of the West to world prominence. Ironically, the religious establishment, which had provided both the impetus and framework for these intellectual achievements, ultimately repressed and repudiated them.

ISLAM IN OTHER PARTS OF AFRICA

The history of Islam in sub-Saharan, West, and East Africa is a history of reception and dissemination. Islam may have come to sub-Saharan Africa as early as the eighth or ninth century. It was first brought in by Kharijites, who settled in oasis towns north of the Sahara, from where it then spread south along trade routes and through migration. The Almohads who later ruled Spain and North Africa may have originally come from Senegal, a possibility that clearly suggests the existence of close relations between North Africa and the rest of the continent. Furthermore, through the Almoravids, the Mālikī legal school was introduced into sub-Saharan and West Africa, where it remains dominant to this day.

The spread of Islam into West Africa took place in three stages. Initially, a small Muslim community would begin to form under a non-Muslim king. This would be followed by the adoption of Islam as the court religion and then, as Islam gained official recognition, its numbers were expanded through mass conversions. By the eighteenth century, Islam was a formidable social and political force in Africa and could provide the framework and principles for social and political reform. Islamic law also increasingly came to compete with traditional legal custom.

Islam's diffusion through Africa followed a pattern similar to that of other places where it became the dominant religion. It was first spread by traders, then on a much larger scale by preachers. Finally jurists came in to consolidate and implement the new faith as a religious and legal system. Sufi orders played an important role in both the spread of Islam and in its use as a motivation and framework for social and political reform.

Islam always had to compete with traditional African religions. The prayers of Islam had to prove their potency as against the magic of the traditional priest, for example, in their efficacy as rain-making prayers. Especially in times of social or family crises, African Muslims even today fall back on their ancient traditions for help. The phenomenon of adapting a new faith to an earlier tradition or appropriating existing customs for new beliefs, so common in both Christian and Muslim history, was observed among the Muslims of the Mali empire and vividly described by the Muslim traveler Ibn Baṭūṭah (1304–1377).[32]

Unlike Egypt and North Africa, the countries of eastern and western Africa were not Arabized, but the Arabic language did penetrate all the local languages; so much so, that at least one third of the Swahili vocabulary is Arabic. Until recently most of the major African languages were written in the Arabic script. Perhaps because of the infiltration of the African languages by Arabic, many African scholars have excelled in Arabic and produced impressive works in that language in all Islamic disciplines. In contrast, a vast and ongoing popular panegyric literature in praise of the Prophet and on other religious themes, continues to appear in the local languages. Thus while Arabic is the language of worship and the religious sciences, the medium of African culture and devotional life remains the vernacular languages.

In East Africa, the cultural and political development of Islam was directly affected by Western colonialism and the slave trade. The arrival of the Portuguese in Africa in the sixteenth century introduced Catholic Christian missionary activity on a large scale. With the coming of the British and other European colonial powers, missionary activity was further intensified and Protestant Christianity was also introduced. Islam therefore had to compete not only with traditional African religions, but also with a variety of Christian sects and denominations.

The success of Islam in Africa has been in large measure due to its ability to accommodate itself to local culture. Islamic rituals have been overlaid with traditional myths and ritualistic practices. Likewise, legal matters, such as dietary restrictions, have often been explained not on the basis of Islamic law but of local custom. Even today, Islam in Africa continues to vacillate between accommodation and reform, between particularism and universalism, and between quietism and political activism. This is due in part to the informality of religious affiliation in African society. People still move freely between Islam and Christianity, and between both and their traditional folk religions.

An important element of East African society has been the Khoja Ismaʿīlī and Twelver Shīʿī community. The Khojas emigrated from India to Africa over a century and a half ago. They are on the whole successful business people with Western educations and close relations with Europe and North America. These relations have been strengthened by the migration of large numbers of the Khoja community to Britain, the United States, and Canada, where they remain prosperous and well organized.

ISLAM IN CENTRAL ASIA

Central Asia, or "the lands beyond the river Oxus" (what is now roughly the republics of Azerbaijan and Uzbekistan) had an urban culture before Islam. Buddhism, Zoroastrianism, Judaism, and Christianity existed side by side in mutual tolerance. The Arab conquest of this region was slow, lasting over a century. It began in 649, less than two decades after the Prophet's death, and was not completed till 752.

Under the Samanid dynasty, which ruled large areas of Persia and Central Asia in the ninth and tenth centuries, the region witnessed an impressive flowering of both Persian culture and religious learning in the Arabic language. The best-known classical *ḥadīth* traditionists, historians, philosophers, and religious scholars flourished in that epoch. And with the first notable Persian-language poet, Rūdakī, who lived in the tenth century, Bukhārā became the birthplace of Islamo-Persian literature. Over time, the celebrated cities of Bukhārā and Samarqand developed into important centers of Islamic learning. Their great prosperity depended largely on industry and trade with India, China, and the rest of the Muslim domains.

In contrast with their neighbors the Buyids, who patronized Shiʿī learning and public devotions, the Samanids firmly established Sunni orthodoxy in Central Asia. Many Sunni theologians and religious scholars lived and worked in Bukhārā and Samarqand under Samanid patronage. Among the great minds who belong to this epoch are the theologian al-Māturīdī (d. 944), the philosopher Ibn Sīnā (d. 1037), the great scholar and historian of religion Abū Rayḥān al-Bīrūnī (d. 1048), and the famous Persian poet Firdowsī (d. *c.* 1020).

In this intellectual environment Islam was spread by persuasion and enticement rather than propaganda and war. The second half of the tenth century witnessed many instances of mass conversions. To a large extent, the rapid spread and consolidation of Islam as a creative religious and cultural system was due to its success in remolding the culture of the people and focusing it around a single unified faith and worldview.

Central Asian Islam was deeply influenced by Sufism and the saint cults it engendered. This, of course, allowed for the importation of old cultic practices from Buddhism, Christianity, and Zoroastrianism. The mystical piety that developed in the Persian cultural environment of Central Asia was largely pantheistic and ecstatic. It expressed itself in rich poetry, music, and dance.

Early in the eleventh century, the Samanids were succeeded by the Seljuq Turks in the Middle East and the Karakhanid Mongols in Persia and Central Asia. The Mongols altered the local situation as profoundly as they would in the Middle East a century later. And, as sea travel to India and China replaced traditional caravan routes, the devastating consequences of the Mongol conquest of Persia and Central Asia were compounded by the region's loss of trade revenues. All this led to a decline in culture and prosperity from which Central Asia never recovered.

ISLAM IN CHINA

The first contacts of Islam with China may have happened shortly after the Prophet's death. Chinese Islamic literary sources, however, do not appear till the seventeenth century. For earlier information, we have to rely on Confucian sources that unfortunately focus on commercial activities and therefore have little to say about the social and intellectual life of Chinese Muslims.

The extent of Muslim presence can often be gauged by the number of mosques in an area. Although Persian and Arab merchants were, from the beginning, allowed to trade freely so long as they conformed with Chinese rules, there is little evidence that there were mosques in China before the reigns of the Mongols and of the Ming dynasty in the thirteenth and fourteenth centuries. This may indicate that the presence of Islam in China before the thirteenth century was limited and transitory. It was not until Muslim traders began to reside in China in reasonable numbers that mosques began to appear.

Our ability to reconstruct the history of Islam in China is hampered by the attitude of the Confucian literati, who looked down scornfully on all foreigners and their cultural and religious practices. Be that as it may, under Mongol rule immigrant Muslims, who were predominantly of Central Asian origin, appear to have enjoyed many privileges. This close collaboration with a foreign regime stirred hostility and mistrust among the Chinese towards Muslims. Nevertheless, Muslims were able to maintain a life of prosperity throughout Mongol (1206–1368) and Ming rule (1368–1644). In the thirteenth century Muslim communities sprang up in all parts of China.

After the Mongol period, Chinese Muslims were culturally assimilated in all but their religious practice. They kept in touch with the rest of the Muslim *ummah* through trade. Hence, the decline of trade with Central Asia in the seventeenth century had devastating effects on the Chinese Muslim community. It was virtually cut off from the rest of the world, so that after the seventeenth century our information about Muslims in China becomes largely a matter of conjecture.

Unsuccessful attempts were made after the seventeenth century to assimilate Islam into the Confucian ethic and worldview. Predictably, this led to Muslim revolts, which led to repression by the authorities. In 1784, religious leaders belonging to the Naqshbandi Sufi order attempted to establish an independent Muslim state in northwestern China. The revolt was put down, though intermittent unrest continued into the twentieth century.

Persistent negative images of Muslims among the Chinese exacerbated an already tense situation. The Muslims of Sinkiang, who were mostly of Central Asian origin, made numerous futile attempts to establish a Muslim state in that province. Islam in fact was never able to establish itself in China as it did in the rest of Asia, perhaps because the Chinese already had an advanced and regimented culture within a closely knit society.

Unlike Buddhism centuries earlier, Islam could not be acclimatized to Chinese society and culture. The situation has not been substantially different in the People's Republic of China. The Muslims under communism have had their share of repression, particularly during the Cultural Revolution. Since 1976, and the end of the Cultural Revolution, things have improved. There are now around 50 million Muslims in China. Their future is as uncertain as the future of Muslims anywhere in today's changing world.

ISLAM IN SOUTH ASIA

Early in its history Islam was brought to India by traders and Arab settlers. In 711, when Muslim armies advanced west into Europe, they also moved eastward into India. The initial incursion was in reprisal for an alleged case of mistreatment of Muslim traders. Since that time Islam has been an integral part of Indian life and culture.

The Muslim conquest of India was a long process. In the second half of the tenth century the city of Ghazna, in what is modern Afghanistan, became the headquarters for the conquest and rule of India. From Ghazna the armies of Sultan Maḥmūd the Ghaznavid (r. 998–1030) and his successors advanced over the famous Khyber Pass into the north Indian plain. By the fourteenth century most of India came under Muslim rule.

The Muslim rulers of India were for the most part foreigners. Thus, maintaining and expanding Muslim power in the vast and diverse subcontinent meant continuous warfare. Yet, in spite of the often repressive Muslim rule of a largely Hindu population, Islam developed a unique and rich religious and intellectual culture in India. Members of local Sufi brotherhoods, such as the Chishti and wandering Qalandar darwishes, interacted with the ascetic sages or yogis of different schools of Hinduism, giving Islam in India a distinct character.

Indian Muslim society remains as diverse as the rest of Muslim society. Besides the Sunni majority, which basically adheres to the Ḥanafī legal school, but is overlaid with a rich tapestry of Sufi popular piety, there is a small but vibrant Shīʿī community. This latter community has made notable contributions to the political and cultural life of India, particularly to Urdu and Persian literature and music.

As we have already observed, Islam was brought to India by Arab and Persian traders, Sufis, and religious scholars. The dominant culture of India was, well into the nineteenth century, the Mughal Persian culture. Arabic nonetheless remained an important language of religious and literary communication. Out of the interaction of these two languages, Persian and Arabic, with Hindi was born an indigenous language called Urdu. The Urdu language has in turn developed its own rich literary heritage. It is the language of educated Muslims in India and the official language of Pakistan.

Around the middle of the thirteenth century, and in response to the Mongol devastation of the Middle East, many well-known religious scholars migrated to India and founded new mosques and religious schools. Such endeavors were encouraged and patronized by the Turkic sultans of Delhi, the present capital of India. Most religious institutions, however, depended not on government patronage or the largesse of rich landholders, but on private pious donations. The general involvement of the masses of Muslims went beyond the devotional and intellectual life of the Muslim community and penetrated to a great depth and extent all of Indian society.

Through the shared culture and social customs of Muslims and Hindus, a sort of caste system developed in Indian Muslim society. Thus the *'ulama'*, or religious scholars, came to constitute a special aristocracy akin to that of the Brahmin priestly class in Hinduism. This high status could also be gained through intermarriage with the *sayyid* class, a Muslim nobility claiming descent from the Prophet through his daughter Fāṭimah and his cousin 'Alī b. Abī Ṭālib.

Alongside the popular Sufi preachers, there arose a type of Muslim gentleman who disdained to speak about Islam in any but one of its official languages, Arabic or Persian. These two languages, therefore, came to occupy a sacred status in Indian Muslim society somewhat resembling that of Sanskrit in classical Hinduism.

Before the modern period, religious thought in South Asia differed little from that in other regions of the Muslim world. The uniqueness of Indian Islam lay in its popular piety, resulting from the interaction with Hindu *bhakti* devotion. This was particularly reflected in the cult of the *shaykh* or preceptor, who could be a Sufi shaykh or a Hindu-Muslim guru. Indeed, Islam in India developed along two distinct lines. There was the official Islamic literary culture of the scholars. Quite different from it was the popular pietistic culture of the masses. The former was enshrined in the classical languages of Islamic learning and the latter in the vernacular languages.

The classical languages of Islam, including Urdu, were completely foreign to the masses of India. In Bengal, for instance, conscious efforts were made to express Islamic devotional ideas in the vernacular. This phenomenon was common to most Indian language groups. It resulted in a rich common Hindu-Muslim religious culture, one of whose expressions is the Sikh religious tradition founded by Guru Nanak (d. 1539). Guru Nanak was the disciple of Kabir, a Hindu-Muslim mystic who is still venerated by Hindus and Muslims alike.

The influence of the Arabo-Persian philosophical and literary mystical tradition can be clearly discerned in the development of Indian Sufism. On the other hand, the Hindu idea of the divine-human guru has, since the fifteenth century, led many Sufi shaykhs to claim prophetic or messianic qualities for themselves. Thus the personality of the Prophet Muḥammad, around which a rich popular cult had developed, was actually shared among local spiritual heroes.

With this rather eclectic piety an equally rich and eclectic culture developed under Mughal rule. The Mughals established a prosperous society and a high culture that reached its zenith under the great emperor Akbar (r. 1556–1605). Akbar used to enjoy gathering Hindu, Muslim, and Christian religious scholars for open debate. Convinced of the narrowness and divisive role of all institutionalized religions, Akbar propounded what he thought to be a universal religion combining the best of Indian and Middle Eastern religions. He called this new faith *dīnī-ilahī*, meaning "Divine Religion."

Akbar's daring religious innovation created conflict and disunity in the Muslim community. His successor Darashikoh attempted to carry Akbar's interreligious work further but was unfortunately deposed and tragically executed by order of the *'ulama'* in 1659. The empire quickly slid into anarchy and Mughal rule was replaced by British rule, which ended in 1947 with the partition of India and the creation of Pakistan.

By the beginning of the nineteenth century the British ruled all of India including Delhi and Agra, the two centers of Mughal culture and authority. This radically changed the Muslim situation, and with it the Muslims' self-image and destiny. Prior to British rule non-Muslims did conquer Muslim lands, but they were themselves eventually assimilated into the Muslim community. Now, however, Western imperialism and aggressive missionary activity sought to undermine traditional Islamic values and authority. Even Islamic law, until this point the sacred domain of the Muslim *'ulama'*, was controlled in its application by the British colonial authorities.

A variety of revivalist movements arose in the nineteenth century, calling Muslims to return to Islam's sacred traditions. Some emphasized the authority of the Qur'ān, others the authority of Prophetic *ḥadīth* tradition, and still others stressed harmony between the two sacred sources. Sometimes revivalists called upon Muslims to rise up in armed struggle, or *jihād*, against all non-Muslim elements. The British colonialists and the Sikhs, who had become bitter opponents of the Muslims in India, were especially targeted.

There were also reformers like Sayyid Aḥmad Khān (d. 1898) who saw in British rule a way for Muslims to survive and reform their own social and political system. He therefore called for cooperation with the British and the Westernization of the Indian Muslim community. Others, like Muḥammad Iqbāl (d. 1938), called for a return to the spirit of classical Islam, but by way of Western philosophical thought in order to provide the modern framework for this important undertaking.

The Indian subcontinent, which is now divided into India, Bangladesh, and Pakistan, has the largest Muslim population in the world. The Muslims of India alone comprise the largest single national population after Indonesia, numbering between one hundred and one hundred and thirty million. Yet the Muslims of India are a minority whose future appears bleak in the face of rising Hindu nationalism. In the 1970s, Pakistan was torn apart and separated into two mutually hostile Muslim countries. Given rapid population growth and the economic hardship of all developing countries, the Muslims of South Asia do not appear to have a very bright future.

ISLAM IN SOUTHEAST ASIA

Islam came to Southeast Asia, not to large urban centers, but to small kingdoms and settlements possessing a wide diversity of languages and cultures. Before Islam, Southeast Asian religious cultures were strongly influenced by the Hindu and Buddhist traditions. This influence is still evident in the ancient Hindu culture of the island of Bali and the great Buddhist monument of Borobudur in Indonesia. In fact most of Southeast Asia was Buddhist, with both Mahayana and Theravada Buddhism represented.

There is no evidence for the presence of Islam in Southeast Asia before the tenth century. Scattered evidence from Chinese and Portuguese travelers, as well as passing references by the Arab traveler Ibn Baṭūṭah, indicate that by the fifteenth century Islam was widely practiced in Southeast Asian society. By the seventeenth century, when British and Dutch trading companies arrived in the region, Islam had become the dominant religion and culture of the Malay Archipelago.

The spread of Islam in Southeast Asia was a slow and modest process, unlike its first great expansions into the Near and Middle East, South and Central Asia, and Africa. It is probable that Arab traders carried Islam into Southeast Asia as they did into China by the eighth century if not earlier. Yemeni traders are reported to have been sailing into the islands of the Malay Archipelago long before Islam's existence. Since Yemenites were among the first to embrace the religion, this fact clearly suggests the possibility of early contact between the Malay people and Islam.

As Muslim merchants settled in the region they intermarried with local women, thus beginning the process of establishing permanent native Muslim communities. These communities were as diverse as the people who initiated them and the cultures in which they grew. Arab and South Asian Muslims, in interaction with the local people, helped shape Islamic culture and popular piety in Southeast Asia.

Socio-political Muslim communities in small states ruled by sultans are widely reported by the thirteenth century. The earliest of these was Pasai, a small kingdom on the east coast of northern Sumatra; other states appeared in the following centuries. Some of the states that arose in the fifteenth century gained considerable prominence. In every case, prosperity attracted Indian Muslim *'ulamā'* to these states. Many may have been of Arab ancestry, giving them an added prestige and religious authority of which they took full advantage.

The isolation and self-sufficiency that had characterized the states of the Malay Archipelago began to give way in the seventeenth century. The Sultan Iskandar Muda of Acheh (r. 1607–1636) ruled the first Muslim state that instituted formal international relations. In his efforts to expand and strengthen his realm, he established alliances with European powers. In spite of this opening to the west, Acheh has always seen itself as the authentic home of Islam in Southeast Asia. It has, furthermore, produced noteworthy Islamic scholarship which remains authoritative in the Malay world.

The expansion of the authority of the Dutch United East India Company, from the seventeenth century on, arrested the recurrent rise and fall of small Muslim kingdoms in the region. The resulting stability helped to establish Islam even more firmly as an indigenous religion. Islam, particularly in Java with its ancient rural cultures, has always been mixed with native ritualistic and ancestral cults. Inspired by the Wahhābī reform movement of Arabia in the eighteenth century, local *'ulamā'* began vigorously to call for reform to purify Islam. Thus in the 1840s a civil war ensued in Java, which in turn led to the expansion of Dutch colonialism in the region.

As elsewhere, and to an even greater extent, Sufi orders played a crucial role in the Islamization and later in the political and social struggle for reform and liberation in Southeast Asia. In the late nineteenth and early twentieth centuries, modernist reform movements in the Middle East inspired similar movements in Indonesia and other countries of the region. The institution that has had the longest and most sustained influence on the intellectual life of Southeast Asia is the Islamic University of al-Azhar in Cairo, Egypt. Al-Azhar continues to graduate the majority of the Islamic scholars of the Malay-Indonesian Muslim community. Most of the Muslims of Southeast Asia follow the Shāfiʿī legal school.

Islam in Southeast Asia did not attain the universal character that it achieved through the Arabic, Persian, and Turkish languages and cultures elsewhere in Asia and Africa, yet Southeast Asia can claim at least one third of the Muslims of the world. Muslim minorities exist in Thailand, Burma, and the Philippines, as well as in other countries of the region. In Malaysia, Indonesia, and Brunei Islam is the majority religion. Indonesia alone has a Muslim population of over one hundred and fifty million, making it the largest Muslim country in the world.

Southeast Asia is far from the sectarian, demographic, ethnic, and political problems that have bedeviled the Near and Middle East and South Asia. Moreover, the gentle disposition and industriousness of the Malay people and their Chinese and Indian compatriots, coupled with the wealth of natural resources, bodes a brighter future for this vast and fascinating part of the world, but God knows best.

7

The Religious Sciences

Our discussion of the initial spread of Islam into areas that now constitute an integral part of the Muslim world was intended to help place the primary sciences of the Islamic faith in their proper cultural and geographic setting. The spread of Islam, as we shall see, did not stop at the areas we discussed, nor was it limited to any specific time-frame. Rather, Islam continues to be the fastest growing religion even today. After the eighteenth century, however, it is more appropriate to speak not so much about the spread of Islam as a social, religious, and political force in society, but about the migration of Muslims into new areas, such as Western Europe and the New World.

As may be inferred from our discussion of the spread of Islam, Muslim geographic expansion far outstripped the development of the religious and political framework within which the vast and newly conquered domains were to be ruled. We also observed that Islamic cosmopolitan cultural centers like Baghdad, Cordoba, and Cairo provided a highly creative pluralistic milieu for the rise of a rich civilization. The religious sciences developed, for the most part, in new cultural centers far from the original Arabian heartland of Islam. Moreover, they were part of a comprehensive philosophical, theological, literary, and scientific efflorescence which began in the eighth century and continued in different parts of the Muslim world well into the seventeenth century.

Muslim life and piety in Arabia were guided by the Qur'ān and the life-example (*sunnah*) of the Prophet Muḥammad and his generation, as represented in the *ḥadīth* tradition. While the Qur'ān was quickly collected in an official and universally accepted codex (*muṣḥaf*), the words and actions of the Prophet were informally remembered and passed on for at least a century before any attempts to record them were made. In fact, *ḥadīth* tradition was not fully codified until the fourth/tenth century for the Sunni community and at least a century later for the Twelver Imāmī Shī'ī legal school.

THE FOUNDATIONS OF LAW AND MORALITY

Islam, as we stressed in our discussion of the five pillars, is a religion of action rather than of abstract speculation about right belief. Hence, the first and most important religious science is Islamic law, which aims at right living, which is, in turn, the essential basis of true faith. The Prophet is reported to have characterized a Muslim as follows: "Anyone who performs our prayers [i.e. observes the rituals of worship], faces our *qiblah* [direction of prayer] and eats our ritualistically slaughtered animals [i.e. observes the proper dietary laws] is a Muslim."[33]

Islamic jurisprudence not only developed before the *ḥadīth* and Qur'anic sciences, it also conditioned them. Yet jurisprudence, both as a theoretical and as an applied discipline, was based on the Qur'ān and Prophetic tradition. Therefore, a proper and comprehensive study of these two primary sources is essential for the understanding of the development of Islamic jurisprudence. With this in mind, we shall briefly examine some of the moral-legislative Qur'anic precepts and the principles and evolution of the science of Prophetic tradition, before discussing the development of the science of jurisprudence and the rise of the legal schools.

Teachings of the Qur'ān

The Qur'ān is not a book of law, theology, history, or science. It is rather a source of moral and religious guidance to the worship of the one God, the creator, sustainer, and judge of all his creatures. The Qur'anic faith in divine oneness (*tawḥīd*) furthermore implies a life of total submission to the one God. On the level of inner personal commitment, submission (*islām*) and faith (*imān*), as we have already observed, are synonymous.

This inner personal submission to the will of God is believed by Muslims to be God's way for all of humankind. On both the personal and the societal levels Islam as a faith and a way of life can only be realized within the framework of divine law, the *sharī'ah*. Yet, properly speaking, the *sharī'ah* is not law but a way of life or conduct based on a set of moral imperatives. These moral imperatives, the Qur'ān insists, must be expressed in a genuine commitment to strive to reform one's life, the life of one's family and immediate society, and the Islamic *ummah* at large. Ultimately, the inward measure of proper observance is the sincerity of a person's intention and faith; the outward, a person's righteous works. To illustrate this important point more clearly, we shall look closely at a few Qur'anic social and economic precepts.

The Qur'ān views humanity as one creation made up of different societies, cultures, races, and languages. It asserts: "Of His signs is the creation of the heavens and the earth and the diversity of your tongues and colors" (Q. 30:22). Because all men and women belong to one humanity, they are all equal before God, regardless of race, color, and social status. They may excel one another as individuals and groups, but only in righteousness and good works. Again, the Qur'ān asserts:

> Humankind, We have created you all of one male and one female and made you different peoples and tribes in order that you may get to know one another. Surely, the noblest of you in God's sight is he who fears God most (Q. 49:13).

The primary concerns of the Qur'ān, and hence of the *sharī'ah*, are social interrelations and the relationship of individuals and societies with God. Social interrelations begin with the most particular and intimate relationship between a husband and wife and move to the interactions of people with their parents and children. They then move farther to include the extended family, then the tribe, and finally the *ummah* and the world. The Qur'ān did not legislate these relationships in a vacuum; rather, it primarily addressed itself to pre-Islamic Arab society and its cultural and moral values, as well as to the day-to-day problems that arose in the process of transforming this society into a normative Muslim community.

Through *zakāt* (the religious welfare tax) and *ṣadaqah* (voluntary almsgiving), the Qur'ān makes care for the poor and needy a social responsibility and a meritorious act. The revenues from these two sources must be distributed among "the poor and needy, those who collect them [the taxes], those whose hearts are reconciled [i.e. non-Muslim sympathizers, with the view of attracting them to the new faith], and for the ransoming of captives of war, for debtors in God's cause, and the wayfarer" (see Q. 9:60). Yet even charity must have its limits. The Prophet is said to have counseled a rich and over-enthusiastic man who wanted to give all he had to the poor that he should not give away all his wealth and leave his children to beg for charity after his death. No more than a third of the wealth of a person who has children or other dependents should go to charity.

The Qur'ān strictly forbids usury as a means of increasing one's wealth. It also forbids illicit profit based on hoarding and speculation.

The ideal is neither voluntary poverty nor total attachment to material possessions. Rather the Qur'ān enjoins, "Seek by means of that which God has bestowed upon you the abode of the hereafter, but do not forget your portion of the present world" (Q. 28:77).

The Qur'ān stipulates harsh punishments for those grave offenses that are considered to be transgressions of the bounds of social conduct set by God. These punishments include amputation of the hand for theft, amputation of the hand and foot for highway robbery, eighty lashes for fornication, and capital punishment for intentional murder. The fundamental purpose of punishment is not to compound suffering, but to protect public order and reform society; its ultimate aim is to lead the offenders to repentance and virtuous conduct.

The Qur'ān does not promulgate absolute laws, even when it strictly demands the severe punishment of the thief, fornicator, or murderer. It is more concerned with moral issues in actual life situations. Among its over six thousand verses no more than two hundred are strictly legislative. In short, the Qur'ān points the way to a good and righteous life and leaves the details of how this goal is to be achieved to those who strive to attain proper understanding of the religion (see Q. 9:122). These are the jurists and *ḥadīth* specialists who have assumed this responsibility with utmost seriousness. Their efforts have shaped the moral and social life of the Muslim community.

The Sunnah of the Prophet

In our discussion of the problem of authority in Islam we observed that obedience to the Prophet is equal to obedience to God. This is because Muslims believe that, whatever the Prophet said or did, he acted on behalf of God and by his command. He could not err because, Muslims believe, all prophets are protected by God from sin and error. With regard to the Prophet Muḥammad in particular, the Qur'ān asserts:

> Your companion did not go astray, nor did he err.
> He speaks not out of capricious desire;
> Rather it is a revelation revealed to him (Q. 53:2–4).

The Prophet is reported to have declared: "I was given the Qur'ān and its equivalent [i.e. the *sunnah*] along with it." Hence the Prophet's actions and sayings are believed by Muslims to be divinely inspired. The Qur'ān asserts that God sent his Messenger with "the Book and the wisdom" (see Q. 62:2). Al-Shāfiʿī, the architect of the science of Islamic jurisprudence and founder of one of the four Sunni legal schools, argued that "the Book" is the Qur'ān and "the wisdom" is the *sunnah*. This view has been generally accepted by Muslims.

It may therefore be argued that the Prophetic *ḥadīth* tradition of Islam is in some ways parallel to the Oral Torah of Judaism. Like the Oral Torah, Prophetic *ḥadīth*s are believed to have been divinely inspired. Again like the Oral Torah, they present a tradition of legal learning in parallel to the community's scripture. In this case, the Prophetic *ḥadīth* tradition represents the oral tradition of the Prophet Muḥammad and his immediate Companions and of the religious science of the scholars who preserved, transmitted and codified it. But most importantly, Prophetic *ḥadīth* tradition played the same role in the development of Islamic jurisprudence as the Oral Torah played in the development of the Jewish halakhic law.

The Prophet's *sunnah* consists of his actions, his tacit consent, and his sayings. His acts are reported as anecdotes of situations or events to which he reacted or in which he participated. Such anecdotal reports may or may not include *ḥadīth* materials. Where they do not include *ḥadīth* materials, that is when no actual words of the Prophet are recorded, the report must go back to an eye-witness of the event. In situations where the Prophet indicated neither approval nor objection, his silence is taken to signify approval. Such anecdotal reports became normative as a source of legal decision for later jurists.

Along with the *sunnah* of action and the *sunnah* of consent, there is the *sunnah* of speech, collectively known as *ḥadīth*. The *ḥadīth*, moreover, is the most important of the three because it expresses more directly the Prophet's opinions or judgments with regard to moral and legal issues.

Contrary to the assertion of some orientalists, namely that *ḥadīth* tradition is essentially a third/ninth-century phenomenon, there is now increasing evidence indicating that interest in *ḥadīth* transmission and compilation began early in the second/eighth century. This interest was based on political, legal, and theological needs. What took over three centuries to develop was not interest in the Prophet's *sunnah*, but the process of evolving the science of *ḥadīth* criticism and of integrating *ḥadīth* into the discipline of jurisprudence.

The aim of the science of *ḥadīth* (*'ilm al-ḥadīth*) is to ascertain the authenticity of a particular *ḥadīth* by establishing the completeness of the chain of its transmission and the veracity of its transmitters. Thus a *ḥadīth* that has three or more complete chains of transmission, all of whose authorities are well known and recognized as pious people who cannot be accused of falsification, is considered a sound (*ṣaḥīḥ*) and universally accepted (*mutawātir*) tradition. A *ḥadīth* that has one complete chain of well-attested authorities going back to the Prophet through a well-known Companion is sound. Where one or more links in the chain of authorities is missing, or one or more of its transmitters is unknown, the *ḥadīth* is considered to be either good or weak, depending on the veracity of its remaining authorities. A *ḥadīth* most or all of whose transmitters are unknown, or known to be untrustworthy, is considered weak (*ḍa'īf*) or fabricated. Finally, *ḥadīth*s transmitted by single authorities are doubted or altogether rejected.

A *ḥadīth* consists of a chain of transmission (*isnād*), beginning with the compiler or last transmitter and going back to the Prophet, followed by the text (*matn*). Although some rules were set for *matn* criticism, they have not been applied as rigorously as those of *isnād* criticism. This is because it is assumed that if the honesty and piety of a transmitter is beyond question, then what he or she says cannot be subject to doubt. Generally speaking, the majority of *ḥadīth* traditions follow a set pattern of expression and subject matter. A *ḥadīth* that deviates from this pattern, but is otherwise considered to be good, is usually called strange (*gharīb*) or rare (*nādir*).

An exception to this norm is the genre known as *ḥadīth qudsī* ("divine" or "sacred utterance"). While Prophetic *ḥadīth* generally deal with legal or moral issues or with legislation, *ḥadīth qudsī* consist of moral or pious exhortations and reflections. *Ḥadīth qudsī* traditions are not the words of the Prophet but of God. Often their *isnāds*, after the Prophet, go through Gabriel and several other angels before they reach God, who is their final authority. Thus *ḥadīth qudsī* traditions are extra-Qur'anic revelations that are believed to have been either communicated to the Prophet by the angel Gabriel, or received by the Prophet in dreams.

These pious divine sayings have been a rich source of solace for Muslims in times of sorrow and adversity. Sufis have freely augmented the *ḥadīth qudsī* literature, making it a means of human colloquy with God and a source of affirmation of his nearness and love for his pious servants.

The following are three typical examples of *ḥadīth qudsī* traditions.

> When God decreed the creation of all things, He inscribed in a book which He keeps always before Him, "My mercy shall overcome My wrath."[34]

> The first of men to be judged on the Day of Resurrection will be a man who died a martyr. He will stand before God and God will make known to him His bounties and the man will acknowledge them. God will ask, "How did you use them?" "I fought in Your cause until I was martyred," the man will answer. But God will say, "You lie! Rather, you fought in order that it may be said of you 'He is brave.'" He shall thus be dragged headlong into the Fire. Another man will be one who acquired much learning and taught it to others and was a Qur'ān reciter. God will remind him of His bounties and he will acknowledge them. God will then ask, "How did you use them?" The man will answer, "I acquired much learning and taught others and I recited the Qur'ān for Your sake." But God will answer, "You lie! Rather, you acquired learning so that others may say 'He is a learned man'; and you recited the Qur'ān so that they may say 'he is a Qur'ān reciter.'" He too shall be thrown headlong into the Fire. Another will be a man upon

whom God bestowed good fortune and granted all kinds of riches. God will, likewise, remind him of His bounties and he will recognize them. God will ask, "How did you use them?" The man will reply, "I never neglected any manner of almsgiving, which You love, but rather I spent much wealth therein for Your sake." But God will say, "You lie! For you did all this only that people may say 'He is a generous man.'" He too shall be dragged headlong into the Fire.[35]

I am at My servant's expectation. And I am indeed with him when he makes mention of Me. If he remembers Me secretly in his mind, I will likewise secretly remember him in My mind. But if he makes mention of Me in an assembly, I will make mention of him in an assembly far better than it. If he draws nearer to Me the distance of a hand's span, I draw nearer to him an arm's length. And if he draws nearer to Me by an arm's length, I draw nearer to him by a phantom's length. If he comes to Me walking, I will come to him running.[36]

EARLY DEVELOPMENTS OF JURISPRUDENCE

Before discussing the development of Islamic jurisprudence, an important distinction must be made between sacred law, or "the law of God" (*sharīʿah*), and jurisprudence, or the process of human comprehension, interpretation, and codification of this law. In Islam, God is the ultimate law giver. Thus the *sharīʿah*, properly speaking, consists of the maxims, admonitions, and legal sanctions and prohibitions enshrined in the Qur'ān, and explained, elaborated, and realized in the Prophetic tradition.

The process of codification of the *sharīʿah* is called *fiqh*, or jurisprudence. The word *fiqh* is derived from the tri-lateral root *f / q / h*, meaning "to comprehend," "learn," or "understand" this divine law. The scholars who specialize in this exacting science are called *fuqahāʾ* ("jurists").

The Qur'ān calls upon Muslims in every community to choose from among them a group that must dedicate themselves to the acquisition of religious knowledge and "instruct their people when they turn to them" (Q. 9:122). This need was felt from the beginning. When the Madīnans that came to negotiate the Prophet's emigration to their city left him, they took back with them a few men that had acquired religious knowledge, so that they might teach the people of Madīnah the rituals and principles of the new faith. As tribal settlements and cities in Arabia, including Makkah, became Muslim domains, governors with special religious knowledge were sent by the Prophet to administer and instruct their people in Islam.

Among these was Mu'ādh b. Jabal, a man of the Anṣār, well known for his religious knowledge. Before he was sent to Yemen, the Prophet is said to have had the following exchange with him. The Prophet asked how Mu'ādh as governor would deal with the People of the Book (Jews and Christians), as most of the people of Yemen were. Mu'ādh answered that he would deal with them "in accordance with the Book of God and the *sunnah* of His Prophet." The Prophet then asked what he would do if he did not find the answer to a problem in either of the two sources. Mu'ādh answered, "I would then use my reason and would spare no effort."[37]

This exchange no doubt reflects much later developments in the science of jurisprudence and in its relationship to the Qu'rān and *sunnah* as its two primary sources. It was invoked to bestow on a developing discipline an aura of Prophetic blessing and authority. Nevertheless, the anecdote is a fitting description of the early stages of the development of Islamic law. Not only Mu'ādh, but other Companions were also known for their ability to deduce right judgments from Qur'anic principles and the acts and instructions of the Prophet.

With the rapid expansion of the Muslim domains through conquest, the need for a uniform body of religious law increased. For some time, Muslims of the first and second generations (the Companions and their successors), particularly those among them who were distinguished as Qur'ān reciters and transmitters of the Prophet's *sunnah*, filled that need and laid the foundations of future regional legal traditions. Until the end of the second Islamic century, these traditions centered in Iraq, especially in Kūfah and Baṣrah, and in the Ḥijāz, particularly in Madīnah and Makkah. It was in these centers that the "living tradition" of jurisprudence was transformed from an oral to a written science with a rich and ever-growing body of literature.

By the middle of the second/eighth century, the process of establishing distinctive legal schools with independent legal systems was well underway. Three men in particular distinguished themselves as the jurists of their time and as founders of the earliest legal schools. These were Ja'far al-Ṣādiq, the sixth Shi'ite Imām (d. 765), Abū Ḥanīfah (d. 767), the son of a Persian slave and founder of the Ḥanafī legal school, and Mālik b. Anas (d. 795), known as the scholar of Madīnah and founder of the Mālikī legal school. All three men knew and respected one another.

Ja'far al-Ṣādiq was especially revered as a descendant of the Prophet and heir to the knowledge of the Prophet's family (*ahl al-bayt*). He lived in Madīnah and was one of its leading scholars. He is regarded as the founder of the Shī'ī legal and religious system that bears his name as the Ja'farī legal school.

After the martyrdom of Ḥusayn b. 'Alī, the grandson of the Prophet and the third Shī'ī Imām, his descendants shunned politics and devoted themselves to religious learning and the task of establishing a new interpretation of Islam. Ja'far and his father Muḥammad al-Bāqir, the fifth Imām and grandson of Ḥusayn, are venerated by Muslims in general for their learning and piety. In spite of the fact that they left no written works, but rather a rich tradition orally preserved and only codified centuries later, they played a seminal role in the development of Shī'ī legal and theological thought and devotion.

Abū Ḥanīfah was the most famous jurist of Iraq; he too left no written sources that can be ascribed to him with certainty. However, his two disciples al-Shaybānī and Abū Yūsuf, who lived during the early and vigorous period of 'Abbāsid rule, developed their master's system into the most impressive and widespread Sunni legal school.

Mālik ibn Anas, the scholar of Madīnah, developed his legal system in the framework of a collection of *ḥadīth* and legal traditions. His book *al-Muwaṭṭa'* ("The Leveled Path") was the earliest such collection and thus reflects the early development of legal thought in Islam. Unlike later jurist-traditionists, Mālik gave equal weight to the Prophet's *sunnah* and the "practice," or "living tradition" of the people of Madīnah. He also showed far greater reliance on the effort to deduce well-considered legal opinions (*ijhtihād*) than did later distinguished religious scholars. He was frequently guided in this effort by the principle of the "common good," or "welfare" (*maṣlaḥah*) of the people.

Abū Ḥanīfah before him also showed greater reliance on rational thinking and living tradition. He resorted frequently to the two principles of analogical reasoning (*qīyās*) and rational preference (*istiḥsān*). The work of both Mālik and Abū Ḥanīfah indicates that the principle of Prophetic tradition (*sunnah*) as a material source of jurisprudence was then in the process of development. This is not to say, as some Western scholars have argued, that the *sunnah* as a material source of law was posterior to the principle that the "living tradition" of any major city or center of learning has force in law. Rather the two principles worked hand in hand, and both were ultimately referred back to the Prophet or the first generation of Muslims.

A decisive stage in the development of the science of jurisprudence came with the crucial work of Muḥammad b. Idrīs al-Shāfi'ī (d. 819). Although Shāfi'ī was closest to the school of Madīnah, he traveled widely and studied in different centers without clearly allying himself with any school. He spent his last years in Egypt where he wrote the first systematic treatise on Islamic jurisprudence. His hitherto unsurpassed work radically changed the scope and nature of this important discipline. Shāfi'ī advocated absolute dependence on the two primary sources of Islamic law, the Qur'ān and *sunnah*. He thus based his own system on a vast collection of *ḥadīth* and legal tradition entitled *Kitāb al-umm*; which he compiled for that purpose.

Shāfi'ī restricted the use of *qīyās*, or analogical reasoning, and rejected both the Ḥanafī principle of *istisḥān* and the Mālikī principle of *maṣlaḥah*. In his insistence on basing all juridical judgments on the

Qur'ān and *sunnah* he preferred, in opposition to the majority of jurists of his time, a *ḥadīth* transmitted on a single authority over personal opinion. His argument was that jurists should not rely on the opinions of men instead of the Book of God and the *sunnah* of his Prophet. Although Shāfiʿī's legal system was later adopted as the basis of the school bearing his name, he himself expressly opposed the idea. He saw himself not as the founder of a new legal school, but as a reformer of Islamic law.

Not long after Shāfiʿī, the well-known traditionist Aḥmad b. Ḥanbal (d. 855) founded the Ḥanbalī legal school strictly in conformity with Shāfiʿī's dictum. He produced one of the now standard *ḥadīth* collections, the *Musnad*, on which his legal system was founded. The *Musnad* of Ibn Ḥanbal was arranged not by subject as were other standard collections, but by the names of primary transmitters, usually the Prophet's Companions and other early authorities. While the *Musnad* of Ibn Ḥanbal is not the first work of this genre, it is by far the largest and most important one.

THE SIX CANONICAL ḤADĪTH COLLECTIONS

The science of *ḥadīth* criticism as outlined above was not perfected and fully implemented until the middle of the third/ninth century. It was actually an integral part of the science of jurisprudence and its crowning achievement. The comprehensive works based on it were intended as sources and to some extent, as manuals to be used by later jurists.

The most important Sunni *ḥadīth* traditionists are Muḥammad b. Ismaʿīl al-Bukhārī (d. 870) and Muslim b. al-Ḥajjāj al-Nīsābūrī (d. 875). They were, as their names suggest, from the cities of Bukhārā in Central Asia and Nishāpūr in the province of Khurāsān in northeastern Iran, respectively. Although contemporaries, the two men did not know one another. Yet each of them journeyed for many years across the Muslim world in search of *ḥadīth* traditions. The two works these long searches produced are amazingly alike, a fact strongly suggestive of an already existing unified and well-established *ḥadīth* tradition.

Al-Bukhārī and Muslim are each said to have collected hundreds of thousands of *ḥadīth*s out of which they selected about three thousand, discounting repetition. Their methodologies and systems of organization became the criteria that all subsequent *ḥadīth* compilers followed. Their two collections, entitled simply *Ṣaḥīḥ al-Bukhārī* and *Ṣaḥīḥ Muslim*, soon achieved canonical status, second in authority to the Qur'ān. Although the *Ṣaḥīḥ* of Muslim is better organized and methodologically superior to that of al-Bukhārī, the latter has achieved first place among all *ḥadīth* collections.

Within less than half a century after Muslim and al-Bukhārī, four other collections, those of Abū Dāwūd al-Sijistānī, Ibn Māja, al-Tirmidhī, and al-Nasā'ī, were produced. It is noteworthy that all four men, like Muslim and al-Bukhārī, were from Central Asia and Iran. Their works are entitled *Sunan* (pl. of *sunnah*) and combine the *sunnah*s of action, consent, and speech. In contrast, the works of Muslim and al-Bukhārī are essentially collections of sound (*ṣaḥīḥ*) *ḥadīth*, as their titles indicate.

The six canonical collections and others modeled on them are organized as legal manuals dealing first with laws governing the rituals of worship, then with the laws regulating the social, political, and economic life of the community. They are divided into books (or sections) beginning with the five pillars of the faith: first, *imān* and *islām*, then the prayers (beginning with the rules for ritual cleansing), followed by almsgiving (*zakāt*), fasting (*ṣawm*), and pilgrimage (*ḥajj*). In addition, they treat dietary laws, marriage and divorce, inheritance and related matters. They also include books on *jihād*, or war, and journeying in God's way. This section includes laws dealing with the status and treatment of *dhimmī*s, that is Jews, Christians, and other protected religious communities. Other sections include rules covering criminal acts, trade, and related matters.

THE NATURE AND SCOPE OF ISLAMIC LAW

The term *sharīʿah* originally signified the way to a source of water. Metaphorically it came to mean the way to the good in this and the next world. It is "the straight way" that leads the faithful to Paradise in the hereafter. The *sharīʿah* is believed by Muslims to be God's plan for the ordering of human society.

As we have been emphasizing, the *sharīʿah* is not an abstract system of ethics or moral philosophy, but a way of life; from the beginning it has been the framework of a positive law of government. In theory, Islam is a nomocracy, a government of laws not of men. Ideally, the purpose of an Islamic government is to ensure the implementation of God's law in human society.

According to the principles of Islamic law, the failure of Muslim governments to meet this ideal does not absolve individuals from the obligation to live their own lives in accordance with the *sharīʿah* and to urge others to do likewise. On the Day of Judgment all will be judged by the extent to which they endeavored to fulfill this purpose in this life.

Within the framework of divine law, human actions fall between those that are absolutely obligatory and will bring good rewards on the Day of Judgment, and those that are absolutely forbidden and will result in harsh punishment. They are classified into five categories as follows:

- lawful (*ḥalāl*) and obligatory;
- lawful and commendable, and therefore recommended (*mustaḥabb*);
- lawful and neutral, and therefore permitted (*mubāḥ*);
- not unlawful yet reprehensible, and therefore disliked (*makrūh*);
- unlawful and therefore forbidden (*ḥarām*).

These categories govern all human actions, acts of worship as well as human interrelations. They regulate personal conduct with regard to food and drink, dress and general behavior. They also cover family and social relationships, business transactions and international and inter-religious relations.

The correctness of an action and the intention that lies behind it define its nature and determine its consequence. This is the reason for the stress in Islam on outward moral conduct rather than on definitions of orthodox belief. Right belief is expressed in right worship, which is one of the chief concerns of the *sharīʿah.*

The two domains of the *sharīʿah* are therefore acts of worship (*ʿibādāt*) and human interrelations or transactions (*muʿāmalāt*). *ʿIbādāt* are essentially the five pillars of Islam and their ancillary rules. The close agreement among all legal schools with regard to *ʿibādāt* reflects the unity and coherence of the *sharīʿah* and its priority in Muslim life. Differences among the various legal schools are for the most part due to different interpretations of the *sharīʿah* with regard to the domain of human interrelations.

Islamic law as it was developed in the legal schools is based on four sources. Two of these, the Qur'ān and the *sunnah* of the Prophet and his generation, are its material and primary sources. The other two are formal sources that represent human endeavor and acceptance. They are the personal reasoning (*ijtihād*) of the scholars and the general consensus (*ijmāʿ*) of the community.

Personal reasoning, the first of the two formal sources of jurisprudence, is the process of deducing laws from the Qur'ān and *sunnah.* These deduced laws became the foundations for the legal schools and explain their diversity. The term "*ijtihād*" signifies a scholar's best effort in executing this process of deduction. It uses *qīyās*, or analogical reasoning, as its instrument.

The process of analogical reasoning consists of four methodological steps. The first is to find a text in the Qur'ān or *ḥadīth* pertinent to a new case or problem facing the jurist. The second is to discern the similarities and differences of the conditions surrounding the two cases. The third step is for the jurist to allow for such differences in making his judgment. The final step is to extend the rationale of the Qur'anic or *ḥadīth* judgment to cover the new case. Needless to say, the elaboration and application of these principles presented many difficulties and differences of opinion among jurists.

While the methodology of personal reasoning may be considered a tool for deriving Islamic law, the principle of consensus (*ijmāʿ*) is meant to be a standard by which the continuity, authenticity, and truth of the three other sources of law are ensured. In its widest sense, this principle embodies the community's acceptance and support of applied *sharīʿah*. More narrowly it has preserved, at least during the creative period of Islamic law, an active interchange of ideas among the scholars of the various schools. Consensus, moreover, has remained the final arbiter of truth and error, expressed in the Prophetic assertion "my community will not agree on an error."

Yet even this important principle has been the subject of much debate and dissension among the scholars of the various schools. One question that arose was whether the consensus of earlier generations is binding on the present one. Another was whether consensus refers to the agreement of the scholars of the different schools or to the consensus of the Muslim community at large. These are only two examples of the many issues involved.

At the heart of the debate have been the sometimes negative consequences of consensus. For, while it preserved the integrity of the *sharīʿah*, the principle of consensus arrested the development of Islamic law at its most crucial stage. This happened because *ijmāʿ* became so sacrosanct that no change after the establishment of the major Sunni legal schools was possible. The result has been that Islamic jurisprudence has become a thick wall protecting the *sharīʿah* while largely depriving it of its dynamic moral and spiritual role in Muslim society.

THE END OF IJTIHĀD AND THE VALORIZATION OF THE SUNNI LEGAL SCHOOLS

The Prophet is reported to have declared: "The best of you are those of my generation, then those who follow them, and then those who follow them ..."[38] This Prophetic judgment aptly expresses the widely held view that after the normative period of the Prophet and the first four "rightly guided caliphs," Muslim society progressively grew corrupt and irreligious. There were exceptions to this rule, men who modeled their lives and piety on that normative period. These were the well-known pious scholars, jurists, and traditionists of the formative period of Muslim history.

By the fourth/tenth century, with the establishment of the major Sunni legal schools and by a sort of undeclared common consensus, the "door of *ijtihād*" was generally considered to be closed. In fact this process of exclusion began earlier and depended not on religious or scholarly considerations, but on the granting of political patronage to some schools and its denial to others. This does not mean that Islamic legal thinking altogether ceased; it simply means that thereafter no new legal systems or schools were tolerated. Thenceforth, *ijtihād* was limited to the jurisconsult (*muftī*) of a city or country. To this day *muftī*s continue to issue legal opinions called *fatwā*s in accordance with the principles of their legal schools. Famous *fatwā*s have been collected into manuals for less creative or less able *muftī*s to draw on.

After a period of often violent conflict, the four Sunni legal schools discussed above gained universal acceptance as true and equally valid interpretations of the *sharī'ah.* They geographically divided the Muslim world among them. The Ḥanafī school was for centuries accorded state patronage, first by the 'Abbāsid caliphate and then by the Ottoman empire. It flourished in all the domains of the two empires: the Indian subcontinent, Central Asia, Turkey, Egypt, Syria, Lebanon, Jordan, and Iraq. Early on, the Mālikī school was carried to Egypt, the Gulf region, and North Africa, and from there to Spain, West Africa, and the Sudan. The Shāfi'ī school took roots early on in Egypt, where its founder lived and died. It spread to southern Arabia, and from there followed the trade routes to East Africa and to Southeast Asia, where it remains the dominant legal school.

Of the four, the Ḥanbalī school has attracted the smallest following; it has also had a disproportionately large influence, especially in modern times. It exists almost exclusively in central Arabia, the present Kingdom of Saudi Arabia, with scattered adherents in other Arab countries. Its conservative ideology, however, has been championed by revolutionaries and reformers since the thirteenth century.

Other minor schools have either died out, or still exist in small and isolated communities. The Ẓāhirī legal school, which was established early by the literalist jurist Dawūd b. Khalaf, ceased with the end of Muslim rule in Spain. The Ibāḍī school, established very early by the Kharijite leader and jurist ʻAbd Allāh b. Ibāḍ, is still represented in small communities in North Africa and Oman.

It should be observed that much of the history of the religious sciences is commonly shared by both the Sunni and Shīʻī communities. However, our account of the development of the Sunni legal schools tells only part of the story of the growth and crystallization of the Islamic religious sciences. Even though numerically the Shīʻī community comprises no more than twenty percent of the Muslims of the world, they have created an impressive system of belief and law. We shall in the following section concentrate specifically on the rise and development of their theological, legal, and *ḥadīth* traditions.

THE SHĪʻĪ TRADITION

It was observed, in our discussion of the problem of authority following the death of the Prophet and the crisis it precipitated, that this crisis created a permanent rift in the Muslim community. The rift began as a political movement or party (*shīʻah*) upholding ʻAlī's right to succeed the Prophet as leader or Imām[39] of the community. It was therefore called, somewhat scornfully, *shīʻat ʻalī* ("ʻAlī's party").

ʻAlī's supporters included some notable Companions from outside the merchant aristocracy of the Quraysh, many of the Anṣār of

Madīnah, and the Arab tribes of Kūfah in Iraq. Generally speaking, the *shī'ah* of 'Alī represented the poorer and under-privileged elements of Muslim society. It quickly attracted large numbers of non-Arab converts known as *mawālī*, who usually belonged to this underprivileged class. The *mawālī* were "clients" or "subordinate allies" of an Arab tribe or clan; a position that gave them quasi-Arab identity and status, as well as protection.

The *mawālī* were conquered people who, by and large, came from cultures superior to that of their Arab conquerors. During Umayyad rule these people were second class members of Arab-Muslim society. Thus it is not surprising that they played a major role in the 'Abbāsid revolution and its subsequent cosmopolitan administration and culture. They, moreover, exerted a great influence on Islamic, particularly Shī'ī, religious and political ideology.

By the tenth century, Sunni Islam had developed a stable and generally uniform legal and theological system. Shī'ī piety, which rests on an ethos of suffering and martyrdom, and hence a revolutionary ideology, has in contrast been a movement of change, instability, and wide diversity. Shi'ism is therefore a broad term covering a large number of disparate religio-political movements, sects, and ideologies. Common to most of these movements, however, is an allegiance to 'Alī and his descendants and their right to spiritual and temporal authority in the Muslim community after the Prophet.

A few short-lived movements either deified the Imāms of 'Alī's descendants, or regarded their own erstwhile leaders as incarnations of the Imāms. These were excessive and unwelcome expressions of what Shi'ism has always signified: an absolute devotion to and love for Muḥammad's family (*ahl al-bayt*). This devotion is based on a number of Qur'anic verses that exalt the families of major prophets, including that of the Prophet Muḥammad. The Qur'ān states: "God has chosen Adam and Noah, the family of Abraham and the family of 'Imrān [the ancestor of Moses and Aaron and of Mary, the mother of Jesus] over the rest of humankind" (Q. 3:33). The Abrahamic descent of

Muḥammad and his family through Ishmael places them in this company. The high status of Muḥammad's family is indicated in the assertion: "Surely, God wishes to take away all abomination from you, O People of the House, and to purify you with a great purification" (Q. 33:33). Furthermore, the Qur'ān commands Muḥammad: "Say, 'I wish no reward for it [i.e. conveying God's revelation] except love for [my] next of kin'"(Q. 42:23). "People of the House" (*ahl al-bayt*) and "next of kin" (*dhawi al-qurbā*) have generally been interpreted to refer to the Prophet's daughter Fāṭimah, her husband 'Alī, and their two sons, Ḥasan and Ḥusayn.

Shi'ite Muslims have based their claim of 'Alī's right to succeed the Prophet as the leader (*imām*) of the Muslim community on the following rather enigmatic Qur'anic verse:

> O Messenger, convey that which has been sent down to you from your Lord, for if you do not, you will not have conveyed His messages; and God will protect you from the people (Q. 5:67).

This verse is reported to have been revealed shortly before the Prophet's death, when he led the Muslims in his farewell *ḥajj* pilgrimage. According to Shī'ī tradition, the command to the Prophet was: "Convey that which was sent down to you from your Lord concerning 'Alī."

In obedience to this divine command, we are told, the Prophet halted his journey back from Makkah at a spot between Makkah and Madīnah called Ghadīr Khumm. Taking 'Alī by the hand, he addressed a large gathering of Muslims saying:

> O people, hear my words, and let him who is present inform him who is absent. Anyone of whom I am the master (*mawlā*), 'Alī too is his master. O God, be a friend to those who befriend him and an enemy to those who show hostility to him, support those who support him and abandon those who desert him.[40]

On the basis of this and other traditions wherein the Prophet is said to have directly or indirectly designated 'Alī as his successor, Shī'ī traditionists and theologians constructed an elaborate legal and theological system of legitimate authority based on the doctrine of *imāmah* and the divine designation of the Imām. (I shall examine this doctrine more fully when I discuss Twelver Imāmī Shiʿism.) Well before the elucidation of the doctrine of the *imāmah*, however, Shiʿism had already developed in several directions.

Following the martyrdom of Ḥusayn in 680, a group of his followers who had deserted him during his fateful battle with the Umayyad army were filled with remorse, and thus became known as "the penitents." Wishing to expiate their sin with their own blood, they rose against Yazīd's governor of Iraq, but were quickly routed and massacred.

This revolt inspired a shrewd and enthusiastic man called al-Mukhtār (*c.* 622–687) to lead a more serious uprising aimed at avenging the blood of Ḥusayn and his fellow martyrs. Al-Mukhtār's revolt plunged the Muslim state into a twelve-year period of chaos and civil strife. It was finally ruthlessly put down by the Marwanids, a new line of the Umayyad dynasty that lasted till the end of Umayyad rule in 750.

Al-Mukhtār introduced a serious innovation into the nascent Shīʿī ideology by claiming Muḥammad b. al-Ḥanafīyah, the son of ʿAlī by a woman other than Fāṭimah, as the rightly guided Imām (*al-mahdī*). He thus removed the condition of Fatimid descent for the Imām; this soon led others to remove the condition of ʿAlid descent altogether. Al-Mukhtār's idea led to the rise of the first extremist Shīʿī sect, al-Kaysānīyah.

This new sect, named after ʿAmrah b. Kaysān (a non-Arab follower of al-Mukhtār), introduced yet another belief, one that would be adopted by many other sects and schools including the Twelver Imāmī legal school: the doctrine of the occultation or concealment *(ghaybah)* of the Imām. The doctrine denied the fact of Muḥammad b. al-Ḥanafīyah's death, asserting instead that he went into occultation on a mountain near Makkah called Mount Raḍwah, and that he would return to vindicate his followers and establish just rule on earth. The sect attracted a large following before it fragmented into many disparate groups and died out.

An important phenomenon common to most Shīʿī movements is that they were born out of bloody but unsuccessful revolts. Thus a pious and highly revered grandson of Ḥusayn called Zayd led a brief uprising in Kūfah against the Umayyad caliph Hisham b. ʿAbd al-Malik in 740. Zayd was betrayed by his fickle followers and met his grandfather's fate.

Zayd's followers established a legal school bearing his name and based on his theological and legal ideas. In contrast to all other Shīʿī schools, the Zaydis accept the legitimacy of the caliphates of Abū Bakr and ʿUmar, although they too hold that ʿAlī was the rightful Imām after Muḥammad. They further hold that the Imām must be a descendant of ʿAlī and Fāṭimah, through either the Ḥasanid or Ḥusaynid line. He must, however, claim the office and support his claim by rising up, with the sword of Islam, against injustice and oppression. The Zaydi school belongs to the moderate wing of Shiʿism, and possesses a rich legal and theological tradition. It predominates to this day in the Yemen along with the Shāfiʿī legal school. The Zaydis are now without an Imām, as their last Imām was overthrown by the Yemeni revolution of 1962 and subsequently died in exile.

We have already noted the important role of Muḥammad al-Bāqir, Zayd's older brother, and of his son Jaʿfar al-Ṣādiq in the development of Shīʿī theology and jurisprudence. These two Imāms lived during a tumultuous period of transition from Umayyad to ʿAbbāsid rule. In the turmoil, a number of their followers claimed divinity for them, or for themselves. Such men were usually denounced by the Imāms and were, with their supporters, executed by the authorities.

The majority of Shiʿites accepted the line of Ḥusaynid Imāms down to Jaʿfar al-Ṣādiq (d. 765) who was the sixth Imām. The first major schism occurred when Jaʿfar's oldest son and successor, Ismaʿīl, died about ten years before his father. Jaʿfar then appointed a younger son, Mūsā al-Kāẓim, as his successor. This was regarded by many as an irregular appointment and was completely rejected by a significant group of Jaʿfar's supporters. They insisted that the imamate should continue in Isma'īl's line and, thus, they came to be known as Isma'īlīs or Seveners.

Basic to Isma'īlī faith and worldview is the doctrine of the divinity of the Imām and his absolute temporal and religious authority. This fundamental doctrine was developed within an impressive neo-Platonic philosophical system of prophetology by a number of famous Isma'īlī philosophers and theologians over the centuries. The doctrine of the divinity of the Imām, moreover, resulted in Isma'ilism becoming an esoteric and secret cult that was widely spread through an active network of missionaries and agents of the Imāms and their deputies.

In spite of their checkered history, the Isma'īlīs have played a conspicuous intellectual and political role in Muslim society. In North Africa, where Isma'īlī missionary activity was strong, the Imām declared himself caliph and successfully extended Isma'īlī rule into Egypt and Syria. As rulers, the Isma'īlī Imāms adopted the title "Fatimid" and declared themselves to be the legitimate caliphs of the Muslim community on the basis of their descent from 'Alī and Fāṭimah.

The third Fatimid caliph al-Mu'izz li-Dīn Allāh (r. 953–975) built the city of Cairo as his new capital. There he established al-Azhar, the first institution of religious learning and the headquarters of his missionary activities. In general, the Fatimid caliphs encouraged the development of an Isma'īlī legal and *ḥadīth* tradition in order to reenforce their own legitimacy. But, even before the end of Fatimid rule, interest in the *sharī'ah* died out altogether in the Isma'īlī community and Isma'ilism has remained an antinomian phenomenon in Islam.

Like most other Shī'ī sects, the Isma'īlī movement broke up into a number of often conflicting secret societies. During the reign of the highly idiosyncratic Fatimid Imām al-Ḥākim bi-Amr Allāh ("the ruler by God's command," r. 996–1021) a group of his extremist followers preached the doctrine of his divinity as the manifestation of God. The group was led for a while by a Turkish missionary called Muḥammad b. Nashtakīn al-Darazī; hence the name of the sect, al-Durūz (the "Druzes").

The Druzes are essentially a chiliastic religious sect holding that their leader Ḥamzah b. ʿAlī, a Persian missionary, is the "Master (*walī*) of the age"; that he is in occultation; and that he and al-Ḥākim, who is regarded as the "One" God, will return at the end of time to rule the world and usher in the end of this eon. They also believe in the reincarnation of the soul in a new-born child immediately after a person's death. The Druzes still exist as a small occult sect in Syria, Lebanon, and Israel.

After the overthrow of the Fatimid caliphate by Salāḥ al-Dīn (Saladin) in the twelfth century, Isma'ilism fell into general obscurity. For centuries Isma'īlīs have lived as members of an occult sect in the Indo-Pakistan subcontinent, East Africa, Syria, and Iran; called Nizārīs, they are the largest faction of Isma'īlīs. Nizārīs carry the line of Imāms through Isma'īl's son Aḥmad and his descendants down to the present. Their leader or Imām came to be known as the Agha Khan, an Indo-Iranian title signifying nobility. The third Agha Khan (d. 1957) initiated a process of reconciliation and reintegration of his followers into the Muslim community. This process has continued under his successor Karim Agha Khan (b. 1936). The Isma'īlīs have emmigrated in large numbers to the West, where they live as a prosperous and well-organized community.

As we have seen, the whole of the Isma'īlī or "Sevener" line of sects began (*c.* 765) with the original rejection by some Shi'ites of the sixth Imam Ja'far al-Ṣādiq's appointment of his younger son Mūsā al-Kāẓim as his successor. The majority of Shi'ites, however, accepted the appointment and followed the line of descent through Mūsā to the twelfth Imām, Muḥammad b. al-Ḥasan (b. 870). With the disappearance of the four-year-old Imām in 874, Shi'ites once again split over the question of succession to the imamate. The largest group to emerge were the "Twelver" or "Imāmī" Shi'ites and they remain the majority to this day.

Twelver Imāmī Shi'ism, as we have already observed, crystallized into a legitimate legal school in the tenth and eleventh centuries under Buyid patronage. It did not, however, begin as a legitimate school intent on setting the criteria for right belief and practice but, rather, largely as a reaction to earlier extremist and highly heterodox movements. These movements, moreover, left a noticeable mark on some of its basic beliefs and on its worldview.

It was within the Twelver Shīʿī tradition that the doctrine of *imāmah* was fully elaborated. According to this doctrine, the Prophet, through divine designation, appointed ʿAlī as his vicegerent or legatee (*waṣī*). ʿAlī in turn appointed his son Ḥasan to succeed him as Imām, and Ḥasan appointed his brother Ḥusayn. Thereafter, each Imām designated his successor, usually his oldest son. And so the line of Imāms continued to the twelfth Imām, who was the ninth descendant of Ḥusayn, and who did not die but went into a lesser occultation at the age of four years in 874. Until 941 the hidden Imām communicated with his Shīʿah through four successive deputies, he then entered into his greater occultation which, Imāmis believe, will last till the end of the world. Before the Day of Resurrection, he and Jesus will return to establish universal justice and true Islam on earth. The Prophet is said to have stated the matter thus:

> Even if only one day remains of the time allotted for this world, God will prolong this day until He sends a man of my progeny whose name shall be my name and whose patronymic (*kunya*) shall be my patronymic; he will fill the earth with equity and justice as it has been filled with inequity and wrongdoing.[41]

In spite of the doctrine of the imamate, Twelver Shiʿism remains, along with Zaydism, the closest legal school to Sunni orthodoxy. Imāmī Shiʿites agree with Sunni Muslims on the centrality of the Qur'ān and *sunnah* as the primary sources of Islamic law. They, however, define the *sunnah* not simply as the life-example of the Prophet Muḥammad and his generation, but as the life-example of the Prophet and those they believe to be his rightful successors, the Imāms. Hence the *sunnah* for Twelver Shīʿī Muslims extends over a period of three centuries, from the time of the Prophet till the end of the lesser occultation of the twelfth Imām Muḥammad b. Ḥasan al-ʿAskarī in 941.

In contrast with Sunni tradition, which first developed a science of jurisprudence and then a canonical *ḥadīth* tradition to buttress it, the Imāmī school based its legal system on the vast *ḥadīth* tradition transmitted from the Imāms. Beginning with the work of al-Kulaynī, who died in 941, at the end of the lesser and beginning of the greater occultation, this tradition was recorded in four major anthologies known as the "four books of *ḥadīth*." Al-Kulaynī compiled the first official *ḥadīth* collection, entitled *al-Kāfī* ("The Sufficient"), which he organized in several books; the first ones deal with the fundamentals of doctrine and worship, the others with legal ancillary matters along the lines of Sunni *ḥadīth* collections.

An important exception to the generally accepted organization of *ḥadīth* collections is the section dealing with the imamate, entitled *Kitāb al-ḥujjah* ("Book of the Proof of God") and included among the books dealing with the fundamentals of faith.[42] In fact, the fundamental belief in the necessary existence of the Imāms, as guardians of the *sharīʿah* and guides to its correct interpretation and implementation by the community, constitutes the essential point of difference between the Shīʿī and Sunni legal tradition. The Imām is believed to be the proof or argument (*ḥujjah*) of God over his human creatures. Hence, the earth cannot be without an Imām, be he manifest and active in the management of the affairs of the community, or hidden from human sight and perception.

Following al-Kulaynī, one of the foremost Shīʿī *ḥadīth* traditionists, Ibn Bābawayh, of the Iranian holy city of Qumm (d. 992), and known as al-Shaykh al-Ṣadūq ("the truthful shaykh"), compiled the second canonical *ḥadīth* collection. This and the two subsequent collections compiled by "the jurist doctor of the community" (*shaykh al-ṭāʾifah*) Abū Jaʿfar al-Ṭūsī (d. 1067), are intended as legal *ḥadīth* manuals. One of Ṭūsī's collections entitled *Tahdhīb al-aḥkām* ("The Proper Ordering of Legal Sanctions") is based on an earlier legal treatise by the famous traditionist-theologian al-Shaykh al-Mufīd, who died in 1022.

With Abū Ja'far al-Ṭūsī the foundations of Imāmī Shī'ī *ḥadīth* and legal tradition were virtually fixed. For Shi'ites the centrality of the doctrine of *imāmah* and the logical necessity of the existence of an Imām were firmly established. However, from the time of the greater occultation in 941, the Imām, though living, remained inaccessible. It was understood that in his absence the scholars of the community were delegated to fulfill his role, however imperfectly, as guardians of the *sharī'ah*. This in turn led to the understanding that *ijtihād*, or personal reasoning, had to go on and consensus had to be limited to the *ijmā'* of the scholars only.

Ijtihād was narrowly defined as the scholar's rational effort not so much to formulate new laws, but to comprehend and interpret the Imāms' rulings in ways that would apply to new situations. For this reason the Imāmī Shī'ī legal school rejected *qiyās*, or analogical reasoning, as an instrument of *ijtihād*. This does not mean that reason came to play a secondary role in the growth of Shī'ī jurisprudence. On the contrary, the primary sources of law were very early defined as the transmitted tradition (*naql*), including the Qur'ān, and human reason (*'aql*). Furthermore, where transmitted tradition and reason conflict, reason takes priority over tradition in a scholar's effort to resolve the conflict.

While *ijtihād* has remained a primary source of law for Shī'ī jurists, the principle of precaution (*iḥṭīyāt*), based on the fear of erring in judgment in the absence of the Imām, has tended to minimize the use of personal reasoning; so much so, that jurists with any measure of originality have, until recently, been few and far-between. Moreover, the principle of *taqlīd*, or the necessity for every Shī'ī man and woman to imitate a recognized jurist in all their legal actions, has had the same effect on the Shī'ī community as the closing of the gate of *ijtihād* has had on Sunni Muslims. The need for courageous and sensitive new approaches to the interpretation and application of the *sharī'ah* is therefore imperative in both communities.

As Imāmī Shi'ism spread into most areas of the Muslim world, becoming in the sixteenth century the state religion of Iran, it interacted with many currents of thought and piety. The result has been the rise on its fringes of a number of antinomian sects and movements. Two major currents of extremist Shiʿism that persisted till the nineteenth century are the Mukhammisah and the Mufawwiḍah. Sects based on the first current of thought deified the five (*khamsah*) personages (Muḥammad, ʿAlī, Fāṭimah, Ḥasan, and Ḥusayn) and held that from eternity they were united in essence and differentiated only in name. Although the five appear throughout human history as different prophets and Imāms, they are in reality one single divine essence.

The Mufawwiḍah ("delegationists") believed that God first created the five holy personages and their descendents, the Imāms; he then delegated to them the creation of the world. They held that God, who is unknowable in his essence, had not only delegated the creation of the world but also all its affairs, including the last judgment, to the Imāms. The notion that the final judgment is delegated by God to the Imāms has had a clear influence on Imāmī Shīʿī messianic eschatology.

After the lesser occultation of the twelfth Imām, such beliefs and ideas produced the extremist sect of the Nuṣayrīs. The sect was founded by Muḥammad b. Nuṣayr al-Namīrī, a companion of the tenth and eleventh Imāms. The Nuṣayrīs are also known as ʿAlawīs, those who regard ʿAlī as an incarnation of God. The Nuṣayrīs exist to this day as a fairly large and influential community in Syria. Other communities holding similar beliefs still exist in Turkey and Iran.

A number of sects mixing popular Sufi and extremist Shīʿī piety appeared between the thirteenth and sixteenth centuries in various regions under Imāmī Shīʿī influence. In the nineteenth century a fascinating theosophical sect known as the Shaykhīs appeared in Arabia. The sect was named after its founder Shaykh Aḥmad Zayn al-Dīn (d. 1826), of the province of Aḥsaʾ in the present kingdom of Saudi Arabia. Under the influence of the theosophical ideas of this school arose the Babi and Bahai faiths in Iran.

Because Imāmī Shi'ism is a *sharī'ah*-based legal school, it has generally been accepted by the rest of the Muslim community. With regard to the fundamentals of faith and worship, the Imāmī Shī'īs may also be regarded as *sunnīs*, that is followers of the *sunnah* of Muḥammad. Moreover, Shī'ī piety, and especially Shī'ī devotion to the Prophet's family, has deeply influenced popular Sunni piety.

Before the Iranian revolution, genuine efforts were made at achieving a meaningful rapprochement among all Islamic legal schools. This noble goal has unfortunately fallen victim to the political turmoil of the last two decades of the twentieth century. It nonetheless remains the hope of many Muslims today.

8

Sufism: The Mystical Tradition

The rise and rapid spread of Islam was, as we have seen, an eminently successful historical process. There was, however, a darker side to this story, manifested in power struggles and tribal loyalties and intrigues, as well as in the wealth and worldliness that naturally resulted from Islam's rapid expansion. Very early, voices that came to represent important movements of protest were raised against the materialism of Muslim society and its rulers. These movements coalesced in Shiʿism, which challenged the political and moral legitimacy of caliphal authority, and Sufism, which condemned the deviation of Muslim society from its spiritual and humanistic ideals.

THE ORIGINS OF SUFISM

The term *taṣawwuf* (Sufism) is derived from the Arabic word "*ṣūf*," meaning wool. In emulation of Jesus, who is represented in Islamic hagiography as a model of ascetic piety, early Sufis wore a garment of coarse undyed wool on their bare skin as a sign of ascetic poverty. In fact, early ascetics sought out Christian desert hermits from whom they learned ascetic practices and ideas. The primary sources of Islamic mysticism, however, are the Qur'ān and Prophetic tradition and the lives of early pious Muslims.

The Qur'anic doctrine of God, which simultaneously affirms God's transcendence as the sovereign Lord, creator, and judge of the universe, and his immanence as its merciful sustainer, has been a rich source of mystical piety. It is a fact that is never forgotten. Indeed, an essential aspect of mysticism is the remembrance of God. The Qur'ān enjoins the pious to "remember God much" (Q. 33:41), to "remember God in the morning and evening" (Q. 76:25), for "in the remembrance of God hearts find peace and contentment" (Q. 13:28). The ultimate purpose of all creation is to worship God and hymn his praise (see Q. 17:44 and 51:56).

Theistic mysticisms of the three Abrahamic religious traditions adore God's majesty as well as his beauty. The Qur'ān proclaims God's majesty in many verses, but one that has captivated the imagination of pious Muslims is "The Throne" verse, which celebrates God's absolute oneness, eternal sovereignty and all-encompassing knowledge, power, and providential care. He is the "Lord of the throne," whose throne encompasses the heavens and the earth (Q. 2:255). God's beauteous qualities are celebrated in another equally popular passage, "The Light" verse:

> God is the light of the heavens and the earth. The similitude of His light is like a niche in which is a lamp. The lamp is in a glass. The glass is like a radiant star, kindled from a blessed tree, an olive neither of the east nor of the west. Its oil is about to shine forth, even though no fire touches it. Light upon light, God guides to His light whomever He will; God strikes similitudes for humankind, and God is knower of all things (Q. 24:35).

Yet in all his majesty and beauty and distance, God, for pious Muslims, is not far. The story of Adam in the Qur'ān shows humankind's proclivity to evil. It also describes how God fashioned this sinful earthly creature with his own two hands and breathed into him his spirit.

And the Qur'ān asserts that God is nearer to every human being "than his own jugular vein" (see Q. 50:16).

The Prophet's night vigils and other devotions, alluded to in the Qur'ān (see Q. 73:1–8) and greatly embellished by hagiographic tradition, have served as a living example for pious Muslims across the centuries. The *ḥadīth* traditions, particularly the divine sayings (*ḥadīth qudsī*), have provided a rich source of mystical piety. Most of all, the Prophet's heavenly journey (*mi'rāj*) has been a guide for numerous mystics on their own spiritual ascent to God.

The Prophet's Companions, especially 'Alī and Abū Bakr, have provided the mystical tradition with good examples of ascetic piety and esoteric knowledge. Like the Prophet, they renounced this world and lived in poverty. Other Companions and their successors have also been presented in Sufi hagiography as great examples of mystical piety for the faithful to emulate.

EARLY ASCETICISM

Islamic mysticism began, as we have already observed, as an ascetic movement. The early ascetics were known as *zuhhād*, meaning "those who shun the world and all its pleasures." One of the earliest champions of this movement was the well-known theologian and traditionist Ḥasan al-Baṣrī, who was born in Madīnah in 642 and died in Baṣrah, in southern Iraq, in 728. He thus lived through both the crises and rise to glory of the Muslim *ummah*. In a letter addressed to the pious Umayyad caliph 'Umar b. 'Abd al-'Azīz (r. 717–720), Ḥasan likened the world to a snake: soft to the touch, but full of venom. He further held that God hates nothing more than this world and that, from the time he created it, he has not looked upon it even once.

The early ascetics were also called weepers, for they wept incessantly in fear of God's punishment and in yearning for his reward. In this, too, they were following a well-attested Prophetic *ḥadīth*, which reads, "Two eyes will not be touched by Hell-fire: an eye that keeps watch at night in the way of God [that is, one who engages in the wars of *jihād*] and an eye that weeps constantly in awe of God."[43]

It is noteworthy that this early ascetic movement began in areas of mixed populations where other forms of asceticism had existed for centuries. These centers were Kūfah and Baṣrah in Iraq, Khurasān in north east Iran (particularly the Balkh region in modern Afghanistan), and Egypt. Iraq had long been the home of eastern Christian asceticism. Balkh was an ancient center of Buddhist ascetic piety. Long before Islam, Egypt was the home of Christian monasticism as well as gnostic asceticism. However, because Islam is essentially a non-ascetic religion, this ascetic movement was soon transformed into a genuine Islamic mystical tradition.

The transformation had its basis in the repudiation by both the Qur'ān and Prophetic tradition of monastic celibacy and their insistence on total involvement in the affairs of this world. Opposition to asceticism for its own sake was expressed by well-known scholars and representatives of early mystical piety. Among these was Ja'far al-Ṣādiq, who argued that when God bestows a favor on his servant, he wishes to see it manifested in the servant's attire and way of life. Ja'far's grandfather 'Alī Zayn al-'Ābidīn is said to have argued that God should be worshiped not out of fear of Hell or desire for Paradise, but in humble gratitude for his gift to the servant of the capacity to worship him.

This latter ideal came to be personified by the woman mystic Rābi'ah al-'Adawīyah of Baṣrah (d. 801), who combined in her own life both asceticism and divine love. Because of adverse family circumstances, Rābi'ah was sold into slavery as a child. Her master was so impressed with her piety that he set her free; she lived the rest of her life alone.

Rābi'ah loved God with no other motive but love itself. Her love was free from either desire for Paradise or fear of Hell. Her prayer was:

> O God, if I worship You in fear of Hell, burn me in Hell, and if I worship You in hope of Paradise, exclude me from Paradise; but if I worship You for Your own sake, withhold not from me Your everlasting beauty.[44]

Mystical love is not a metaphysical principle, but an outpouring of passionate love. Mystics of all religious traditions have used the language of erotic love to express their love for God. Rābiʿah was perhaps the first to introduce this language into Islamic mysticism. She loved God with two loves, a passionate love (*hawā*) and a spiritual love worthy of him alone, both of which came to be important expressions of love of God.

FORMATIVE HISTORY

The ninth to eleventh centuries constitute the formative period of Sufism during which most of its basic principles, beliefs, and practices were developed. An important figure of the ninth century was Dhū al-Nūn al-Miṣrī ("the Egyptian"; d. 859), who was the first to distinguish between *maʿrifah*, or divine gnosis, and *ʿilm*, knowledge acquired through discursive reasoning. In his aphoristic sayings, Dhū al-Nūn speaks tenderly of the love of God, whom the true gnostic hears and sees in every sound and phenomenon of nature.

Dhū al-Nūn speaks of God in terms of opposites, which coincide in him alone. God is the one who gives life and causes death, the one who loves his servant and afflicts him with pain and torment. Dhū al-Nūn was also the first to elaborate the theory of the stations and states that the mystic experiences on the spiritual journey to God.

The love of which Rābiʿah and Dhū al-Nūn spoke was the devotional love of the worshipful servant for her or his Lord. It did not imply an absolute union of the devotee with God. Such ideas belong to mystical ecstasy, of which there were many well-known and controversial proponents.

Bayazīd Bistāmī (d. 874), about whose life little is known, was one of the best representatives of ecstatic Sufism. Bayazīd saw the quest of the mystic lover as the attainment of absolute union and hence total annihilation in God. In this union only God exists, for the attributes of the mystic lover are completely annihilated in the divine attributes. In this state of annihilation (*fanā'*), it is not the lover who speaks when he speaks, but God who speaks through him.

Bayazīd couched his mystical theories in pithy theopathic utterances known as *shaṭaḥāt* ("fantastic utterances") that shocked his uninitiated hearers. His intoxicated cries of "Glory be to me, how great is my majesty!" and "There is none in this garb save God" were regarded as utter blasphemy by the *'ulama'*. For the initiated mystic, however, such utterances are excusable because they are uttered in the state of mystical intoxication.

Bayazīd was a pious scholar of the religious sciences and strictly observed the rituals of worship and other requirements of the *sharī'ah*. In his mystical life, however, he represented intoxicated Sufism, in contrast with his near contemporary Abū Qāsim al-Junayd of Baghdad (d. 910) who typified sober devotional mysticism.

Ḥusayn b. Manṣūr al-Ḥallāj, another intoxicated Sufi, was brutally executed by the 'Abbāsid authorities in 922 for his theopathic utterances. Al-Ḥallāj was initiated into Sufism early in life. He traveled widely and studied with the best-known Sufi masters of his time, including al-Junayd. After some time, al-Ḥallāj broke away from his teachers and embarked on the long and dangerous quest for self-realization. It all began when he went one day to see al-Junayd, who asked who was at the door. Al-Ḥallāj answered, "I, the Absolute [or Creative] Truth" (*anā al-ḥaqq*). *Al-ḥaqq* is one of the ninety-nine names of God mentioned in the Qur'ān. Al-Junayd is reported to have sharply reprimanded his wayward disciple and predicted an evil end for him.[45]

After a period of travel that took him as far as India, where he came into contact with sages of other religious traditions, al-Ḥallaj returned to Baghdad and became an itinerant preacher with great charismatic appeal. He attracted many disciples, but also many enemies among the *'ulama'* as well as moderate Sufis. He was suspected by the authorities of secretly allying himself with the Qarmatians, an extremist Ismaī'lī sect that posed a considerable threat to the central government of Baghdad.

While the core of al-Ḥallāj's message was moral and deeply spiritual, his seemingly incarnationist theology and at times antinomian behavior shocked most of his Muslim contemporaries. In contrast with Bayazīd who preached annihilation of the mystic in God, al-Ḥallāj preached total identification of the lover with the beloved. This is clearly expressed in the following ecstatic verses:

> I am He whom I love, and He whom I love is I.
> We are two spirits dwelling in one body.
> If you see me, you see Him
> And if you see Him, you see us both.[46]

In these verses al-Ḥallāj speaks of God dwelling in a human body. To the *'ulama'*, this meant incarnation. The term *ḥulūl* ("indwelling") used by al-Ḥallāj is one of the terms used by Arabic-speaking Christians to signify the incarnation of Christ, the eternal logos, in a human body. He was therefore accused of spreading a Christian heresy.

Most probably al-Ḥallāj had no theological or metaphysical theories in mind but, rather, spoke under the influence of divine intoxication. Furthermore, both he and his later defenders were well aware that the secret of love must not be divulged to the uninitiated, who would rightly be scandalized by it. But al-Ḥallāj, who continuously remained in a state of intoxication (*sukr*), could not keep his love for God a secret.

Like Jesus on the cross, al-Ḥallāj, too, forgave his executioners. Unlike Christ, he did not pray God to forgive them because "they know not what they do," but because they rightly condemned him to death in defense of God's religion. After an extended imprisonment and much controversy, al-Ḥallāj danced in his chains to the gallows. He begged his executioners:

> Kill me, O my trusted friends, for in my being killed is my life.
> My death is in my life and my life is in my death.[47]

Al-Ḥallāj lives on in the piety and imagination of many Muslims as the martyr of love who was killed for the sin of intoxication with the wine of the love of God by the sword of the *sharī'ah* of God.

THE CRYSTALLIZATION OF SUFISM

Although ecstatic mysticism contributed substantially to the intellectual and spiritual maturity of Sufism, it was too esoteric for the masses and highly suspect for the religious establishment. Devotional sober Sufism, however, continued to appeal to Muslims who found the hair-splitting arguments of the jurists and theologians irrelevant to their spiritual needs.

With the spread of Sufi spirituality, there was a pressing need for a body of literature that could explain Sufism and legitimize it as one of the religious sciences. To meet this need, a vast literature consisting of manuals, biographical dictionaries, Qur'ān commentaries, theosophical writings, and mystical poetry was produced. The manuals especially were used to explain esoteric ideas and sayings of ecstatic mystics, to place Sufism in the framework of the Qur'ān, Prophetic tradition, and the *sharī'ah*, and to present it as a universal and non-sectarian way to God, open to all Muslims.

The mystical life is in reality a spiritual journey to God. The novice who wishes to embark on such an arduous journey must be initiated and guided by a master, a *shaykh* or *pir*. The *shaykh* of a disciple (*murīd*) is a spiritual parent. So intimate is the relationship between masters and disciples, that disciples must absolutely obey their master. As Sufism grew and many well-recognized masters attracted too many disciples to allow for a one-to-one relationship, teaching manuals became necessary to help in imparting the ideas of great masters to eager disciples.

The crystallization of Sufism and its general acceptance as a legitimate mode of Islamic piety reached a high point in Abū Ḥāmid Muḥammad al-Ghazālī (d. 505/1111), who was born in Ṭūs, near the modern Iranian city of Mashhad. According to a widely accepted Prophetic tradition, at the start of every century God will raise a scholar who will renew and strengthen the faith of the Muslim community. Such a man is known as a *mujaddid* ("renovator") of the faith.

Al-Ghazālī has been regarded as the *mujaddid* of the sixth Islamic century. His work went far beyond mysticism to cover all the religious sciences.

In 1091 al-Ghazālī was appointed as a professor of theology and law at the prestigious Nizāmīyah college in Baghdad. There he tirelessly defended mainline Sunni Islam against the innovations of the theologians and the heresies of the philosophers and of the occult Ismaī'lī doctrines. Four years later al-Ghazālī underwent a deep psychological crisis. He gave up his teaching and embarked on a long quest for true knowledge. Absolutely certain knowledge (*yaqīn*), he came to realize, could be attained neither through the senses nor through the rational sciences, but only through divine light, which God casts into the heart of the person of faith.

Having regained his reason and achieved enlightenment, al-Ghazālī produced one of the most ambitious and indispensable works on the religious sciences, appropriately entitled *Iḥya' 'ulūm al-dīn* ("The Revivification of the Religious Sciences"). This *magnum opus* deals with all the religious sciences from a deeply mystical point of view. Through this work and al-Ghazālī's own impeccable Sunni orthodoxy, Sufism secured a place of honor in Muslim piety. Thenceforth, many jurists have also been noted masters of the mystic way.

STATIONS AND STATES

The Qur'ān enjoins Muslims to "journey in the earth and observe the end of bygone generations." Mystics have taken this injunction both figuratively and literally. Thus, they have been great spiritual as well as physical wanderers.

Sufi disciples are called "travelers" (sing. *sālik*). Their spiritual journeys consist of many stations or stages (*maqāmāt*; sing. *maqām*) and psycho-spiritual states or conditions (*aḥwāl*; sing. *ḥāl*). Once attained, a station remains with the traveler, who must then progress to the next stage. A state (*ḥāl*), on the other hand, is a divine gift, a momentary flash of spiritual insight or a psychological condition. Mystical states are alternating psychological conditions through which the mystic passes on the spiritual journey. States of extreme depression or contraction of the self (*qabḍ*) may alternate, without any apparent reason, with states of extreme elation or expansion (*basṭ*). In their spiritual strivings, mystics may alternate between moments of intoxication (*sukr*) and sobriety (*ṣaḥw*) but they do not remain in any state permanently.

The first step on this spiritual journey is the intention of the traveler to turn to God with sincere repentance (*tawbah*). The second is poverty or absolute self-insufficiency (*faqr*). The third is steadfastness or patience (*ṣabr*) in all things. The fourth is gratitude (*shukr*) for whatever God decrees, be it good or ill. The fifth is absolute trust (*tawakkul*) in God. The sixth is complete acceptance of, or contentment (*riḍā*) with whatever God decrees for his servant. The seventh station is bewilderment or utter confusion (*ḥayrah*) in the presence of the beloved. These stations express the Sufi quest for God and the Sufi's effort to realize it.

The next four stations are the states of intimacy of the lover with the beloved, which culminate in a new life in God. The first is love (*maḥabbah*), which is a divine favor; it is the capacity to respond to God's love. This is understood to mean that God's pious servants can love him only in answer to his love for them. The Qur'ān says concerning them, "those whom God loves and who love Him" (Q. 5:54). The second is nearness to God (*qurb*), as true love always impels the lover to seek the company of the beloved. The third is happiness or bliss (*uns*) in the company of the beloved. The fourth station of this journey to God has often been explained by Sufi poets through the simile of the moth that flutters around a lamp in a state of total absorption until it plunges into the flame and is consumed, thus becoming one with the light. The stations of love, proximity, and blissful companionship inevitably lead to this last station or state of annihilation (*fanā'*) of the self of the lover, and all its attributes in God's attributes. This state is based on the Prophetic injunction: "Emulate in your morals God's moral characteristics."

Since God is the final quest of the mystic, even the station of *fanā'* must be renounced so as not to stand as a veil between the lover and the beloved. Hence, the final station of the journey is the annihilation of annihilation (*fanā' al-fanā'*). When, like the moth, the lover no longer exists, then God grants the lover a new life or subsistence (*baqā'*) in God. Thus transformed, the mystic lover returns to the world to show others the way.

THEOSOPHICAL SUFISM

The term "theosophy" means "divine wisdom." In contrast with philosophy, which aims at knowledge of God or ultimate reality through rational wisdom, theosophy seeks divine knowledge through esoteric gnosis or divine illumination.

The journey to God follows different paths depending on the spiritual and intellectual potential of the traveler. These paths are the ways of illumination and of contemplation. But since God, the ultimate goal of the journey, is in his essence beyond human conception and knowledge, a third way, the way of negation, must always guide the traveler along the middle course between divine immanence and transcendence, between extreme monism and pantheism. The way of negation, which speaks of God as "not this, not this," to use a Hindu mystical phrase, insures a proper relationship between the worshipful servant and his or her Lord.

The way of illumination was elaborated by the great master of illumination (*shaykh al-ishrāq*) Shihāb al-Dīn Suhrawardī (d. 1191). Drawing on the Qur'anic "Light" verse and Ghazālī's interpretation of it in his famous treatise *Mishkāt al-anwār* ("The Niche of Lights"), and on ancient Iranian and neo-Platonic wisdom, Suhrawardī constructed an impressive cosmos of light and darkness populated by countless luminous angelic spirits. The source from which this divine cosmos emanates is God, who is veiled from the human soul by veils of light and darkness. The soul's ultimate quest is to penetrate these veils through the power of intellect, until it returns to its original heavenly source. While in the body, the soul is in the exile of the west, the realm of darkness. The body is likened to a deep well into which the soul falls and out of which it seeks to escape and return to the east, the source of light.

Suhrawardī belongs to the ancient gnostic tradition, which had its source in Greco-Iranian wisdom. Gnosticism, which was rejected by the ancient Church, was accepted in its Islamic form by Shīʿī theosophy as *ʿirfān* ("divine gnosis"). Thus Suhrawardī's theosophy has had a deep and lasting influence on Shīʿī esoteric wisdom.

IBN ʿARABĪ, THE GREAT SHAYKH

By far the most important master of Islamic theosophy was Muḥyī al-Dīn Ibn ʿArabī. Ibn ʿArabī was born in Muslim Spain, where he received his early Islamic education. He thus belonged to its eclectic mystical tradition. He traveled widely in the Middle East, finally settling in Damascus where he died in 1240.

The core doctrine of Ibn ʿArabī's theosophy is "the unity of being" (*waḥdat al-wujūd*), which he elaborated in numerous books and treatises. According to this doctrine, God in his essence remains from eternity in "blind obscurity." However, he makes himself known in his creation through an eternal process of self-disclosure or manifestation (*tajallī*). According to Ibn ʿArabī therefore, human beings need God for their very existence, but God also needs them in order to be known.

This means that all beings are in reality manifestations of God's attributes of either majesty or beauty. Beings that represent harmony, love, compassion, and mercy manifest God's beauteous attributes, which are supremely expressed in Paradise. On the other hand, beings that represent disharmony or overwhelming power and judgment manifest God's attributes of majesty, which are fully expressed in Hell. It follows from this that if Muḥammad, as a guide to God, represents God's attribute *al-hādī* ("he who guides aright"), then Satan, who leads into error, represents God's attribute *al-muḍill* ("he who leads astray"). This means that there is in reality no good or evil, but only God, the highest Good.

Ibn 'Arabī's doctrine of the unity of being had many implications. For instance, if God alone really is, then all ways ultimately lead to him. This means that the various religions are mere names, for the reality is one. Ibn 'Arabī says:

> My heart has become capable of every form, a pasture for gazelles and a cloister for monks, a temple for idols and a pilgrim's Ka'bah, the tablets of the Torah and the scroll of the Qur'ān. It is the religion of love that I hold: wherever its caravan turns, love shall be my religion and my faith.[48]

Between the material world of multiplicity and the divine realm of unity stands the "perfect man" (*al-insān al-kāmil*); his existence is necessary for the world's existence. This perfect man is the Prophet Muḥammad, whose light, or Muḥammadan reality, was the first to be created by God. Thus Muḥammad becomes the divine creative logos, for whose sake all things were created. He is the seal of the prophets, while the perfect man after him is the seal of the saints (*awlīyā'*).

Little of Ibn 'Arabī's thought is new or original. Yet, as a great systematizer, he remains one of the greatest mystical geniuses of all time. In the poetry of ecstatic mystics, his idea of the unity of being led to the cry of Persian Sufis of "All is He!" (*hamā-ūst*). His idea of the perfect man raised Muḥammad to a divine status high above mortal man. In fact, the Muḥammad of Ibn 'Arabī is more like the Christ of Christianity than like the all too human Prophet of the Qur'ān. Ibn 'Arabī's theosophical system is the most creative product of the multireligious society of Muslim Spain.

EPIC POETRY

The thirteenth century was one of the most troubled and also one of the most creative periods of Muslim history. Like Ibn 'Arabī, other great Persian and Arab poets imparted the mysticism of love in a rich variety of themes and expressions. The Egyptian poet 'Umar b. al-Fāriḍ (d. 1235) presents the spiritual journey to God in exquisite verses unsurpassed in Arabic poetry. Another poet, the Persian Sufi Farid al-Dīn 'Aṭṭār, presents the same journey in touching allegorical tales. In his allegory "The Conference of the Birds" (*Manṭiq al-ṭayr*), 'Aṭṭār tells of thirty birds (*sīmurgh*) setting out on a long and arduous journey in search of the legendary phoenix (*simurgh*), the king of birds.[49] Having passed through the various mystical states and stations, they arrive at the realization that the object of their quest was in reality within them.

The most creative poet of the Persian language is Jalāl al-Dīn Rūmī (d. 1273) who, like Ibn 'Arabī, was the product of a multi-religious and multicultural environment. Rūmī was born in Balkh, but as a child fled with his parents before the advancing Mongols. Finally the family settled in Konya, the ancient Byzantine city Iconium, in central Anatolia.

In 1244 Rūmī met Shams of Tabriž, a wandering Sufi. The two men developed a relationship of closest intimacy, such that Rūmī neglected his teaching duties as he could not be separated from his friend for a single moment. In the end Shams disappeared and Rūmī poured out his soul in heart-rending verses expressing the love he held for the "Sun (*shams*) of Tabrīz."

Rūmī's greatest masterpiece is his *Mathnawī* ("Book of Couplets") consisting of over thirty thousand verses. The spirit of this vast poetic panorama may be clearly discerned in its opening verses which portray the haunting melodies of the *neyy*, or reed-flute, telling its sad tale of separation from its reed-bed. In stories, couplets of lyrical beauty, and at times even coarse tales of sexual impropriety, the *Mathnawī* depicts the longing of the human soul for God.

SUFI BROTHERHOODS

The institution of religious fraternities is an ancient and widespread phenomenon. The Sufi idea of the friendship (*ṣuḥbah*) of kindred spirits provided the framework for this phenomenon in Muslim piety.

The Islamic emphasis on communal life and worship was no doubt another determining factor. The earliest Sufi brotherhoods date back to the late eighth century. Small ascetic groups gathered on the island of Abadan in the Persian Gulf away from the allurements of city life. With its harsh climate, Abadan was well suited for ascetic austerities.

As has already been observed, the Buyids, who patronized Shiʿite religious and philosophical learning, were succeeded in the eleventh century by the Seljukids, a staunch Sunni dynasty. To promote Sunni orthodoxy, Seljuk rulers encouraged Sufi brotherhoods as a counterweight to Shīʿī, and particularly Ismaʿīlī, missionary activities. This patronage made Sufi fraternities an important social and spiritual force in Muslim society.

By the thirteenth century, these fraternities became institutionalized in "mystical paths" (*ṭarīqahs*), or Sufi orders. They began as teaching and devotional institutions centered in *khānqāhs* and *zāwiyahs* in Persian and Arab urban centers. A Sufi order was usually founded by a famous shaykh, or a disciple in his shaykh's name. A *zāwiyah* or *khānqāh* was often a large compound consisting of a school, a mosque, and the disciples' humble dwellings surrounding the residence of the shaykh, or head of the order.

Sufi orders often attached themselves to craft or trade guilds in a city's main bazaar. It is still a widely accepted custom for Muslims to associate themselves with a Sufi order. Lay associates provide the order with a good source of income and receive in return the blessing (*barakah*) of the shaykh as they participate in the order's devotional observances.

The truth and authenticity of a shaykh's claim to spiritual prominence depends on his spiritual genealogy. By the thirteenth century, Sufi chains of initiation, similar to chains of *isnād* in *ḥadīth* transmission, were established. A Sufi *silsilah*, or chain of initiation, begins with the shaykh's immediate master who invested him with the Sufi patched frock (*khirqah*) and goes back in an unbroken chain to ʿAlī, one of his descendants, another Companion of the Prophet, or one of the Successors. It is not unusual for a famous shaykh to be initiated by several well-known masters, thus greatly enhancing his prestige and *barakah*. Some shaykhs claim to have received their patched frock from al-Khiḍr, the mysterious green prophet who lives forever as a wandering ascetic initiating spiritual adepts into the Sufi path and helping the pious who call upon him in times of danger or difficulty.

Generally speaking, two main chains of initiation came to be recognized. The first goes back to al-Junayd and typifies sober Sufism, the other to Bayazīd Bistāmī and typifies intoxicated or ecstatic mysticism. From these two, hundreds of *silsilah*s have evolved.

Out of the ecstatic branch of Sufi *silsilah*s arose the order of the Malāmatīyah ("self-deprecating" or "reproaching" Sufis). The Malāmatī Sufis eschewed all forms of ostentation, thus rejecting both Sufi initiation and the guidance of a shaykh, and lived in continuous self-examination. Although they were meticulous in their observance of the *sharī'ah*, the Malāmatī Sufis often intentionally brought blame and sharp reproof upon themselves through strange and unsanctioned behavior. An extreme form of the Malāmatīyah are the wandering dervishes known as Qalandarīyah, who impudently spurned all religious laws and practices.

VENERATION OF THE AWLĪYĀ'

The term "*walī*" (pl. *awlīyā'*) means "intimate friend" or "ally." The Qur'ān uses the term to refer to God, who is the protecting friend or patron (*walī*) of the people of faith. The Qur'ān also uses the term to refer to the righteous who are the intimate friends (*awlīyā'*) of God.

The epithet "*walī*" has been applied to Sufi shaykhs, particularly the heads of Sufi orders. Through his spiritual lineage, a Sufi shaykh inherits the grace, or *barakah*, of his masters, who inherited it from the Prophet. In turn, the shaykh bestows his *barakah*, or healing power, on his devotees, both during his life and, with even greater efficacy, after his death.

The concept of Sufi saintship (*walāyah*) developed out of the idea of the perfect man, as elaborated in Ibn 'Arabi's cosmic hierarchy. This doctrine was further developed by the great shaykh's successors, particularly 'Abd al-Karīm al-Jīlī (d. 1428) in his famous treatise *al-Insān al-kāmil* ("The Perfect Man").

The perfect man must exist in every age. He is the intimate (*walī*) of God and repository of his blessing. He is thus known as the great succor or refuge (*ghawth*) and the pole or axis (*quṭb*) around whom the existence of the world revolves. The perfect man is assisted by a large hierarchy of lesser saints whose presence in the world preserves its stability and well-being.

As this high office came to be claimed for many shaykhs simultaneously, it led to great rivalry among some of the more popular Sufi orders. It also led to exaggerated forms of saint veneration, manifested in pilgrimages to the tombs of famous *walī*s to whom prayers for healing, prosperity, and intercession continue to be directed.

The shaykhs of Sufi orders are like the saints of the Catholic Church in that miracles as divine favors (*karāmāt*) are ascribed to them. But unlike the saints, they are recognized through popular acclaim during their lifetimes, rather than by official canonization after death.

DEVOTIONAL PRACTICES

Besides the acts of worship embodied in the five pillars of Islam, Sufis observe additional devotional prayers, night vigils, and fasts. The purpose of such ritual practices is to draw the devotee closer to God. In a well-known *ḥadīth qudsī* God declares:

> My servant continues to draw nearer to Me through additional personal prayers (*nawāfil*) until I love him. When I love him, I become his eye with which he sees, his ear with which he hears, his hand with which he grasps and his foot with which he walks. Thus through Me he sees, hears, grasps and walks.[50]

The most characteristic Sufi devotional practice is the *dhikr* ("remembrance") of God, which may be a public or private ritual. The congregational *dhikr* ritual is usually held before dawn or evening prayers. It consists of the repetition of the name of God, *Allāh*, or the *shahādah*, "There is no god except God" (*lā ilaha illā allāh*). The *dhikr* is often accompanied by special bodily movements and, in some Sufi orders, by elaborate breath control techniques akin to those of Indian yoga.

Often the performance of the *dhikr* is what distinguishes the various Sufi orders from one another. In some popular orders it is a highly emotional practice, similar to charismatic ritual practices in some Pentecostal churches, intended to stir the devotee into a state of frenzy. In the widespread sober Naqshbandī order (founded by Bahā' al-Dīn al-Naqshbandī, d. 1388) the *dhikr* is silent, offered as an inward prayer of the heart.

In fact, true *dhikr* must progress from the audible remembrance of the tongue to the silent remembrance of the heart and finally to the recollection of the innermost being of the pious Sufi. At this stage *dhikr* becomes a constant state of the devotee, so that every breath or heart beat is an inward utterance of God's name.

Another distinctly Sufi devotional practice is the *samā'*, meaning "hearing" or "audition." It consists of listening to often hypnotically beautiful chants of mystical poetry accompanied by various musical instruments. As instrumental music is legally not allowed in the mosque, the *samā'* sessions are usually held in halls adjacent to the mosque, or at the shrine of a famous shaykh.

In the Mevlevi (*mawlawī*) order, so called after Mawlānā ("our master") Jalāl al-Dīn Rūmī, and founded by his son shortly after his death, music and dance constitute a vital element of the order's devotional life. Here the dance is a highly sophisticated art symbolizing the perfect motion of the stars, where the haunting melodies of the reed flute and large orchestra accompanying the chants of mystical poetry in praise of the Prophet and the great founder of the order echo the primordial melodies of the heavenly spheres. It is this primordial music that the soul heard on the day of the primordial covenant, "the day of *alastū*" ("Am I not your Lord?"), and that it recollects in the music and dance of the Whirling Dervishes, as the Mevlevis are called.

This elevated use of music is not, however, typical of all orders. In some cases music led to wine drinking and the use of drugs to induce a state of heightened consciousness. Among popular and antinomian Sufis, it also led to the neglect of regular worship. Furthermore, the beautiful face of a beardless boy, which figures prominently in Sufi poetry as a symbol of divine beauty, became an actual object of erotic love as such boys adorned the *samāʿ* sessions. This of course led most jurists to ban or greatly restrict the use of music. Nevertheless, music remains an integral part of Sufi devotions.

SUFI ORDERS AND THE DECLINE OF SUFISM

The decline of Sufism in modern times can be attributed to some external, as well as to many internal, causes. Perhaps the most important of the latter is the actual growth of Sufi orders from small spiritual fraternal societies into large international *ṭarīqah*s. Leadership in these orders was transformed from a system of spiritually transmitted authority to one of hereditary office, passed from father to son with little regard to leadership qualities or spiritual attainments.

This development reached a high point by the mid-fourteenth century. Thenceforth, Sufi brotherhoods have generally been centers not of spiritual training, but rather of cultural adaptations of Islamic faith and piety in places as far apart as North Africa and Southeast Asia. This in turn has led to the introduction of strange shamanistic practices into the rituals of some Sufi orders.

Among the major external causes for the decline of Sufism are the rise of reform movements, such as the Wahhābī movement in the eighteenth century, and the strong influences of Western secularism and rationalism on Muslim thought in the nineteenth and twentieth centuries. Such political and intellectual religious movements rejected

Sufism as an irrational and world-renouncing distortion of what was held to be true Islam. Of course, exaggerated practices of saint veneration have been a determining factor in this generally negative attitude towards Sufism.

It is often claimed by educated Muslims that Sufism is by nature an other-worldly religious movement that neglects the social, political, and military requirements of *jihād*. This claim is completely unfounded. From the beginning, well-known Sufi ascetics died in battle and the military Sufi fraternities (collectively known as the *ribāṭ*[51]) of the middle ages were a widespread and highly important phenomenon. In fact, the well-known Western military monastic orders such as the Templars and Hospitallers were patterned on the Sufi *ribāṭ*. The motto of such fraternities is "Be monks (*ruhbān*) by night and knights (*firsān*) by day." Moreover, Sufi orders, such as the Sanūsīyah (founded by Muḥammad b. 'Alī al-Sanūsī, d. 1859) in North Africa and the Tījānīyah (founded by Abū al-'Abbās Aḥmad al-Tījānī, d. 1815) in North and West Africa, played a primary role in the struggle of these regions against Western colonialism and for the preservation of the indigenous religion and culture.

In spite of its many ups and downs throughout Muslim history, Sufism has always shown an amazing aptitude for self-reform and regeneration. It was the Sufis who preserved Islamic learning and spirituality after the fall of Baghdad; the Sufis and Sufi piety that carried Islam to Africa and Asia; and now it is Sufi piety that is exerting Islam's deepest spiritual influence on the West. While present-day Sufism lacks the vitality and creativity of earlier centuries, it is experiencing a real revival in many parts of the Muslim world.

9

Theology and Philosophy

The Islamic religious sciences may be divided into two categories: the transmitted sciences (*al-ʻulūm al-naqlīyah*) and the rational sciences (*al-ʻulūm al-ʻaqlīyah*). The first category includes the sciences of the Qur'ān, *ḥadīth*, and jurisprudence, and their ancillary branches, treated in chapter 7. The second includes primarily theology and philosophy, which are the subject of the present discussion.

THEOLOGY: SCOPE AND SOURCES

Theology is the science of the knowledge of God's existence and attributes, as well as his relationship to the universe in general and humankind in particular. Theology is called *ʻilm al-kalām*, meaning the "science of speech" or theological discourse. It is discourse about God, his attributes, and his teleological acts of creation and nurturing of all things. It is also concerned with human free-will and predestination, moral and religious obligations (*taklīf*), and return to God on the Day of Resurrection for the final judgment.

Inasmuch as theology deals with human faith and moral conduct, it is part of the science of *fiqh*, or jurisprudence. Inasmuch as it is concerned with the rational investigation of God's existence, creation, and theodicy, theology is more akin to philosophy, whose principles and rationalistic methodology were employed in the formulation and argumentation of theological principles. During the formative period, theology and law were indistinguishable; after their consolidation into two independent fields of religious knowledge, they were again combined in a comprehensive religious science known as the knowledge or study of "the fundamentals of the religion" (*uṣūl al-dīn*).

Like jurisprudence, the primary sources of theology are the Qur'ān and Prophetic tradition. Likewise, its formal sources are the personal effort (*ijtihād*) of the scholars and the broad consensus of the community (*ijma*ʿ). The Qur'ān defines itself as the speech (*kalām*) of God (see Q. 2:75 and 9:6). Thus the "Arabic Qur'ān," which Muslims believe to be literally the revealed word of God, has itself been the subject of much theological debate. Furthermore, the Qur'anic theology (or teachings about God and his nature and attributes) and the Qur'anic anthropology (or teachings about human beings and their creation, purpose, and destiny) have provided the source and framework of theological thinking.

Indirect sources were Christian theology and Iranian Manichean or Mazdakian dualism. Early Muslim contacts with Nestorian, Jacobite, and Malkite Eastern Christian theologians raised new theological questions regarding God's attributes and essence, particularly his attribute of speech and its relation to the Qur'ān. The question at issue was whether the Qur'ān is co-eternal with God or created in time. Contacts with ancient Iranian dualistic concepts of good and evil – personified in cosmic powers locked in an eternal conflict that is manifested in human good and evil behavior – brought into sharp focus such questions as God's responsibility for good and evil human conduct and, inevitably, the issue of free-will and predestination.

Greek philosophy, both as a logical and as a metaphysical discipline, provided an important rational framework for a rich and sophisticated Islamic theological and philosophical system. Besides providing the necessary tool for analytical thought, Greek philosophy introduced important theological issues, such as the eternity or creation of the universe and the relationship of reason to revelation. But, although the interaction of Muslim theology with other faiths and ideologies left a mark on its development, in the end Islamic theology rests on the Qur'ān and Prophetic *sunnah.*

In our discussion of the concepts of *islām* ("submission") and *imān* ("faith"), we saw how Muslim thinkers used Prophetic *ḥadīth* tradition to precisely define these concepts. Included in the definition of faith is "faith in divine decree, be it good or evil." Through a politically motivated process of common consensus, such traditions became the basis of a broad Sunni Muslim orthodoxy affirming God's ultimate responsibility for both good and evil in the world, and his ultimate predestination of humankind, some for Paradise and others for Hell. In its extreme form, this concept left no room for human initiative and made God look like a capricious tyrant. It was therefore challenged through an emphasis on God's justice by Muʿtazilī and Shīʿī theologians and traditionists.

Theology and Politics

The political crisis occasioned by the Prophet's death resulted in great schisms in the community. Apart from the Shīʿah and Kharijites already discussed, there appeared two other theological schools, the Muʿtazilah (so called because they isolated themselves theologically from what came to be mainline Sunni orthodoxy) and the Murji'ah. All four schools arose in response to the great sedition (*fitnah*) in the community, which began during the reign of ʿUthmān (r. 644–656), the third of the four rightly guided caliphs, and ended in his murder, the assassination of ʿAlī four years later, and the establishment of the Umayyad dynasty by Muʿāwīyah b. Abī Sufyān (r. 661–680). In light of the historical circumstances, it is not surprising that major differences between the schools arose in response to the question of how grave sinners were to be judged.

The Shi'ites considered 'Alī and his descendants to be the sole legitimate heirs of the Prophet in all things except prophethood. Thus Abū Bakr, 'Umar, and 'Uthmān (the three caliphs who preceded 'Alī) were considered to be usurpers of his rights and those caliphs who came after 'Alī were seen as usurpers of the rights of his descendants. This view eventually crystallized in the doctrine of the imamate. According to this doctrine, the Imām is a manifestation of divine grace, mercy, and justice in the world. God must, as a just and merciful God, ensure that the earth is never without an Imām. The gravest of sins is for one to die not knowing the Imām of his time. Such a person, the Prophet is said to have declared, "dies the death of pre-Islamic ignorance and folly (*jāhilīyah*)."[52]

The Kharijites regarded both 'Alī and Mu'āwīyah as grave sinners and, therefore, as rejecters of faith: 'Alī because he accepted human arbitration instead of God's judgment; Mu'āwīyah because he rebelled against the Imām ('Alī) of the Muslims. This extreme position and its violent political consequences raised the basic question of the status in this and the next world of a Muslim who commits a grave sin.

The term "*murji'ah*" means "those who postpone," in this case judgment regarding the ultimate fate of a Muslim who is a grave sinner. In contradistinction with the Kharijites, the Murji'ites held that Muslims remain believers in spite of their sins and that it is up to God to forgive or punish them on the Day of Judgment. They therefore argued that so long as a Muslim continues to profess the faith of Islam, he or she should be treated both socially and legally as a Muslim. In its moderate form, Murji'ism came to represent the official Sunni position.

Mu'tazilī Theology

The Mu'tazilites dealt with the issue of a reprobate Muslim in the context of their well-known five fundamentals. The first three of these are

God's oneness (*tawḥīd*); God's justice (*'adl*); and God's promise (*wa'd*) of rich reward for the people of faith and his threat (*wa'īd*) of eternal punishment for grave sinners. The fourth concerns the reprobate Muslim, who is regarded as neither a person of faith (*mu'min*) nor a rejecter of faith (*kāfir*), but as one who is in a state (*manzilah*) between the two. The fifth and final fundamental principle is the Qur'anic injunction of commanding good (*ma'rūf*) and forbidding evil (*munkar*) conduct.

Mu'tazilī theology was from the beginning deeply rationalistic. It was influenced by Greek rationalism as well as Christian theology, thus, in contrast with Christian trinitarianism, Mu'tazilite theologians argued that God's absolute oneness necessitates that his attributes (*ṣifāt*) be one with his essence (*dhāt*). Otherwise, there would be God and his word, God and his power, God and his knowledge, and so on, which would imply a multiplicity of gods, an error worse than the Christian doctrine of the trinity.

For Mu'tazilites attributes such as speaking and creating are not eternal, rather, they are attributes of actions and come into being only when such acts take place. Therefore, in contrast with the general Sunni belief that the Qur'ān is the eternal word of God, Mu'tazilites held the Qur'ān to have been created as it was being sent down to Muḥammad by the angel Gabriel.

The Mu'tazilī view of divine oneness also requires that all anthropomorphic assertions about God in the Qur'ān are to be taken metaphorically. Hence, references to God's hands and face, his sitting upon the throne, and his coming down with the angels for the final judgment must be interpreted metaphorically. The Mu'tazilites denied the frequent assertion in both the Qur'ān and Prophetic tradition that the faithful will see God in the hereafter. The possibility that one might literally "see" God, they argued, would mean that he is a body limited in time and space, which is impossible.

The Mu'tazilī explanation of divine justice centered on questions of good and evil and led to some controversial conclusions. God's justice, they maintained, implies that he cannot wish evil, let alone be its cause in any way. He is constrained by his justice to wish for his servants only what is best for them. This means that human beings are themselves the creators of their own acts and hence are fully responsible for the consequences.

Muʿtazilites defined good and evil not in any metaphysical sense but as rationally recognizable states of goodness (*ḥusn*) and badness (*qubḥ*). As such, they are equally knowable by God and human beings. This in turn means that what humans recognize as good and evil God must also recognize as such. God becomes an absolutely just judge, incapable of either mercy or forgiveness, subject to human reason in all his dealings with humankind. This view goes against one of the most fundamental principles of popular Muslim piety: the hope of the faithful that the Prophet will intercede with God on their behalf, on the Day of Judgment.

According to Muʿtazilī thought, since God promises eternal bliss in Paradise for the obedient and threatens eternal chastisement in Hell for the rebellious, he would not then impose predestination; thus, human beings are free to make their own destinies. A sinful Muslim is simply, within the scope of our limited knowledge and judgment, in an intermediate state between faith and rejection of faith. But, as such a person freely plots the course of their own destiny, God will judge him or her on the last day. All that Muslims can and must do is to enjoin the good and dissuade from evil.

Muʿtazilī theology was vehemently opposed by the mainline Sunnī *ʿulama'*, particularly the "people of the *ḥadīth*," as the traditionists or jurists were called. However, during the reign of the ʿAbbasid caliph al-Ma'mūn (r. 813–833), and with his support, Muʿtazilites attempted to impose their theological beliefs on the rest of the community. They established a sort of inquisition known as the *miḥnah* ("test" or "ordeal"), whereby traditional Sunni scholars had to publicly profess the doctrine of the createdness of the Qur'ān, or suffer harsh punishment. The great traditionist and founder of the Ḥanbalī legal school, Aḥmad b. Ḥanbal, was a notable victim of the *miḥnah*. He was publicly flogged and imprisoned for insisting that the Qur'ān was the eternal word of God, preserved in the well-guarded Heavenly Tablet (see Q. 85:21–22).

The caliph al-Mutawakkil (r. 847–861) reversed this policy, reaffirmed Sunni orthodoxy, and persecuted the Muʿtazilites. Muʿtazilism thus gradually lost its vitality as a rationalist school of Islamic theology and not long thereafter it died out. But its basic tenets of divine unity and justice have been preserved in Zaydī and Twelver Imāmī Shiʿism.

Ashʿarism and the Triumph of Sunni Orthodoxy

A major contributing factor to the decline of Muʿtazilism was the rise of Ashʿarite theology. Abū al-Ḥasan al-Ashʿarī (d. 935) was a prominent Muʿtazilī thinker. He, however, abandoned Muʿtazilism and, using Muʿtazilī dialectical reasoning, set himself the task of refuting Muʿtazilī theology and establishing his own orthodox school.

Ashʿarī argued that God is one, the sole creator and sustainer of all his creation. Nothing happens except by his will and eternal decree. His attributes "are neither He, nor are they other than He." Hence, God is not life, knowledge, power, and so on, as the Muʿtazilī position would imply. Rather, God knows, lives, and wills by a knowledge, life, and will that are other than his essence; the same is true of all his attributes.

With regard to God's hand, face, and his sitting upon the throne, Ash'arī argued that to deny these would amount to nullifying (*taʿṭīl*) God's attributes. Yet if these attributes were taken literally, it would amount to making God a body like any other body. This is *tashbīh*, literal anthropomorphism. Hence, both positions are erroneous. The solution is that such Qur'anic statements must be accepted, but "without asking how" (*bilā-kayfā*).

Ashʿarī rejected the Muʿtazilī view of divine justice, arguing instead for God's absolute freedom to will and act as he chooses, without being answerable to any of his creatures. God is just because he wills to be just; were he to will otherwise, his actions would still be right and good.

Similarly, good and evil are what they are, not in themselves, but because God decrees them to be so. Nor are they determined by human reason, but again simply by God's legislation. Good and evil are not rational or even moral in essence, but legislative. Were God to stipulate in the *sharī'ah* that lying, adultery, and theft were good, they would be allowed in spite of the fact that human reason may judge them to be evil. God only allows human beings to discern good and evil, not to legislate or determine them.

Just as extreme Mu'tazilism circumscribed God's power to will and to act by insisting on absolute free-will for human beings, extreme Ash'arism rendered human striving to do good or evil meaningless. In order to ensure God's absolute freedom, some Ash'arites like al-Ghazālī went so far as to deny causality altogether. He argued that each time God wills an act by a human being, he creates both the act and its cause. For example, if God willed that a person murder another, he would occasion the cause for the act, cause the making of the knife or gun to be used as an instrument of killing, and then cause the murderer to walk to his victim, raise his hand and kill him. In fact, the murderer would have done nothing more than fulfill what God had decreed for him from eternity.

Ash'arī himself avoided such an extreme predestinarian position by arguing that God creates all actions, but also gives human beings the capacity to act or not and thus to earn the rewards and punishments for their acts. This is known as the doctrine of *kasb* (earning good reward through meritorious deeds) and *iktisāb* (accruing evil recompense through evil acts). This doctrine is based on the Qur'anic assertion: "God does not charge a soul beyond what is in its capacity. To it belongs [the good] it has earned and against it shall be [the evil] it has accrued" (Q. 2:286).

The following debate between Abū al-Ḥasan al-Ash'arī and his famous Mu'tazilite teacher Abū 'Alī al-Jubbā'ī succinctly depicts the split between the two schools over the issue of human free will and divine predestination.

> It is related by scholars that Abū al-Ḥasan asked his teacher about three brothers, one of whom was righteous and God-fearing, the second a reprobate and wretched rejecter of faith, the third a child. All three died. How would their end be? Al-Jubbā'ī answered: "As for the righteous man, he will be in the high stations [of Paradise]. As for the rejecter of faith, he will be in the lowest circles [of Hell]. But the child will be of the people of happiness and well-being." Al-Ash'arī said, "What if the child wanted to attain to the stations of his righteous brother, would he be permitted to do so?" "No," answered al-Jubbā'ī, "because he would be told 'your brother reached these high stations as a reward for his many acts of obedience, but you did not perform such acts.' " "What if this child," al-Ash'arī argued, "protests to God saying 'this incapacity is not my fault, for You did not allow me to live, nor did You grant me the capacity to perform acts of obedience.'?" "The Creator would say to him," countered al-Jubbā'ī, " 'I knew that had you lived on you would have committed acts of wickedness, and thus you would have deserved painful chastisement. I therefore did what was best for you.' " Al-Ash'arī retorted, "What if the wicked brother were to say, 'O Lord of all beings, as You knew well his situation [here on earth], so You knew mine. Why did You then do what was best for him and not what would have been best for me?' " Al-Jubbā'ī angrily said, "You are a mad man!" "No," al-Ash'arī answered, "rather the donkey [the response] of the master has stalled on the steep road."[53]

The Qur'ān itself is not a systematic theological treatise. It affirms, at one and the same time, divine predestination and human free-will and responsibility. There are, in fact, verses that can be used to support even extreme Mu'tazilī and Ash'arī positions. Nonetheless, the Muslim community divided into two theologically distinct camps, the Qadarites and the Jabrites, which in their extreme forms were placed outside the pale of Islamic orthodoxy. The former either minimized or denied altogether divine decree (*qadar*), the latter affirmed it absolutely as divine predeterminism (*jabr*). The first camp included Shi'ites, Mu'tazilites, and philosophically inclined thinkers; the second comprised the Sunni majority.

In the end, it was Ash'arism that triumphed. To this day, Sunni Friday prayer leaders affirm belief in divine decree, be it good or evil, from mosque pulpits around the world. They warn their faithful listeners: "Of all things, the most evil are novelties, for every novelty is an innovation, every innovation is an error, and every error leads to the Fire."[54]

While Christians considered theology to be "the queen of the sciences," some Muslims, like al-Ghazālī, considered it to be the work of Satan. They argued that theology confused the generality of Muslims, discouraged any kind of innovative thinking, and occupied intellectuals with unsolvable questions.

The gate of theological creativity was, like the gate of *ijtihād*, virtually closed in the Sunni community until the end of the nineteenth century. Then, in his treatise entitled *Risālat al-tawḥīd* ("The Message of Divine Oneness"), the Egyptian reformer Muḥammad 'Abduh (d. 1905) reviewed traditional positions and judged them irrelevant. In the Shī'ī community, however, both theology and philosophy have continued to flourish and have occasional moments of originality.

PHILOSOPHY

Greek philosophy was introduced to Muslim society in the Umayyad period, early in the eighth century. Thus the two disciplines of theology and philosophy developed concurrently; but, while the motivation for theology was indigenous, philosophy was an altogether foreign discipline. Furthermore, while theological discourse (*kalām*) is concerned with God's existence and attributes and with human destiny, philosophy (called in Arabic *falsafah*) is concerned with rational truth, being and non-being, and the nature of things, of God, and of the cosmos. Nevertheless, the two disciplines share a common goal: human happiness in this and the next world.

The rapid spread of Islam out of Arabia into Syria and Mesopotamia brought Muslims in touch with Helenized Syriac

Christians, Jews, and people of other faiths and ethnic backgrounds. Such contacts stimulated an already existing love of knowledge. Soon, interest in Greek scientific and medical work grew and translations into Arabic from either the original Greek or from Syriac translations began to appear.

With the rise of the 'Abbasid dynasty, interest in Greek philosophy and science increased, such that the court of al-Manṣūr (r. 754–775) attracted a large number of Muslim theologians and traditionists, as well as Christian, Jewish, and Mandaean[55] scholars. This quest for knowledge reached its peak under the caliph al-Ma'mūn (r. 813–833) whose Bayt al-Ḥikmah ("House of Wisdom") was the first institution of higher learning in the Islamic and Western worlds. Nestorian and Jacobite Christian scholars had already translated into Syriac, and commented on, many Greek medical, philosophical, and theological treatises. They were able to carry on their work with greater exactitude at the House of Wisdom, which possessed an impressive library of Greek manuscripts. Families of translators, such as that of the well-known scholar Ḥunayn b. Isḥaq (d. 873) and his son Isḥaq b. Ḥunayn worked in teams, rendering into Arabic the ancient treasures of Hellenistic science and philosophy. Already existing centers of philosophical and medical studies in the Syrian city of Ḥarrān and the Iranian city of Jundī-Shāpūr also made their notable contributions.

Muslim Philosophers

The Islamic worldview, as presented in the Qur'ān, rests on the principle of the unity of truth. Muslim philosophers assumed this principle in the study of Greek philosophy, particularly that of Plato and Aristotle and their commentators. For a long time a philosophical work, comprising a paraphrase of parts of the *Enneads* of the great third century C.E. mystical philosopher Plotinus (d. 270) and a work of the well-known Alexandrian neo-Platonist Proclus (d. 485) dealing with "the highest good," was mistakenly ascribed to Aristotle and known as "the theology of Aristotle." Thus, in spite of major differences in the actual philosophical systems of Plato and Aristotle, the two were considered to have been in total harmony. This mistaken ascription gave Islamic philosophy a distinct character. It was Aristotelian in its logic, physics, and metaphysics; Platonic in its political and social aspects; and neo-Platonic in its mysticism and theology. Muslim philosophers also studied Greek medicine, notably the works of Galen; science and astronomy, including Ptolemy's *Almajest*; and mathematics, including Euclid's *Elements.*

The two first major philosophers were Abū Yūsuf Ya'qūb al-Kindī (d. 870) and Abū Bakr Zakarīyā al-Rāzī (d. 926). Al-Kindī was a theologian-philosopher who, at least intellectually, belonged to the Mu'tazilī rationalist school. Using philosophical principles and methods of reasoning, al-Kindī defended fundamental Islamic beliefs, such as God's existence and oneness, the temporal creation of the universe by God's command out of nothing, the necessity for prophets, and the inimitability (*i'jāz*) of the Qur'ān. Unlike the philosopher, who acquires his knowledge through rational investigation and contemplation, the prophet, argued al-Kindī, receives his knowledge instantaneously, through divine revelation.

In contrast, Rāzī was a thoroughgoing Platonist. He rejected the Qur'anic view of creation out of nothing, presenting instead a view based on Plato's theory as elaborated in the *Timaeus.* The universe evolved, according to Rāzī, from primal matter floating as atoms in an absolute void. God imposed order on this primeval chaos and thus the universe or cosmos came into being. Moreover, because it is in the nature of matter to revert to its primeval state, at some distant point in the future chaos will set in again.

In this scheme of creation, since neither the existence of the world nor humankind has moral or religious basis or purpose, there is no need for prophets or even religion. Human souls, which come down to the body from the celestial realm of the universal soul, will all in the end despise this material body and return to their original source.

Salvation, or eternal happiness, can be attained through wisdom and the contemplation of higher things, but in any case, all will be saved in the end.

Rāzī was a humanistic philosopher for whom religion was the source of social strife and conflict. He was therefore considered a heretic by both theologians and moderate philosophers. For this reason, the works of this fascinating thinker were lost and the little that is known about his thought is derived from extensive quotations of his writings in the works of his detractors.

In spite of Rāzī's originality, it was al-Kindī's system of relating philosophy to faith that was most influential. His two most notable successors were al-Fārābī and Ibn Sīnā. These two encyclopedic minds dominated the philosophical scene of the tenth and eleventh centuries.

Abū Naṣr al-Fārābī (d. 950) was a great philosopher, a musical theorist, and an accomplished instrumentalist. His Platonic philosophical system was comprehensive and universal. According to al-Fārābī, God is pure intellect and the highest good. From God's self-knowledge and self-contemplation emanated the first intellect. From its self-contemplation and contemplation of God, the first intellect emanated a series of intellects that govern the various heavenly spheres, as well as the intellects of the planets including the sun and moon. The lowest, and hence least perfect in this hierarchy of being, is the active intellect (*'aql*) which governs this world and links its rational elements, the human souls, to their celestial source.

For al-Fārābī, therefore, human society would realize its full potential goodness if it were ruled by a prophet-philosopher. On this basis he constructed a universal political system, presented in a work modeled on Plato's *Republic* and entitled "The Views of the People of the Virtuous City."

Agreeing with al-Kindī, al-Fārābī held that a prophet is gifted with a sharp intellect capable of receiving both philosophical and religious verities naturally and without any mental exertion. He then communicates these truths to the masses, who are incapable of comprehending them on the philosophical level. Religion, for al-Fārābī, is therefore the imitation of philosophy. Since, moreover, the essential truth of religion and philosophy is one, all religions are one in essence. Thus, because the Truth, the ultimate object of philosophy and religion, is one, religious differences are due to the diversity of languages and cultures, not to a diversity of truths.

Al-Fārābī was called "the second teacher," Aristotle being the first. He was, however, excelled by "the great master" Ibn Sīnā (d. 1037). Ibn Sīnā was a self-taught genius who at the age of ten mastered the religious sciences and at the age of eighteen became a leading physician, philosopher, and astronomer. His encyclopedic manual of medicine (*al-Qanūn fī al-ṭibb*) and his philosophical encyclopedia *al-Shifā'* ("Book of Healing") were part of the curricula of European universities throughout the Middle Ages.

Using al-Fārābī's neo-Platonic ideas, Ibn Sīnā built a comprehensive system of mystical philosophy and theology. He accepted and developed al-Fārābī's emanationist theology, placing it in a more precise logical and philosophical framework. He argued that all existents must be either necessary or possible in themselves. There must be one, and only one, being whose existence is necessary in itself and who bestows existence on all other beings and things. This being is God, on whose existence the existence of all things is contingent. Following Aristotle, Ibn Sīnā argued that God must be the first and necessary cause of all existence, otherwise there would be either an infinite regress of causes or a situation of circular causality, both of which were considered to be logical absurdities. Thus, he reasoned, God is the sole and necessary cause or creator of all things.

The process of creation, or more precisely emanation of the universe, begins with God's eternal self-knowledge. This necessitates the creation of a first intellect that is possible in itself, but necessary through another being, namely God. This first intellect then undergoes a threefold act of cognition: knowledge of God, knowledge of itself as necessitated by him, and knowledge of itself as only a possible being.

This act in turn produces three beings: a second intellect, a universal soul, and a body (the outermost sphere of the universe). This threefold act is repeated by each successive intellect until the active intellect, from which emanates the world of generation and corruption, is produced.

The human soul emanates from the active intellect. It is non-material and only becomes individuated as it enters the body. Ibn Sīnā mystically compares the soul to a beautiful heavenly bird that descends into the body after great reluctance. The body is like a cage out of which the soul seeks to escape. Good souls return to their celestial abode to exist eternally in the great bliss of beholding God and contemplating him. Bad souls, on the other hand, exist in eternal misery, deprived of this beatific vision but forever seeking it.

Ibn Sīnā accepted al-Fārābī's view of religion as the imitation of philosophy. He affirmed the prophethood of Muḥammad and the revelation of the Qur'ān. He also affirmed the immortality of the soul, but he denied both the resurrection of the body and the reward of Paradise and punishment of Hell, as depicted in the Qur'ān and Islamic tradition.

Reference has already been made to al-Ghazālī's critique of philosophy. In his book "The Incoherence [or Collapse] of the Philosophers," (*Tahāfut al-falāsifah*) Ghazālī criticized the philosophers on twenty counts, seventeen of which he considered errors of judgment and three as expressions of rejection of faith (*kufr*). These latter are the pre-eternity of the world, Ibn Sīnā's assertion that God knows only universals and not particulars, and the denial of bodily resurrection. As an Ash'arī theologian, al-Ghazālī rejected the philosophical view of causality and denied the necessity of the world, countering it with his theory of occasionalism, which denies causality altogether. Al-Ghazālī's critique was itself criticized by the Andalusian Aristotelian philosopher Ibn Rushd.

Philosophy in North Africa and Spain

As philosophy began to decline in the eastern lands of the Muslim empire, it experienced a veritable flowering in the West. This decline was due to several important factors. Among these were Ghazālī's scathing critique, which strengthened an already strong anti-rationalist reaction among the traditional *'ulamā'*; the tumultuous political, religious and intellectual situation; and the Seljukid patronage of Sunni orthodoxy. Still another important factor was that Ash'arī theology had by then adapted the philosophical rationalist method for its scholastic purpose, and thus could easily dispense with formal logic and metaphysics, the two fundamental elements of philosophy.

Islamic philosophy in Spain began as a somewhat eclectic mystical movement initiated by Ibn Masarrah (d. 931), a shadowy figure who had no appreciable influence on the development of philosophy. The first true philosopher and heir to al-Fārābī's political and metaphysical thought was Ibn Bājjah (d. 1138). But the two most important philosophers of the twelfth century in Muslim Spain were Ibn Ṭufayl (d. 1185) and Ibn Rushd (d. 1198).

Ibn Ṭufayl was a physician, philosopher, and astronomer of the Almohad court. His numerous philosophical and scientific writings are lost, except for the well-known allegorical story of Ḥayy b. Yaqẓān (meaning "the alive, son of the awake"). First recounted by Ibn Sīnā, this allegorical tale seeks to explain the natural relation of religion to philosophy.

On a lush tropical desert island an infant boy called Ḥayy b. Yaqẓān mysteriously comes into being. He is suckled and cared for by a female gazelle whom Ḥayy takes for his mother. As Ḥayy grows older, he discovers how to clothe and protect himself. In time the gazelle dies, and Ḥayy tries to bring her back to life by dissecting her. Finally he comes to know through his unaided reason that his true mother was a spirit and not the gazelle. Through ascetic and spiritual exercises, Ḥayy arrives at the knowledge of God and the highest metaphysical truths.

On a neighboring island live two brothers, Absāl and Salāmān, and a community of non-philosophical religious people. Salāmān is their religious teacher; his brother Absāl, a philosopher, tries in vain to teach them the higher truths of philosophy. Discouraged, Absāl gives up and seeks solitude on a desert island, which turns out to be Ḥayy's island.

Absāl teaches Ḥayy language and the two live a life of contemplation and asceticism. Finally, they decide to go back and try again to teach Salāmān's people philosophy, again to no avail. Ḥayy then enjoins the people to remain as they are and he and his companion return to the desert island to spend the rest of their days.

The story of Ḥayy resembles in some ways the Qur'anic account of how Abraham arrived at the knowledge of God through his native rational and religious disposition (*fiṭrah*). But it also is meant to affirm the view that religion is the imitation of philosophy, as elaborated by al-Fārābī and Ibn Sīnā. In fact, the story was offered as an allegorical explanation of Ibn Sīnā's mystical philosophy.

Ibn Ṭufayl's contemporary and teacher, Ibn Rushd, was the greatest Muslim commentator on Aristotle. He came from a long family line of Mālikī jurists and was himself a noted scholar of Islamic law. His legal training decisively influenced his philosophy.

Ibn Rushd's critique of Ghazālī, entitled "The Incoherence of the Incoherence" (*Tahāfut al-tahāfut*), methodically criticizes both Ghazālī and Ibn Sīnā; the former for his misapprehension of philosophy, the latter for his misunderstanding of Aristotle. Ibn Rushd was the first to reject the "theology of Aristotle" as an authentic work of the Greek philosopher and to thus construct a true Aristotelian philosophical system.

Ibn Rushd essentially shared his eastern predecessors' views of the relation of religion to philosophy. He, however, elaborated this view in his famous double truth theory, which affirmed the equality of the two approaches to the truth. Nonetheless, for Ibn Rushd religion is still meant for the masses, while philosophy is meant for the intellectual elite. His views of the hereafter are ambiguous. While he affirms bodily resurrection, for example, his actual philosophy of the soul leaves little room for this and other Islamic eschatological ideas.

Ibn Rushd was the last great systematic philosopher of Sunni Islam. After him the thirteenth century witnessed only a few other Sunni philosophical thinkers of note, among them the great philosophical mystic Ibn 'Arabī, who has already been discussed, and his systematic Aristotelian expositor Ibn Sab'īn (d. 1270). A more empirical philosopher was the Tunisian born 'Abd al-Raḥmān Ibn Khaldūn (d. 1406).

Through his extensive travels and the positions he held as a jurist and political theorist, Ibn Khaldūn gained great insights into the workings of nations and political and religious institutions. This led him to write a universal history. In the important prolegomena (*Muqaddimah*) to this work, he presents the first social philosophy of history in either the Islamic or the Western world.

The ninth through twelfth centuries, the period from al-Kindī to Ibn Rushd, was a great epoch of philosophical thinking. It had a long-lasting influence on Western medieval and renaissance philosophical and theological thought. Islamo-Hellenistic philosophy, although greatly curtailed after this period, did not end with Ibn Rushd. In the Shī'ī community of Iran especially, philosophy has continued to grow and prosper. For the most part, however, Shi'ite philosophy is heir to Ibn Sīnā's mystical thought and Suhrawardī's illuminationist mystical philosophy.

Since the mid-nineteenth century, the Arab and Muslim worlds have been philosophically influenced by the West. Only a few Islamic thinkers during this period can be truly considered as philosophers. The future does not seem to promise any real revival of this noble discipline.

10

Women and Men

The Qur'ān views the Muslim community as an organic body made up of different, but interrelated, religious, social, economic, and political units. These units consist primarily of individual men and women who are the basic units that make up the nuclear family. A collection of such families constitutes the extended family or clan. Individuals, families and clans related by blood or marriage form a tribe, and all these together constitute a people, nation or community.

In pre-Islamic Arabia, the largest social entity was the tribe, or *ḥayy*, meaning a quarter wherein one or more related tribes lived. There was no concept of a community bound by a particular faith, ideology, common history, or destiny. While the Qur'ān and classical Muslim tradition maintained the same social units, the whole organic body was now viewed as an *ummah* or community of faith. Nevertheless, in this faith-community it is still the family that constitutes the basic social and economic unit that defines the place of the individual in society, be it the wife, husband, or child. I shall therefore discuss the relationship between women and men within the framework of family relations.

WOMEN AND THE FAMILY IN PRE-ISLAMIC ARABIA

The women and men of seventh-century Arabia lived by the norms and values of a nomadic society. This was true even of settled societies in agricultural or trading towns, such as Makkah and Madīnah. Often children and young adults were sent to the desert to live with nomadic tribes either to be nursed by their well-nourished women or to imbibe their norms and habits.[56] Among the most important pre-Islamic social values and customs were those governing family relations, such as marriage, divorce, and attitudes towards male and female children.

In general, the situation of the female in pre-Islamic Arab society was precarious and paradoxical. For instance, the honor of a family or tribe depended on the honor of its girls and women; therefore much value was placed on the female's honor. But because the female could easily be the cause of dishonor to the family, she was also seen as a weak link and a drain on the family's meager resources. Since the family was vulnerable through its women, the protection of females from capture and forced concubinage was of paramount concern. To guard against such an eventuality, families often buried alive one or more of their female infants.

This custom may have had its roots in the ancient Semitic practice of offering human sacrifices to the gods; or it may have been merely the outcome of the difficult nomadic life led by the Arabs. In this setting, women were not considered to be as productive as they were (and are still considered to be) in agrarian and urban societies. In itself, the life of a female was of little worth; she was often considered a burden and a liability. The Qur'ān graphically portrays and strongly condemns the tendency of the head of the family in these times when the birth of a female was announced to: "turn gloomy and become agitated." We are told that such a person would either reluctantly allow the child to live, or bury her in the dust (Q. 16:58–59).

Islam strictly forbade female infanticide and demanded that those who had killed their daughters in the time of *jāhiliyyah* make expiation for their heinous act. On the Day of Resurrection, the Qur'ān states, "The female buried alive will be asked for what sin was she slain" (Q. 81:8–9). This is understood to mean that such females will be vindicated and recompensed on the Day of Judgment for the terrible wrong done to them.

TYPES OF MARRIAGE

Before Islam, marriage in Arab society was essentially of two types.[57] The first was determined by female, and the second by male kinship relations. Marriages based on female kinship were known as *ṣadīqah*, since they were based on a gift called *ṣadāq*, which the man gave directly to his bride herself at the time of marriage. A variant of this type of marriage was based on the *mahr*, a negotiated gift between the groom and his tribe and the tribe of the bride, which the husband gave to the bride's parents or other close relatives as a bride price.

The *ṣadīqah* marriage was generally based on the mutual consent of the man and woman involved. It is likely that the importance this type of marriage accorded the woman's opinion in the choice of her spouse gave it a special place in the Qur'anic reform of marriage and the family, as will be demonstrated below. The *ṣadīqah* marriage was in turn of two kinds: a permanent union called *binā* and a temporary marriage known as *mut'ah*. The *binā* marriage allowed the woman to remain attached to her tribe and enjoy its protection. While giving her considerable power in the marriage, the arrangement left her utterly dependent on her tribe. Her husband would pay conjugal visits, but they did not live together as a family or household, nor was the husband responsible for the maintenance of his wife and child.

Another type of marriage based on female kinship was called *mut'ah*. The term "*mut'ah*" means enjoyment; hence *mut'ah* union is a marriage of desire or pleasure. It is contracted by the man and woman without the two witnesses presently required for ordinary, permanent marriages. Temporary marriage was practiced in early Islam, but later repudiated by the Sunni legal schools. It was, however, regulated, and continues to be sanctioned by the Shi'ite or Ja'farī legal school as a legitimate form of union.

Standing in contradistinction to the *ṣadīqah* types of marriage, which reflected ancient matrilineal practices, were the *ba'l* marriages, based on male domination. The term *ba'l* means both lord and husband. It is in this latter sense that the term is used in the Qur'ān.[58] *Ba'l* marriage was either imposed by the man on female war captives, or arranged between the would-be husband and the bride's family. In the second case, a *mahr*, or bride price, was given to the father or guardian of the woman in return for losing both her and her offspring to the husband's tribe. The *ba'l* marriage was in fact a transaction of sale or barter between the husband and the father or guardian of the bride. Once the sale was concluded, a woman who was once, effectively, the property of her tribe became the property of her husband to do with as he pleased. Often women captives were not married but kept as concubines. It was not uncommon for slave girls to be sold as concubines to men other than their captors or forced by their masters to work as prostitutes.

In *jāhiliyyah* times polygyny was unregulated, so that a man could marry an indefinite number of women, whom he could divorce, remarry, and divorce again as often as he wished. His freedom in this regard was, however, often curtailed by the status of the woman and prestige of her tribe. Once divorced, a woman had no security or power of her own. If she returned to her tribe, her life would be one of shame and degradation. Here again, there were exceptions based on a woman's social position, looks, or personal initiative, all of which could play an important role in improving her marital and personal status.

THE MUSLIM FAMILY

We have dwelt at some length on pre-Islamic Arab marriage practices and customs because they were the types of marriage known to the first generation of Muslims, who practiced them until they were superseded by Qur'anic legislation. The Prophet's marriage to Khadījah, which was contracted not long before the rise of Islam, is a good case in point. Khadījah's economic independence, her direct marriage proposal to a man many years younger than herself and apparently without the mediation of a male guardian, as well as her monogamous marriage all reflect the free and unrestricted *jāhiliyyah* practices of a prominent Arab noblewoman, rather than later Islamic precepts and norms. It is noteworthy that early Islamic sources are silent regarding Khadījah's business activities after her marriage to the Prophet, which may suggest that she gave them up. Be that as it may, Khadījah's case was by no means a unique one. The Prophet's wife 'Ā'ishah, his daughter Fāṭimah and his great-granddaughter Sukaynah, daughter of Ḥusayn, are only a few of numerous prominent women in early Islam. I have designated pre-Islamic marriages as types rather than fixed practices or institutions because nomadic and semi-nomadic Arabs were highly individualistic and free people, who may have respected time-honored social values and customs, but did not feel strictly bound by them, an attitude which no doubt influenced their marriage customs as well. Arab society before Islam lacked any developed family or marriage institutions. The fact that the children of a *ṣadīqah* marriage belonged to the tribe of the mother and those of the *ba'l* marriage to the tribe of the father, rather than to the wife and husband as a family, clearly illustrates this point. The Prophet Muḥammad himself was the child of a tribal *ṣadīqah* marriage, so that his mother remained with her clan after her marriage to his father 'Abd Allah, who died before Muḥammad's birth. Muḥammad's paternal relatives took custody of him only after his mother's death.

The Qur'ān adopted neither the *ṣadīqah* nor *ba'l* types of marriage, but formulated its own rules which reflected them both. It maintained the *mahr* or bride price, but stipulated that it be given to the wife as her exclusive property. According to the Qur'ān itself (Q. 4:26), the husband can enjoy his wife's property only if she is willing to share with him. Likewise, the bride's custodian is not her tribe, but her father or nearest of kin, who are bound to act in her interest, and that only after she consents to the marriage. The Qur'ān, in addition, recognized the special authority of the husband as the head of the family but gave the wife the sole right to own and dispose of her property, whether her *mahr* or inheritance.

The male marriage partner is charged in Islam with well-defined responsibilities both as a husband and as a father. It appears that the religion wanted to curb the previous tendency of Bedouin males toward irresponsibility in their relations with women. Thus the husband is bound, by both moral standards and the law, to properly maintain the wife, while the wife is, according to strictest law, not obliged to contribute to her own maintenance. The Qur'ān and Islamic law also lay much emphasis on paternity and the duties of the father to his offspring. The basic assumption of the law is that a child belongs to the man who is in a legal sexual relation with the mother; and it is difficult for a man to refute paternity, but very easy for him to acknowledge it. It is the father and the father alone – or, if he is somehow incapacitated or deceased, his male relatives – who are responsible for maintaining the child. In order to insure the integrity of paternity, the Qur'ān and subsequent Islamic law also prohibited adoption. Muslims are urged to care for the destitute and needy, including orphaned or illegitimate children, but they cannot give such children their family names. The Qur'ān insists: "[God] did not render those you claim [as adopted sons] your actual sons," and tells the believers to "call them after their fathers" (Q. 33:4–5).

The great stress of the tradition on the integrity of paternity and female chastity was not simply an assertion of patriarchal authority, but a repudiation of the polyandrous types of marriage practiced in some Arab tribes. Bukhārī reports on the authority of 'Ā'ishah, the Prophet's wife, that the Arabs before Islam practiced four types of marriage; two of the four were polyandrous unions and one was the type known and practiced by Muslims in her own time. The Qur'ān absolutely forbade all forms of polyandry, which it equated with adultery.[59] In the noted women's collective oath of allegiance (*bay'ah*), alluded to in Q. 60:12 and known as the *bay'ah* of women, the women involved were required to refrain from *zinā*, or adultery, and we hear that some protested that the liberty of a free woman would be compromised if polyandrous unions were now to be classed as *zinā*.

The Qur'ān made marriage the foundation of a strong and well-defined family institution. Marriage is a contract between husband and wife, based on mutual consent. The father or guardian of the girl, "he in whose hand is the tie of marriage" (Q. 2:237), is expected to act on her behalf, and ideally in her interest. With regard to divorce, the Qur'ān makes it a last resort, to be used only after all efforts, including attempts at arbitration (Q. 4:35), have failed. The Prophet warned: "The lawful act most hateful to God is divorce."[60]

The law of divorce as outlined in the Qur'ān and developed by the scholars of Islam gives the man exclusive and free right to divorce, but also attempts to slow or stop abusive or hasty divorce. In response to the pre-Islamic custom of repeatedly marrying, divorcing, and remarrying a woman, the Qur'ān limits revocable divorce to two times. Following divorce, a woman enters a period of sexual abstinence for three menstrual cycles in order to ascertain whether or not she is pregnant; if she is pregnant, her period of abstinence extends till the time of delivery and the child in her womb necessarily belongs, as noted above, to her former husband. During the time of abstinence, the couple is encouraged to reconcile. Once a third divorce is pronounced by the man, however, reconciliation is not possible unless the woman has married and been divorced by another man in the interim (see Q. 2:230). This Qur'anic legislation is meant to safeguard the woman's welfare. It aims at preventing the husband from keeping the woman hanging by marrying her one day and divorcing her the next, until she buys her freedom with her marriage gift. It is, however, always open to abuse, as the husband could himself arrange a formal marriage and divorce, so that he can take his wife back should he regret a hastily pronounced repudiation of their marriage. This legalistic subterfuge is known as *taḥlīl*, that is "making lawful" a remarriage after a third divorce.

While the Qur'ān does allow polygyny, it also places two significant restrictions upon it. First, it limits a man to four wives at one time, in contrast to the unlimited number of wives allowed before Islam. Secondly, it demands strict justice and equality from the man in the material and emotional care of all his wives. If this is not possible, the Qur'ān stipulates, "then only one." The Qur'ān further warns, "You cannot act equitably among your wives however much you try" (Q. 4:3 and 129). The Qur'ān, in fact, shifted the emphasis with regard to polygyny from a man's unrestricted right to sexual gratification to social responsibility in such arrangements. The passage dealing with polygyny opens with the proviso, "If you [men] are afraid that you will not act justly towards the female orphans [in your care], then marry what seems good to you of women: two, three, or four" (Q. 4:3). This statement can be interpreted in two ways. The verse could mean that a man may marry the widowed mothers of such orphans in order to provide a family situation for them. It could also mean that a man may marry two, three, or four orphan-girls after they have attained to marriageable age, again to provide a home and family for them. In either case, marriage to more than one wife is allowed by the Qur'ān in order to deal with the problem of female orphans and widows in a traditional society beset with continuous warfare. In fact, the verses of Sūrah Four that deal with the issue of polygyny are reported to have been revealed shortly after the Battle of Uḥud in which numerous Muslim fighters fell, leaving many widows and orphans behind. In such a society, a woman could only have found the love and security she needed in her own home, provided by a husband.

The Qur'ān provides a measure of security and personal worth for women in allowing them to own property and to dispose of it as they please. Women may acquire property through bequest, inheritance, or bride dowry (*mahr* or *ṣadāq*). To be sure, judged by today's social and economic needs and circumstances, these rights may seem inadequate. Yet it cannot be denied that the Qur'ān bestowed on women a social personality and a sense of human dignity denied them in many societies until modern times.

Islamic law and especially social custom, however, have been far less generous and forward-looking than the Qur'ān. In general, they have tended to either restrict these rights or render them virtually inoperative. It may therefore be useful to review briefly some of the conditions and limitations the Qur'ān and classical Islamic law placed on marriage and divorce, and then examine a few modern reforms of family law and some of the discourses that led to these reforms.

MARRIAGE AND DIVORCE IN CLASSICAL ISLAMIC LAW

In pre-Islamic Arab society, only males who could fight in defense of their tribe were entitled to the inheritance of their father's property. This included the father's wife, whom the son either married (if the woman was not his mother) or kept in a state of suspense, neither marrying her himself nor allowing her to marry someone else – particularly if she had any wealth that he might eventually inherit. In contrast, the Qur'ān regulated inheritance for both males and females, the male receiving twice the portion of the female (Q. 4:11). This apparent inequity is predicated on the responsibility of the husband as the sole maintainer of the family, and on the fact of the female's bride dower, which can be considerable.

The Qur'ān also strictly regulates the degrees of kinship in marriage. It absolutely forbids a man to marry his own mother as well as his deceased father's wife or stepmother. It further prohibits marriage with one's daughters, sisters, paternal and maternal aunts, as well as the daughters of one's brothers and sisters. Also disallowed are foster mothers, foster sisters, the mother of a man's wife, or his stepdaughter who is under his care, after he had conjugal relations with her mother (though if the marriage with her mother was never consummated, then she is lawful for him to marry). Other forbidden unions are with daughters-in-law, as well as with two sisters simultaneously. Unions with married women are forbidden, except for slave-girls, whose captivity legally separates them from their former husbands.

Family law in the *fiqh* or jurisprudence of the legal schools (*madhāhib*) is based in part on Qur'anic reforms and in part on customary social practice. Marriage, according to the Qur'ān and subsequent legal tradition, is essentially a mutual agreement between a woman and a man to live together as husband and wife and make a family. It is based on a request of marriage (*ījāb*) by the man and acceptance, or consent (*qabūl*) by the woman. This agreement must include a *mahr* or *ṣạdāq*, that is a marriage gift to the woman, and should be witnessed by two upright men. If the *mahr* requested by the woman or her guardian (*walī*) is beyond the man's means, then the judge can fix the amount or value of the *mahr* to fit the suitor's social position and circumstances.

Like all the major religious traditions, Islam arose in a patriarchal society. It inherited patriarchy from its original Arab cultural milieu and wider Semitic heritage. Child marriages were a common occurrence in all patriarchal societies, including Arab society before Islam and, until recently, in the Muslim community as well. Classical legal tradition instituted child marriage, so that a boy of twelve and a girl of nine can be married. Where the marriage agreement is concluded by the primary or authoritative (*mujbir*) guardian, it becomes binding on the ground that the wise judgment of a father or grandfather must not be questioned. But if the marriage contract is later proven to be fraudulent, or if it was concluded by other guardians, then the boy can indicate his assent to the marriage by the *mahr* payment to his bride or cohabitation with her, or repudiate it. The girl, however, can contest the marriage within a reasonable time; otherwise her silence is taken as a sign of assent. It is preferred that the marriage contract is in writing, but oral witness to the terms of the contract is sufficient for its validity.

The function and authority the Qur'ān assigns to the *walī*, or guardian, is far more limited than that which was given him by later Islamic law. The guardian was originally supposed to represent female minors who could not comprehend the intricacies of marriage and family life. The *walī* holds "in his hand the tie of marriage," but only after the mutual consent of the bride and groom to be married (see Q. 2:233). The Qur'ān warns both the husband and guardian not to use coercion against women seeking divorce to keep them married against their will, or to keep them hanging, neither married nor unmarried (Q. 2:231–232). The greater power of the guardian seen in actual Islamic law is a result of the influence of long-standing custom and the force of patriarchy in general.

Islamic law is not a rigid legal system of absolute prohibitions and sanctions, but a sacred moral law or way of life. Thus all acts, be they acts of worship or social and economic transactions, move between five degrees of moral probity or repudiation. They can be obligatory or forbidden, recommended or reprehensible, or, finally, neutral. The same method of classification applies to marriage and divorce.[61] Thus we see that a marriage can be good or sound (*ṣaḥīḥ*), or conversely completely unlawful, and thus void (*bāṭil*). Between these two extremes is a marriage which is valid in its foundation (*aṣl*), but flawed in its attributes, and thus corrupt (*fāsid*). The degree of validity of a marriage may be determined by several factors. These are the number of spouses, religious affiliation, degrees of kinship, the period of waiting (*'iddah*) and equality between the husband and wife (*kafā'ah*) in economic and social status. As for the number of spouses, it should not exceed four wives for the man and only one husband for the woman. With regard to religion, a Muslim man may marry women of the people of the Book, but he cannot marry an idolatrous woman. Because of the law of paternity, a Muslim woman can marry a non-Muslim man only if he embraces Islam, which would insure the Muslim paternity of the children. I have already discussed the degrees of family relationships in a valid marriage; suffice it to say here that these Qur'anic sanctions and prohibitions have been minutely studied and codified by later jurists and Qur'ān commentators.

The primary conditions and duration of *'iddah*, or waiting period, have likewise been examined. It must be emphasized here that the *'iddah* period is another important Qur'anic measure to help ascertain true paternity and thus preserve the integrity of the family. *'Iddah* is of two kinds: after divorce, and after the death of the husband. The former, as has already been mentioned, is three menstrual cycles or the delivery of a child, while the latter is four months and ten days, or until the birth of the child of the deceased husband. During the *'iddah* of divorce, the couple should ideally live under one roof. They should practice genuine privacy (*khalwah saḥīḥah*) in order to allow for reconciliation through intimate sexual relations. A third type of *'iddah* is observed during the prolonged absence of the husband, which is until he returns or is presumed to be dead. Here the legal schools have differed widely, but all have been unfair to the wife who might be forced to endure economic hardship and emotional suspense for many decades as she waits in vain for her disappeared husband.

The Qur'ān abolished social status, wealth or tribal prestige as criteria for family unions. Thus a Muslim man or woman should prefer a faithful slave in marriage to a free man or woman who is a rejecter of faith. It explicitly enjoins Muslim men and women not to make poverty an impediment to marriage: "Marry such of you who are maid-servants and pious among your slaves, for if they are poor, God shall enrich them of His bounty" (Q. 24:32).

Yet social custom prevailed, as classical law decreed that a man should always maintain a woman in accordance with her own social station. It stipulated further that social and economic disparity between husband and wife could be used by the judge (*qadī*) as grounds for the annulment (*faskh*) of the marriage.

Marriage in Islam is a contract of rights and responsibilities. The duties of the wife include maintaining the home, caring for the children, and obeying her husband. The husband's duties are to provide food, lodging, and clothing for his wife and her children, and to live amicably with her. Obedience to the husband, as defined by classical law and elaborated by medieval jurists, meant above all the total restriction of the wife's movement outside the home without her husband's permission. It was institutionalized in the law of seclusion of women, in order to protect the man's family honor (*'ird*) and give him absolute control over all the women of his household. This social custom, buttressed by the authority of the sacred law, virtually deprived women of the right to share public space with men, or even to participate in public worship. Until modern times, the debate over the veil or *ḥijāb* centered not on dress but on the seclusion of women.[62]

In some legal schools, notably the Ḥanbalī and Jaʿfarī *madhhabs*, the woman can lay down far-reaching conditions in the marriage contract. These include restricting the husband's right to contract a second marriage, allowing her greater freedom of movement, and giving her some possibility to divorce, if the husband agrees that this will happen should he violate the stipulated conditions. Until the husband signs the marriage contract and thus approves these clauses, however, they are not binding. Furthermore, they can all be sabotaged by the husband's right to divorce – although modern reforms have also tried to put further restrictions, in addition to those of the classical law, on this male power, for instance by requiring that the husband pay large amounts of money if he wishes to divorce. Enforcing this type of marriage contract has been one of the most important reforms in modern times.

In no area of Muslim law has social custom prevailed over the spirit and letter of Qur'anic legislation as in the law of divorce. The reason may be that divorce presents the ultimate challenge to male authority for, regardless of its form and consequences, divorce forces the man to relinquish his power over the woman.

Like marriage, divorce is of different types and degrees of moral and religious probity. The two broad categories are divorce through repudiation and divorce through juridical process. Under these two categories, there are five types of divorce: simple repudiation (*ṭalāq*), delegated repudiation (*ṭalāq al-tafwīḍ*), irrevocable divorce by mutual consent (*khul‘* or *mubāra'ah*), divorce through an oath of imprecation (*li‘ān*) and annulment (*faskh*), and separation by reason of apostasy.

Divorce by simple repudiation could be the best (*ahsan*) or good (*hasan*), depending on the extent to which it adheres to the spirit of the Qur'ān and Prophetic *sunnah*. It takes place during a woman's state of ritual purity, and consists of a single pronouncement of repudiation followed by the *'iddah* period. It may be revoked either by cohabitation or arbitration, in accordance with the Qur'anic dictum: "... their husbands have priority in taking them back" (Q. 2:228). Where proper compliance to the Qur'ān and *sunnah* is lacking, then this form of divorce becomes an innovation (*bid‘ah*) divorce, but does not lose its validity. It is a triple repudiation uttered at one time, "I divorce you," or "You are divorced," after which *taḥlīl* is necessary. If either the husband or wife dies during the *'iddah* period, the other has the right to inherit the deceased spouse, as stipulated by the Qur'ān (Q. 4:12).

Delegated (*tafwīd*) divorce is a process by which the husband delegates the authority of divorce to the wife through the formula, "Divorce yourself," or "Choose to divorce yourself." In such a case the wife would give up all or part of her dower, if divorce takes place at her initiative. The *khul‘*, or irrevocable repudiation, is similar in purpose, though not in form. The major difference is that this type of divorce is done through juridical process. It is initiated at the instigation of the wife, often in return for her *mahr*, in full or in part. When separation is chosen by both spouses, it is called *mubāra'ah*, that is total dissociation between the two spouses, but without the exchange of any property.

Adultery is a major offense (*ḥadd*) in Islam; the most severe punishment is death by stoning. Yet the charge of adultery can only be established on the testimony of four men who have seen the actual sexual act of penetration. Otherwise, the accusation becomes a calumny (*qadhf*), with severe consequences to the guilty party. The Qur'ān states: "As for those who falsely accuse chaste women [of adultery], but cannot bring four witnesses, deal them eighty lashes and never accept their testimony henceforth" (Q. 24:4). As for men who falsely accuse their wives of adultery but are unable to produce any witnesses except themselves, then the testimony of one equals four affirmations by God that he is telling the truth. In a fifth affirmation he should invoke God's curse upon himself, if he is a liar. The woman can avoid punishment by making four oaths that her husband is lying. Her fifth oath should invoke God's wrath upon herself if her husband is telling the truth (Q. 24:6–9). Following this dramatic ordeal, the judge would irrevocably dissolve the marriage.

Another form of irrevocable divorce mandated by the *sharī'ah* law is when either of the two spouses renounces Islam and adopts another religion, including the monotheistic religions of the Book where intermarriage is allowed. Two legal justifications of this form of divorce have been advanced. The first is that religion is the framework of Muslim society, and hence of family relations. When therefore this framework is no longer intact, the marriage union itself is rendered illegitimate (see Q. 2:233). Secondly, since a non-Muslim cannot legally inherit a Muslim, whether between husband and wife or child and parents, then safeguarding the integrity of the family requires dissolution.

One final issue of classical law which continues to be subject to much debate and acrimony is child custody. Since, according to the Qur'ān, the child belongs to the father, most legal opinion agrees on the right of the father to the custody of his children. They disagree, however, on the age of transferring custody from the mother to the father. The point at issue here is the need of the child to remain with the mother, which ranges from only the two years of nursing as enjoined in the Qur'ān till the age of seven for boys and until puberty and beyond for girls. During this period, both mother and child are entitled to maintenance. In case of the father's death or inability to support the child, then the grandfather, or other relative within the degrees of consanguinity of inheritance, must assume that responsibility. This issue also has been subject to discussion and reform in modern times, with the idea of custody "according to the best interests of the child" currently gaining ground in some jurisdictions.

WOMEN AND THE FAMILY: MODERN DISCOURSES AND REFORMS

If the primary goal of feminism is to assert the independence of women, their distinct identity and their equal social and legal rights with men, it may be cogently argued that feminism in the Muslim community began during the life of the Prophet. It is reported that the Prophet said: Prostration (*sujūd*) should be offered to God alone. But were I to command anyone to make prostration before another person, I would command the wife to prostrate herself before her husband." Hearing this, a woman protested, "By Him who sent you as a prophet with the truth, I will let no man control my neck."[63] Feminism as a discipline or public forum for the debate of women's issues, however, is a distinctly modern phenomenon belonging to the modernist reform movements of the nineteenth and twentieth centuries, discussed in the following chapter.

The first prominent thinker seriously to engage in this debate was the Egyptian reformer Muḥammad 'Abduh (1849–1905). 'Abduh opposed polygyny on the grounds that it contradicts the principle of love and compassion which the Qur'ān (Q. 30:21) presents as the framework of the relation of husbands and wives. He further argued that it is impossible to have good relations of love and kindness between the children of different mothers. For good social and psychological reasons, polygyny should, in 'Abduh's view, be abolished.

'Abduh may have been far more radical than what appears in his writings and legal opinions. It is probable that he was the author of at least part of the book of the Egyptian journalist and radical reformer Qāsim Amīn, *Taḥrīr al-mar'ah* (The Liberation of Woman), which appeared in 1899. Among the reforms Amīn advocated was the abolition of the veil and a complete cultural and moral transformation of Egyptian society, following European models. Amīn's thought, in the work under discussion, his many articles, and another seminal book entitled *al-Mar'ah al-jadīdah* (The New Woman) mark the beginning of feminism in the Arab world. From the late nineteenth century until the Second World War, most Arab thinkers, and particularly feminist reformers, were deeply influenced by Muḥammad 'Abduh and his rationalist school. 'Abduh's influence extended into many Muslim lands, from Morocco to Indonesia.

After the colonial period in the first half of the last century, most Middle Eastern countries, including Turkey and Iran, adopted European law codes and constitutional models instead of the *sharī'ah* law. The only law that was preserved was family law. The remaining family law, however, was subjected to far-reaching reforms. These varied from officially abolishing polygyny completely, as in Tunisia and Turkey, circumscribing it, as in Iraq and pre-revolutionary Iran, or simply discouraging it, as in other countries.

One of the most important reforms was to place both marriage and divorce under the jurisdiction of the *sharī'ah* courts, that is to put it under official control rather than letting it be a private matter. This gave the courts a good deal of control over the abuse of the rights of women and children by restraining male authority. To give one example, Ḥanafī law, which is applied in many Muslim countries from South Asia to Central Europe, allows the man to divorce his wife under any circumstances, even in a state of drunkenness, by simply pronouncing the divorce formula. Without the *sharī'ah* courts, such laws leave the wife's fate subject to the husband's capricious whims. Unfortunately, as forces for the return to the *sharī'ah* law gained the upper hand since the 1970s, some of these reforms have been reversed.

Muslim feminist discourses have centered on two broad issues, namely the veil and male authority, both of which are treated in the

Qur'ān. A third important but unrelated issue, which lies beyond the scope of this book, is the influence of Western feminism, which has been welcomed by some Muslim feminists as a good model and rejected by others as an expression of Western intellectual neo-colonialism. Whatever the case may be, Muslim feminism must be viewed as part of the modern Islamist reform movements.

As for the veil, the Qur'ān calls on both women and men to behave modestly in both dress and decorum. Men must lower their gaze and avoid temptation. Women should cover their private parts and other parts of their bodies which, if exposed, will lead to temptation and sin. Such parts of the bodies of men and women are called *'awrah*, meaning nakedness. More specifically, women must draw their shawls *(khumur)* over their bosom. They should not entice men by stamping their feet, so as to jingle their anklets, or show their ornaments except to their husbands and other close blood relatives with whom they could not be united in marriage (see Q. 24:30–31).

Nowhere does the Qur'ān use the word *ḥijāb* to mean dress, or head cover, as it is used today. The word is used to signify a curtain which is to separate the Prophet's wives – the "mothers of the faithful" (Q. 33:6) – from other men, who are told to "speak to them from behind a curtain" (Q. 33:53). Prophetic tradition and subsequent jurisprudence were more concerned with the seclusion of woman than with her dress. This was no doubt meant to protect women from invading soldiers and other strangers who frequented the abode of Islam. From the end of the nineteenth century, and especially in urban societies, women became increasingly free to leave the home. The veil thus became the dress that would give women a place in the public space of men. Typical is the example of the Iranian *chador*, a term meaning tent, which in fact serves as a protective covering in which the women can move around as lawyers, physicians, teachers, nurses, and even religious scholars.

The legal and moral issues of the veil have been politicized beyond recognition. Those who call for the abolition of the veil can find good proof texts. Likewise, those who advocate returning to the veil can use both texts and the authority of consensus to back their arguments. It is time for these issues to be depoliticized and thus be discussed by men and women within the moral and religious context of personal commitment of Muslim women and men to their faith and tradition.

The discourse of male authority has generally focused on a single Qur'anic verse (Q. 4:34). The verse in question reads: "Men are set over (*qawwāmūn*) women in that God has preferred some of them over others, and in that they spend of their wealth. Thus righteous women are those who are obedient [to God], keeping their faith in the unseen, as God had decreed it to be kept. As for those women whom you fear may step out of line, admonish them, then desert them in the beds, then hit them. But if they listen to you, do not seek any recourse against them." The verse must be read as advice for men to carry out their responsibilities towards their wives. Similarly, it enjoins women to keep their commitments to their husbands, to live in harmony, and to preserve their chastity. The term "*qawwāmūn*" (set over) signifies responsibility and service rather than despotic authority. The priority of men over women is neither physical, spiritual, nor moral, but social, that is within the patriarchal family. This includes their economic priority, as they spend of their wealth for the upkeep of their families. If, however, women possess the same economic and social qualities, then the prerogative of responsibility and service should be shared equally between wives and husbands. Men's fear that women may "step out of line (*nushūz*)" is expressed with regard to men as well (Q. 4:128). In both cases, the Qur'ān enjoins harmony and amicable living.

The Qur'ān instituted marriage for the sake of the family. It is in the family that the sanctity of marriage resides. The family begins with the two spouses and includes the children, all of whom must practice love and mercy towards one another. The Qur'ān places kindness and respect towards one's parents next in importance to the worship of God. Muslims are enjoined to care for their parents in old age, without showing any sign of annoyance or displeasure; rather, they must show humility and compassion to them and pray God to bestow mercy upon them (see Q. 17:23–24). Feminist discourses in the Muslim community should not be bogged down in the rhetoric of apologetics and polemics, but should be used as a dynamic tool to strengthen good and harmonious family relations. Divergent concerns and ideas should be debated in the spirit of constructive dialogue between men and women to preserve the social, moral, and spiritual integrity of the family which is the basic unit of a healthy Muslim *ummah*.

11

Islam and Modernity

Islam is a tradition of social and religious reform and personal commitment. Furthermore, since Islam has no official priesthood, every person is responsible not only for their own moral probity, but for the moral reform of the entire Muslim *ummah*. The Qur'ān enjoins:

> Let there be of you a community that calls to the good, enjoins honorable conduct (*ma'rūf*), and dissuades from evil conduct (*munkar*). These are indeed prosperous people (Q. 3:104).

Throughout Muslim history, there have always been individuals and groups who took it upon themselves to reform the rest of the community. Prophetic sanction was early secured for this responsibility in the *ḥadīth* tradition "God shall raise at the head of every hundred years for this community a man who will renew for it its faith."[64] Since no characteristics of such renovators of the faith are specified in this *ḥadīth*, many have been honored with the title of *mujaddid* ("renewer") of Muslim faith and conduct.

This sanction of an active personal involvement in the reform of society is further specified in the oft-quoted Prophetic injunction:

> Anyone of you who sees something lewd or dishonorable (*munkar*), let him change it with his hand. If he is unable, then with his tongue, and if he is still unable, then let him change it with his heart, but this is the weakest of faith.[65]

This *ḥadīth* has been taken as a call for social and religious *jihād* for the purification of society. Heeding this call with utmost seriousness, the Kharijites became an extreme example of reform through violent means, but by no means the only one. In fact many later movements, as we shall see, resembled them in many respects.

An external impetus for reform has been Muslim interaction with, and reaction to, Western Christendom. The first major Western challenge to Muslim power and to Islam's great capacity to rally its people in a universal *jihād* for the defense of the integrity of its domains was the Crusades. Fired by a spirit of Christian *jihād*, or holy war, for the liberation of Jerusalem from Muslim domination, the armies of the first Crusade were able to capture the Holy City in 1099 after a great massacre of its Jewish and Muslim inhabitants. For nearly two centuries, Frankish Christian kingdoms existed side by side with Muslim states along the eastern Mediterranean shores, sometimes peacefully, but most of the time at war.

Although in the end the crusaders returned home and those who remained were assimilated, the spirit of the Crusades and the distorted images of Islam and its followers that the crusaders took back with them live on. Conversely, the equally distorted images of Christianity and Western Christendom that the Crusades left in Muslim lands have been reenforced and greatly embellished through Muslim reactions to Western imperialism and its aftermath. We shall therefore examine Islam in the modern age from two perspectives: internal reform and the challenge of the West.

PRE-MODERNIST REFORM MOVEMENTS

Common to all reform movements has been the call to return to pristine Islam, the Islam of the Prophet's society and the normative period of his rightly guided successors (*al-khulafā' al-rāshidūn*). Among the men who championed this cause was the great religious scholar Ibn Taymīyah (d. 1328). Ibn Taymīyah was a neo-Ḥanbalī jurist who fought relentlessly against Shi'ite beliefs and practices, Sufi excesses of saint veneration and esoteric doctrines, as well as against the blind imitation by the masses of established legal schools and the general reluctance to revive the practice of *ijtihād*. Ibn Taymīyah exerted a powerful and long-lasting influence on all subsequent reform movements.

The first to adopt Ibn Taymīyah's ideas as the basis of its reform program was the Wahhābī movement, so called after its founder Muḥammad Ibn 'Abd al-Wahhāb. Significantly, this powerful and uncompromising revivalist movement began in the highlands (Najd) of Arabia. Ibn 'Abd al-Wahhāb's long life (1703–1792) allowed him to establish his movement on firm ideological and political grounds. He allied himself with Muḥammad Āl Sa'ūd, a local tribal prince, with the understanding that the prince would exercise political power and protect the nascent movement, which would hold religious authority. This agreement remains operative to the present, as the kingdom of Saudi Arabia is a Wahhābī state ruled by the descendants of Āl Sa'ūd.

Like the Kharijites before them, the Wahhābīs regarded all those who did not share their convictions to be either misbelievers (*kuffār*) or persons gone astray. They thus waged a violent campaign aimed at purging Muslim society of what they considered to be its un-Islamic beliefs and practices. They tried to destroy the Prophet's tomb in Madīnah and level the graves of his Companions. They attacked the Shi'ite sacred cities of Najaf and Karbalā', massacred their inhabitants, and destroyed the shrines of 'Alī and his son Ḥusayn. They also went on a rampage of Arab cities, desecrating the tombs of Sufi saints and destroying their shrines.

The Wahhābīs preached a strictly egalitarian Islam based solely on a direct relationship between the worshiper and God. They regarded saint veneration, including veneration of the Prophet, as a form of idolatry. They likewise repudiated the universally cherished hope of intercession by the Prophet and other divinely favored *walī*s with God on behalf of the pious for blessing and succor in this life, and salvation in the next. They even advocated the destruction of the sacred black stone of the Kaʿbah, as it too stood as an idol between the faithful Muslim and his Lord.

Again like the Kharijites, the Wahhābīs equated "Islam" with "Arab," and like them limited their activities to Arab society. This accounts for the fact that the Wahhābī movement has survived only in Arabia, where it remains the ideological framework for an increasingly unpopular regime.

This is not to say, however, that the Wahhābī ideology has had no influence elsewhere. On the contrary, its basic ideals continue to have great appeal to reformist and revivalist groups and individuals everywhere. Especially significant was the Wahhābī influence on Sufi reforms in the eighteenth and nineteenth centuries.

ISLAMIC REVIVALIST MOVEMENTS IN THE NINETEENTH CENTURY

The nineteenth century witnessed the rise of a number of Sufi *jihād* movements. These movements arose in part as a Sufi answer to Wahhābī reform and in part as a reaction to European colonialist encroachments on Muslim domains. Several of these movements were able to establish short-lived states, such as those of ʿUthmān dan Fodio (d. 1817) in Nigeria, Muḥammad al-Sanūsī (d. 1859) in Libya, and Muḥammad Aḥmad al-Mahdī (d. 1885) in the Sudan. Common to all these movements was an activist ideology of militant struggle against outsider colonialism and internal decadence. They also strove for reform and the revival of *ijtihād*.

Because of their broad-base appeal, these Sufi reform movements exerted a lasting influence on most subsequent reform programs and ideologies. In North Africa in particular, Sufi shaykhs and religious scholars spearheaded a long and bloody struggle against French and Italian colonialism. They also helped preserve the religious, linguistic, and cultural identities of the North African countries they led to independence. The Sufi shaykh 'Abd al-Qādir of Algeria, for example, played an important political role in the long struggle for Algeria's independence. King Muḥammad V of Morocco was a Sufi shaykh and a venerable descendant (*sharīf*) of the Prophet. Likewise, the grandson of al-Sanūsī, Idrīs I, ruled Libya as king until the September revolution of 1969.

The Sanūsīyah movement spread in North and West Africa, where it worked for reform and Muslim unity. In contrast, the Mahdiyyah of the Sudan was an eschatological movement. Its founder saw himself as God's representative on earth sent to reestablish the Prophet's paradigmatic state. He thus called his own companions Anṣār, or helpers, as Muḥammad had called his Madinan supporters. He regarded the Ottoman-Egyptian rule of the Sudan as an irreligious occupation and waged a war of *jihād* against it. In 1885, he triumphed over Egyptian forces and established an Islamic state based on a strict application of the *sharī'ah* law, which lasted till 1889.

MODERNIST REFORMERS

When Napoleon landed on Egyptian shores in 1798, he brought with him not only soldiers, but also scholars and the printing-press. Through Napoleon's oriental adventure, the Middle East discovered Europe. Furthermore, the great Ottoman empire which in the early decades of the sixteenth century had threatened Vienna, had by the nineteenth become "the sick man of Europe." With the British empire ruling India and controlling much of the Muslim world, Muslim thinkers everywhere were awed by the West and resentful of the state of somnolence into which the Muslim *ummah* had fallen.

In spite of Muslim political inertia, the nineteenth century witnessed an intellectual and cultural revival in many areas of the Islamic east. Egypt, for instance, was the home of an Arab intellectual renaissance. Due to unsettled social and political conditions in the Levant, a number of Western-educated Syro-Lebanese Christians emigrated to Egypt, where they established newspapers and cultural journals and actively participated in the recovery of the Arabo-Islamic heritage.

The Arab renaissance of the nineteenth century was largely stimulated by a Western cultural and intellectual efflorescence. With the breakup of traditional church-dominated regimes and institutions as a consequence of the Protestant Reformation and the Enlightenment, secularism and romantic nationalism largely supplanted religious faith and institutions in nineteenth-century Europe. These ideas appealed to secular Christian and Muslim Arabs alike and in the end led to the rise of Arab nationalism. The same ideas also influenced other Muslim peoples, so that nationalist identities came to compete, and in some cases even supersede, Islamic identities.

These and other Western cultural and intellectual influences were strengthened by Western Christian missionary schools and institutions of higher learning, which greatly proliferated throughout the Muslim world. Islamic reform of the nineteenth and twentieth centuries in Asia, Africa, and the Middle East must be viewed in the light of this great cultural and intellectual ferment.

Afghānī and ʿAbduh

The second half of the nineteenth century was dominated by two figures, the Iranian Jamāl al-Dīn al-Afghānī (d. 1897) and the Egyptian Muḥammad ʿAbduh (d. 1905). Afghānī had a traditional Shīʿī philosophical and theological as well as a Western education. He was a religious humanist who cherished an idealized vision of a pan-Islamic *ummah* inhabiting a vast area stretching from Southeast Asia to North and West Africa.

True to his pan-Islamic vision, Jamāl al-Dīn adopted the epithet Afghānī in order to obscure his Iranian Shīʿī identity. Like a number of other reformers of the time, he tirelessly worked for the realization of an Islamic cultural, religious, and political revival in a rejuvenated international Ottoman state. He traveled far and wide, from India, through the main centers of Islamic culture in Asia and Africa, to Europe, preaching his pan-Islamic ideology.

Afghānī introduced a new approach to the West that continues to be upheld, in one way or another, by reformers to the present. He admired the vigor, industry, and seriousness of Europeans, but argued that these were in fact Islamic values that Muslims had lost and had to recover. Science, he argued, is not the exclusive property of the West, but a universal field of knowledge open to all peoples, regardless of religious and cultural identity.

Islam, for Afghānī and his followers is a rational religion that is in full accord with science. In contrast, Christianity is irrational, Afghānī asserted, as it is based on mysteries that people are enjoined to believe without understanding. Therefore, when Europe was most Christian it was most backward, while the Muslim community was most advanced when it was most Muslim.

Afghānī and his disciple Muḥammad ʿAbduh were for some years exiled from the Middle East by the Ottoman government, in response to British pressure. They lived in Paris, where they began an international journal entitled *al-ʿUrwā al-wuthqā*, an expression borrowed from the Qur'ān, meaning "the firm handle" (see Q. 2:256). In this journal they continued to urge reform, the resumption of *ijtihād*, and the adoption of Western science and technology but not Western materialistic values. They further urged all Muslims to overthrow their corrupt and despotic regimes and unite in a pan-Islamic state capable of freeing the *ummah* from European domination.

Afghānī was, however, more of a political agitator than a thinker. His legacy of active reform provided the needed motivation for twentieth-century reform and revivalist movements. Afghānī spent the last years of his life as a virtual prisoner in Istanbul, strictly confined to a comfortable home.

In contrast with Afghānī's public and dynamic personality, Shaykh Muḥammad 'Abduh was a quiet, introspective, and mild character. He grew up in the small Egyptian town of Ṭanṭā, whose shrine to the popular saint Sayyid Aḥmad al-Badawī remains to this day the home of a rich tradition of Sufi folk piety. 'Abduh was brought up by his uncle, himself a noted Sufi adept. Although 'Abduh in the end repudiated both popular and theosophical Sufism, his Sufi upbringing left its mark on his personality.

While sharing Afghānī's view of the superiority of Islamic faith and civilization over Christianity and Western civilization, 'Abduh was a pragmatic reformer. He was convinced that for reform to be effective, it had to begin from within. He therefore began a series of reforms of religious education that transformed Cairo's al-Azhar University from a traditional into a modern institution, where both religious and secular subjects were taught. He used his office as the Grand Mufti, or jurisconsult, of Egypt to implement his educational reforms and embark upon an ambitious project of editing and publishing the primary sources of Islamic philosophy, theology, history, and jurisprudence. 'Abduh had a far greater and more lasting influence on Arab and Islamic thought in general than any reformer before or after him.

The Indian Subcontinent

The religio-political situation prevailing in India in the eighteenth and nineteenth centuries was the consequence of a unique set of circumstances. A Muslim community, while remaining a minority, ruled most of the subcontinent and its largely Hindu population for a prolonged period. From this emerged a Hindu-Muslim society with a rich Perso-Indian culture. From the tenth century, there were sharp differences between the traditionists (*ahl al-ḥadīth*), who insisted on basing everything on the Qur'ān and *sunnah*, and the more Sufi-oriented syncretistic mystics and poets, who served as a bridge between

Hindu and Muslim piety. With the demise of the Mughal empire in the seventeenth century, calls for reform on traditional lines grew more vocal. One of the strongest voices for reform was that of Aḥmad Sirhindī (d. 1724). Sirhindī called for a return to the *sharīʿah* and condemned Sufis as deviants and Ibn ʿArabī in particular as a misbeliever (*kāfir*).

Shah Walī Allāh of Delhi (d. 1762) initiated the most important movement of Islamic reform in the Indian subcontinent in modern times. Although he was a disciple of Ibn ʿAbd al-Wahhāb, unlike his mentor he was a Sufi who did not reject Sufism, but sought to reform it. Shah Walī Allāh was a moderate reformer with encyclopedic learning. He rejected the principle of blind imitation (*taqlīd*) and called for the revival of active *ijtihād*. He also sought to reconcile Shīʿī-Sunni differences, which have always been a source of great friction in the community, particularly in the Indian subcontinent.

Shah Walī Allāh's grandson Aḥmad Barelwi (d. 1831), however, transformed his program into a *jihād* movement against British rule and the Sikhs. In 1826, he established an Islamic state based on the *sharīʿah* and adopted the old caliphal title "commander of the faithful." Although he was killed in battle in 1831, his movement lived on as a *jihād* movement.

For Aḥmad Barelwi, India ceased to be an Islamic domain after the end of Mughal rule. Hence, Muslims had to wage a *jihād* to liberate it. If independence from infidel sovereignty proved impossible, Muslims would have to depart, in an act of religious migration (*hijrah*), to an area ruled by Muslims.

The shock that Indian Muslims suffered through the consolidation of British rule was intensified by the fact that the British tampered with Islamic law itself. The result was the interesting but short-lived code known as Anglo-Muḥammadan law. This code was a mixture of Islamic law and Western humanistic rulings.

On one end of the spectrum of reaction to British rule was the *jihād* movement of Aḥmad Barelwi and others like it, on the other, the apologetic approaches of Sayyid Aḥmad Khān (d. 1898) and Sayid Amīr 'Alī (d. 1928).

Like Muḥammad 'Abduh, Aḥmad Khān was a thorough rationalist. But while 'Abduh typified Mu'tazilī rationalism, Khān followed medieval Muslim philosophers, notably Ibn Rushd, and the deists of his own time. 'Abduh held the basic principles of religion to be eternal verities that could not be questioned, even when they seemed to disagree with the laws of nature. For Aḥmad Khān, on the other hand, nature followed a strict system of causality that allowed for no exceptions.

Revelation, "God's word," and nature, "God's work," argued Khān, could not contradict one another. Therefore, where revelation contradicted science, it had to be interpreted such that the inner harmony between the two was revealed. Aḥmad Khān's rationalism was in large measure a consequence of his Westernization.

Like all reformers, Khān called for modern *ijtihād*, or the rethinking of Islamic tradition. Unlike most of them, he rejected *ḥadīth* tradition as a legitimate source of modern Islamic living. He founded the Aligarh Muḥammadan College (later Aligarh Muslim University) in India. There he attempted to implement his ideas in a modern Western program of education.

Muḥammad Iqbāl

Sayyid Aḥmad Khān's ideas and those of his fellow apologists culminated in the philosophy of Muḥammad Iqbāl (d. 1938), the greatest Muslim thinker of modern India. Iqbāl argued for an inner spirit that moves human civilization, a spirit akin to the nineteenth-century French philosopher Henri Bergson's idea of the "vital urge" (*élan vital*). Iqbāl actually constructed a theory of Islamic civilization on the thought of Western philosophers (including, besides Bergson, Nietzsche), as well as on the dynamic Sufism of Jalāl al-Dīn Rūmī.

Like Afghānī and 'Abduh before him, Iqbāl argued for the acquisition of Western science and philosophy, as rightfully belonging to the Islamic heritage. He, however, argued for a process of integration of these fields of knowledge into a fresh *Reconstruction of Religious Thought in Islam*, which he gave as the title of his only major work in English. This call for a dynamic rethinking of Islamic faith and civilization is frequently repeated in Iqbāl's philosophical-mystical Urdu and Persian poetry.

Although Iqbāl did not wish to meddle in politics, he is regarded as the father of Pakistan. He suggested to Muḥammad 'Alī Jinnāḥ, the chief founder of Pakistan, the idea of an autonomous Muslim state in northwest India. It is doubtful whether he actually conceived of an independent Muslim country in the Indian subcontinent.

TWENTIETH-CENTURY MODERNISM AND SECULARISM

However diverse and idealistic nineteenth-century reform movements may have been, they nonetheless represented a dynamic and courageous spirit of reform and progress. Perhaps due to the international upheavals of two world wars and the breakup of the Ottoman empire, Islamic reform experienced a loss of nerve in the twentieth century. Another reason for the premature stifling of this spirit may have been the lack of a coherent program of reform for post-colonialist Muslim thinkers to implement or build upon.

Afghānī, 'Abduh, and their fellow reformers were at one and the same time liberal modernists and traditional thinkers. They are known as *salafīs*, that is reformers who seek to emulate the example of "the pious forebears" (*al-salaf al-ṣāliḥ*). This important ideal of equilibrium between tradition and modernity was lost by the third decade of the twentieth century. The result was the transformation of nineteenth-century ideas of liberal reform into traditional revivalist movements, apologetics, or secularism.

Muḥammad 'Abduh was succeeded by his Lebanese disciple Muḥammad Rashīd Riḍā. Before his death, 'Abduh established *al-Manār*, an important religio-cultural journal that Riḍā continued to publish until his death in 1935. Chiefly through this journal, 'Abduh's rationalist school continued to play a significant, but increasingly diminished, role in shaping Arab thought in the first half of the twentieth century. However, not only this school, but the whole ideology of reform was radically transformed by new political, social, and economic realities.

After the Ottoman defeat in the First World War, a young army officer, Muṣṭafā Kamāl Ata-Turk, led a revolutionary movement that transformed the Ottoman state from a traditional Islamic empire into a modern secular Turkish republic. In 1923, he abolished the caliphate and a year later assumed official leadership as the first president of the new republic. Although it had been for centuries a shadowy office without any power, the caliphate still symbolically embodied Muslims' hopes for a viable pan-Islamic state. This action therefore had far-reaching effects on Islamic political thought.

Muṣṭafā Kamāl banned Sufi orders, dissolved Islamic religious institutions, substituted the Latin for the Arabo-Ottoman alphabet, and waged a nationwide campaign for literacy in the new script. His express aim was to thoroughly Westernize the Turkish republic and completely cut it off from its Islamic past. While his ideology remains official state policy, his aim has largely failed. The Turkish people's Islamic roots could not be easily destroyed. Islamic faith and practice remain strong among the people, and Turkey has its own powerful revivalist movements.

On the eve of the abolition of the caliphate in 1923, Riḍā published an important treatise on the Imamate or Supreme Caliphate. In it he argued for the establishment of an Islamic state ruled by a council of jurists or religious scholars. In such a state nationalist sentiments and aspirations would be recognized, but as much as possible subordinated to the religio-political interest of the larger community.

Since his Islamic-state idea remained an unrealized political theory, Riḍā became increasingly nationalistic and traditional in his thinking. Riḍā's ideas of Islamic revivalism and Arab nationalism came to represent one of the main trends in twentieth-century revivalist thinking. His political idea was realized in Imam Khomeini's theory of the "guardianship" or "authority of the jurist" (*walāyat al-faqīh*), which provided the ideological framework of the Iranian Islamic revolution of 1978–1979.

CONTEMPORARY REVIVALIST MOVEMENTS

Although the ideal of Islamic reform remains the establishment of a transnational Islamic caliphate, the reality has been the rise of local movements reflecting local needs and ideas. Even at the local level, however, the ideal of an all-inclusive and self-sufficient Islamic order is common to most revivalist movements of the second half of the twentieth century.

This ideal has its roots in the social and educational organization of the Muslim Brothers. In 1929 Ḥasan al-Bannā, an Egyptian school teacher, founded the Society of Muslim Brothers (*jam'iyyat al-ikhwān al-muslimīn*). The aim of this society was to establish a social, economic, and political Islamic infrastructure through which the total Islamization of society might in time be achieved. Thus, through the schools, banks, cooperatives, clinics, and other social and educational facilities, the Society of Muslim Brothers penetrated all levels of Egyptian society.

The political and militaristic aspects of the revivalist movements likewise have their beginnings in the Society of Muslim Brothers, particularly in the Society's development after the assassination of its populist and generally pacifist founder in 1949. Al-Bannā was succeeded by hard-line leaders who advocated active *jihād* against the Egyptian state-system, which they regarded as un-Islamic.

Among the products of the ideology of the Muslim Brothers were the young officers who successfully led the 1952 Egyptian socialist revolution, which abolished monarchical rule. Gamal Abd al-Nasser, the leader of the revolution and charismatic proponent of Arab nationalism in the 1950s and 1960s, then clashed with the Brothers. He imprisoned, exiled, or executed most of their leaders in the mid-1960s and thus drove the movement underground. This led to the Society's loss of power and status in Egypt. Following the Arab defeat in the Arab-Israeli six-day war of June 1967 and the death of Nasser three years later, the Muslim Brothers were superseded by other and more powerful revivalist movements under Anwar Sadat (d. 1981) and his successor Husni Mubarak.

Vis-à-vis Egypt, without its social infrastructure the Society exists as a largely ineffectual ideological movement in exile. It has, however, spread into other Arab countries, where it remains active. It is, moreover, showing some signs of revival in its country of origin.

In 1943 a similar organization, the *Jamā'at-i islāmī* (Islamic Society), was founded by Mawlana Sayyid Abu-l A'la Mawdudi (d. 1979). Like Ḥasan al-Bannā, Mawdudi was committed to pan-Islamic unity. But also like Bannā, he concentrated his efforts on his own society, in this case the Muslims of India and later Pakistan. The influence of both organizations spread far beyond their original homes.

While most contemporary revivalist movements, including the two organizations under discussion, have been open to modern science and technology as well as the reform of Muslim society, they reject such social ideals as women's liberation, capitalist democracy, Western forms of entertainment and styles of dress, and the free mixing of the sexes as decadent Western values and practices. Therefore, unlike nineteenth-century reformers who looked to the West for ideas of reform, contemporary revivalist reform movements look for Islamic alternatives. Mawdudi, for example, wishing to distinguish his Islamic state model from Western democracies, described it as "theo-democracy," based on the broad Qur'anic principle of consultation (*shūrā*) and the *sharī'ah* law.

STATE ISLAM AND THE ISLAMIC REVOLUTION

Besides the nineteenth-century Islamic states of Muḥammad Aḥmad al-Mahdī in the Sudan and Aḥmad Barelwi in India, a number of attempts to create Islamic states based on the *sharī'ah* law were made in the second half of the twentieth century. Such attempts were in part reactions to the secular nation-states of the Muslim world that came into being after the First and Second World Wars. In the majority of cases, these states adopted European law codes for all areas of social and economic life except family and personal-status law.

In the Sudan, Ja'far Numayri (r. 1971–1985) plunged that agriculturally rich country into deep conflict between the generally Christian south and Muslim north because he insisted on applying the *sharī'ah* as the law of the land. The tragic results continue to be famine and bloodshed under short-lived and unstable governments. Likewise, General Mohammad Ziya' al-Haqq (d. 1988) attempted to transform Pakistan into an Islamic state governed by the *sharī'ah.* Here too, the result has been social and political unrest. In Egypt and Algeria revivalist movements continue to resort to violent means in their quest for Islamic states. The results are similarly social strife and instability.

In practically every Muslim country there is at least one revivalist movement striving for some form of an Islamic state. In some cases like Malaysia and Indonesia, the governments themselves espouse Islamic national policies aimed at forestalling such attempts and silencing extremist voices calling for radical reform. Nevertheless, in most Muslim countries tensions continue to run high between Islamic movements made up of middle class educated men and women and despotic regimes determined to hold on to power at any cost.

In such highly charged social and political conditions, religion serves as a powerful moral, social, and spiritual expression of discontent not only for Islamic activists, but for a broad spectrum of the community as well. It was upon this mass discontent that Imam Khomeini and his fellow Shi'ite *mullahs*, or popular religious leaders, built the Iranian Islamic republic.

The roots of the Islamic revolution of Iran lie deep in the ethos, worldview, and history of Twelver Imāmī Shi'ism. The cruel death of Ḥusayn b. 'Alī gave the Shī'ī community an ethos of suffering and an ideal of martyrdom as means of rectifying an errant Muslim society in the absence of the twelfth Imām. Until the Imām returns to right all wrongs, his oppressed community must struggle against all rulers, for all rulers are regarded as usurpers of his divinely instituted authority.

In view of the dichotomy between an ideal legitimate divine authority and an illegitimate human rule, a religious hierarchy of scholars and jurists came to represent the Imām's authority during his long absence. Headed by a supreme *mujtahid* (jurist) regarded as a sign of God (*āyat allāh*) in learning and religious authority, this highly organized religious hierarchy dominates the social, political, economic, and religious life of the community.

Throughout the long period of Shi'ite secular rule in Iran (1501–1978), the authority of the religious *'ulama'* operated in more or less continuous tension with the secular authorities. This tension was greatly exacerbated during the reign of the late Shah Muhammad Riza Pahlavi (r. 1941–1979) who sought to Westernize the country and obscure its Islamic identity by asserting Iran's pre-Islamic cultural past.

In 1963, during the Muḥarram observances of Ḥusayn's martyrdom, matters came to a head between the Shah and the religious establishment. The Shah's dreaded secret police, the Savak, ruthlessly put down mass demonstrations led by the *'ulama'* and sent Khomeini, an already prominent religious leader, into exile. Secretly, a broad alliance between religious elements, student activists, and leftist groups was formed to oppose the Shah's regime.

In a series of lectures to a group of religious students in one of the seminaries of the holy city of Najaf in Iraq, Khomeini elaborated his religio-political theory of *walāyat al-faqīh*. The question of the role of the jurist as the Imām's representative during his absence is an old one. For most Shi'ite religious scholars even today, the jurist's authority is limited to religious and legal affairs. But on the basis of a number of *ḥadīth* traditions from the Imāms, Khomeini argued for the all-embracing authority of the jurist in the community. Thus *walāyah*, or guardianship, came to mean for Khomeini actual rule by the jurist.

After a brief period of exile in France, Khomeini returned to Iran in February 1979 as the head of the Iranian Islamic revolution. The Islamic republic he founded has so far had a turbulent history. It fought an eight-year-long war with Iraq (1980–1988), out of which it emerged greatly weakened but still intact. The dramatic assassinations and other acts of sabotage that the Mujahidin-e-Khalq opposition carried out have also had their effect. But in the absence of an alternative program, and with the popular support that the religious establishment in Iran still enjoys, the "authority of the jurist" remains largely unchallenged.

The Iranian Islamic revolution and the state it engendered is a unique and highly significant phenomenon in modern Islamic history. For the first time, an indigenous revolution succeeded, not by armed resistance but by the will of people who triumphed over guns with their bare chests. While the Islamic republic has not been able to export its revolution to other Muslim countries, it has inspired innumerable groups and individuals around the world to reaffirm their confidence in the ability of Islam to transform their own lives. Among the movements influenced by the Iranian Islamic revolution are the first and second Palestinian *intifadahs* in 1986 and 2000 respectively, as well as the Algerian Islamic uprising, which has devastated that country since 1992.

ISLAM IN WESTERN EUROPE

The presence of Islam in Western Europe began early and in a variety of ways. After the establishment of Muslim rule in southern Spain in 711, commercial, political, and cultural relations were also established with both Latin and Byzantine states. But medieval Europe did not tolerate a permanent Muslim community on its soil and so the establishment of actual Muslim communities in Western Europe is a recent phenomenon.

Some Muslims migrated to Europe from the colonies as students, visitors, and merchants. After the devastation of the two world wars,

Muslims came in large numbers to rebuild Britain, France, and other European countries. Many Muslims also came as menial laborers and factory workers, especially after the Second World War.

The ethnic makeup of Muslim immigrants in Europe was largely determined by European colonial rule. Furthermore, the majority of immigrants were male workers ranging from teenagers to forty-year-olds. Immigrants from French colonies in North Africa and elsewhere went to France. Indian and, later, Pakistani and Bangladeshi Muslims tended to go to Britain. Turkish and Turkic Muslims from the former Soviet republics went to Germany and the Netherlands, and Bosnians went to Austria. Such migrations began in the early decades of the last century and have continued in spite of many restrictions.

Muslim communities in Europe tend to form along ethnic and linguistic lines rather than sectarian affiliations. With the recent establishment of hundreds of mosques, centers, and religious and cultural organizations in every European city, Muslim communities have become a dynamic religious and intellectual force in European society. In France and Britain, where many Muslims are citizens, Muslims are no longer confined to the status of "guest workers." It is in fact estimated that within the early decades of the present century, Muslims will constitute fifty percent of the population of France.

After the Islamic revolution of 1978–1979, many Iranians also migrated to Europe, thus adding yet another ethnic and religious component to the already wide diversity of European Muslims. Likewise, the fifteen-year-long Lebanese civil war of 1975–1990, as well as the disturbances in other Arab countries, including the Gulf War of 1991, sent many political and economic refugees to the West. Intermarriages and conversions have also infused new blood into the Muslim community in the Western world.

Since the mid-1980s most European countries have taken legal measures to limit immigration; some have even repatriated some of their Muslim immigrants. Such actions may have been prompted by economic considerations, but perhaps equally by nationalistic fears that Muslim immigrants would alter the social and ethnic character of these countries. So, while European-born Muslims of foreign parentage are increasingly assimilating into European society and culture, European discrimination against ethnic minorities and the Islamic awakening caused by the Islamic revolution of Iran have made Muslims more aware of their own religious and cultural identity.

An important factor contributing to the integration of Muslims into European society is interfaith dialogue. Very useful and sophisticated discussions are being sponsored by the Catholic Church, the World Council of Churches, the Islamic Council of Europe, as well as by local church and Islamic organizations. It is hoped that honest and constructive dialogue between Muslims and people of other faiths and ideologies will promote a spirit of mutual respect and acceptance in an increasingly pluralistic world.

ISLAM IN NORTH AMERICA

It is a matter of conjecture as to when the first Muslims arrived on American shores. The evidence that Muslims from Spain and West Africa sailed to America long before Columbus should not be discounted, but it is far from being conclusive. It is very likely that the fall of Granada in 1492, and the harsh Inquisition against Muslims and Jews that followed, led many to flee to America soon after Columbus's historic voyage. Scattered records point to the presence of Muslims in Spanish America before 1550.

In the sixteenth and seventeenth centuries hundreds of thousands of slaves were brought mainly from West Africa to the Spanish, Portuguese, and British American colonies. At least twenty percent of these slaves were Muslims. Among the slaves brought from the coast of Senegal, Niger, and the Sudan the majority were Muslims, and many were well educated in Arabic and the religious sciences. They were able to preserve their faith and heritage, and some tried to maintain contacts with Muslims in their places of origin. But Muslims were quickly absorbed into American society, adopting their masters' religion and even family names.

Islamic customs and ideas can still be traced in the African-American community. The Islamic history of these early slaves in the United States is being reconstructed from slave narratives, oral history, and other archival materials, including notices by white travelers of some Islamic activities in the mid-nineteenth century.

Beginning in the late nineteenth century, African-Americans have been making conscious efforts to recover their Islamic heritage. In the 1920s Elijah Muḥammad (d. 1975) founded the Nation of Islam in America. He saw Islam as the religion of the Blacks only, thus misrepresenting the universalistic and non-racial nature of Islam. However, his sons and successors, after traveling in the Muslim world and observing the international and multiracial character of the *ḥajj* pilgrimage, have returned to mainstream Sunni Islam. Islam continues to be the fastest growing religion in America, particularly among African-Americans.

Prior to the revival of Islam in the African-American community early in the twentieth century, small numbers of mainly Syrian and Lebanese Muslims came to the United States and Canada. These early immigrants were uneducated men who came to North America to make money and return home. Instead, many married Canadian and American wives and were soon completely assimilated.

The first Muslim missionary in America was Muḥammad Alexander Webb, a jeweler, newspaper editor, and diplomat who embraced Islam during his travels in India. On his return to America, Webb founded an Islamic propaganda movement. He wrote three books on Islam and established a periodical, *The Muslim World.* He traveled widely spreading the new faith and establishing Islamic study circles or Muslim brotherhoods in many northeastern and midwestern American cities. Webb died in 1916 and his movement died with him.

Immigration to Canada and the United States increased markedly during the twentieth century. Moreover, many of the new immigrants came as students who chose to stay, or as well-educated professionals who came in search of better opportunities. Others came to escape persecution in their homelands on account of their religious or political activities. Interestingly, many in recent years were staunch anti-Western Muslim revivalists but, once they arrived in Canada or the U.S.A., they reassessed their previous hostilities and now live as peaceful, responsible, and law-abiding citizens.

While these and other religiously committed Muslim immigrants may have toned down their political convictions, they have retained a high degree of religious zeal, which they put to good use in the service of their own community and the society at large. They have played a crucial role in preserving the Islamic identity of fellow immigrants and promoting a better understanding of Islam through media activities and academic conferences and symposia.

The first mosque in the United States was built in Detroit in 1915 by Albanian Muslims, another followed in 1919 in Connecticut. Other mosques were established in the 1920s and 1930s in South Dakota and in Cedar Rapids, Iowa. In 1928, Polish Tatar Muslims built a mosque in Brooklyn, New York, which is still in use. Now, in every American city at least several mosques or centers exist.

The first Canadian mosque, the al-Rashid Mosque, was built in Edmonton, Alberta, in 1938. Others soon followed as the community grew and became better organized. At present, metropolitan cities like Toronto and Montreal each have at least ten mosques or centers. Even in small farming communities like Swift Current, Alberta, small Muslim groups are recovering their heritage and building mosques for themselves and their children.

The exact number of Muslims in Canada and the U.S.A. is a matter of great debate. It is estimated that in 1951 there were between two and three thousand Muslims in Canada. By 1983 the number had risen to well over 100,000. It is now estimated at somewhere between 500,000 and a million. Some estimates go much higher and much lower, the widest range being from 200,000 to 2.5 million. The United States has not had a religious census since 1936. Estimates for the 1980s run between 2 and 8 million and even higher. The current numbers are still in dispute, ranging from 3 to 14 million. Whatever the numbers may be, Islam in North America is no longer the strange religion of a strange people. Rather it is the faith of the neighbors of Jews, Christians, and other North Americans.

It is hoped that Muslims will find a new home for Islam in the West. It is also hoped that they will use their Western technology and democratic institutions to revitalize the Muslim communities in their countries of origin as well as in the rest of the Muslim *ummah.* No doubt, modern communications, international relations, and the easy transfer of knowledge will aid in this process. It is further hoped that the end of the Cold War will allow for better relations between the Western and Muslim worlds.

A new era of Muslim and even world history began on September 11, 2001. The consequences of this tragic event are still unfolding and therefore it is too soon to predict the final outcome. But whatever the outcome may be, North American and European Muslims, immigrant and native born, have no other home or destiny than those of their non-Muslim compatriots and neighbors. It is imperative, therefore, for Muslims to play a vital Islamic role in making their new homes an abode of peace and their destiny a good and positive one for them and their children.

Muslims can do much in the West if they promote Islamic humanism and a spirit of trust that would allow them to work with their non-Muslim neighbors for greater social justice and moral consciousness. There is still a great need to change old images and ideas if future generations of Muslims in the West are to remain Muslims in an integrated society of Muslims and non-Muslims. We can only pray that the dark night of September 11 will soon end with the dawn of a new day of peace for us all.

Epilogue: The Muslim Ummah and the Modern World

It has been repeatedly argued in this small volume that the Muslim community is not simply a collection of individuals, but an organic body transcending all racial, geographical, and social differences. Although God will hold each individual man and woman accountable for their personal behavior here on earth,[66] the community will also have to account for its conduct and face the consequences. The Qur'ān asserts that on the Day of Judgment not only every individual woman and man will have to give an account of her or his earthly life, rather God "shall question those [communities] to whom messengers were sent and ... [He] shall surely question the messengers as well" (Q. 7:6). Since this important Qur'anic teaching has already been discussed, I need only briefly restate the argument here, namely that individual moral and religious responsibilities and obligations can be properly discharged only in a communal setting. Therefore, unless the faith of the individual is manifested in works of righteousness in society, it remains a hypocritical and dead faith. This implies that not only every individual man and woman must choose between being a person of faith or a rejecter of faith, but every nation or community (*ummah*) is faced with the choice of righteousness or wickedness. It can choose either blessing and prosperity or destruction, in this world, and either eternal blessedness or damnation, in the world to come.

Like the individual, the *ummah* is an organic being with definite rights and responsibilities towards God and the rest of his creation. Again like the individual, it is subject to rewards and punishments in this world and the next. This organic worldview extends to beasts and birds as well, as has already been observed.[67] The Qur'ān accords the term "*ummah*" a variety of social and temporal meanings. Abstractly, the word means a period of time, as in Sūrah 12:45, where we read: "He [one of the two prisoners with Joseph] who was spared when he remembered, after a space of time (*ummah*) ..." It also means social custom or customary belief or practice, as the Makkan opponents of the new faith are said to have insisted: "We have found our forefathers upon a practice [or belief] (*ummah*), and we are following in their footsteps" (Q. 43:23). In these and similar occurrences, the term "*ummah*" signifies an entity, a period of time, or a specific way of life or conduct.

In its basic etymology, the word "*ummah*" is derived from the same root as the word for mother, *umm*. It denotes an assemblage of individuals, families, and tribes bound together by a common identity or a particular real or symbolic space or time. Abraham, as the prototypical man of faith and father of nations, is symbolically called in the Qur'ān "*ummatan qānitan*" (Q. 16:120), that is, an *ummah* "obedient to God and constant in prayer." The term is sometimes used to designate only a few people, but in its widest sense, it refers to a nation or community. Hence, the *ummah* is a social grouping of people bound together by a common destiny, language or culture, faith or ancestry.

Muslims everywhere must, in the view of the Qur'ān and Prophetic tradition, strive to be one single body,[68] a worldwide community bound by a common faith that is meant to supercede all other racial, cultural, linguistic ties, or relationships. Ideally, the unity of the *ummah* must reflect God's oneness, as the Qur'ān emphatically declares, "This *ummah* of yours is one *ummah* and I am your Lord, therefore, serve Me."[69] It is to strive to be a community calling others to the good: "the best *ummah* brought forth for humankind, enjoining good and decent conduct and dissuading from evil and reprehensible conduct and having true faith in God" (Q. 3:104 and 3:110).

This ideal of the "best *ummah*" does imply a kind of divine election, not, however, on the basis of ethnic descent, or even religious affiliation, but rather on the basis of faith and righteous conduct. It also implies a clear mission, that is the call (*da'wah*) of all human beings to God. While this noble ideal inspired many Sufi masters and their disciples, as well as countless other pious men and women peacefully to carry the faith of Islam to all the regions of the globe, it has often been used to justify political domination over non-Muslims in the name of "the call to God." It has also fostered narrow religious exclusivism and supersessionism.

From the beginning of Muslim history, we witness a growing misunderstanding of the Qur'anic view of election. The call to Islam, with which Muslims are charged, does not mean a monopoly of the truth, but a call to the way of God "with wisdom and fair exhortation" (Q. 16:125). In their modern expressions, misinterpretations of the Qur'anic vision of the *ummah* and its mission in the world are by and large nineteenth- and twentieth-century ideological reactions to Western colonialism and neo-colonialism.

In contrast to such narrow interpretations, the world in the view of the Qur'ān is a pluralistic world of many races, languages, cultures, and religions.[70] This richness, moreover, is one of the signs of God's wisdom, second in importance to the creation of the heavens and the earth (Q. 30:22). This diversity should, the Qur'ān asserts, spur human individuals, faith-communities, and nations to compete not for the exclusive claim to the truth, divine grace, and salvation; rather they should compete in the performance of righteous works. This is because the truth in its fullness cannot be known here on earth, but only in the hereafter, as the Qur'ān insists: "To everyone We have appointed a way and a course to follow. For, had your Lord so willed, He would have made you all one *ummah*; rather He would try you by means of that which He gave you. Compete therefore with one another in good deeds, for to God shall be your return, and He will inform you of the things in which you have differed" (Q. 5:42).[71]

The claim to an exclusive special status, divine election, or favor of one religious or racial community over all others, is found in different forms in most of the major religions of the world. It is often justified through narrow interpretations of sacred scriptures and buttressed by conquest and domination of others in the name of God, primordial sacred wisdom, or the will of heaven.[72] The empire for Christians and the *dawlah* for Muslims, expressions of worldly power, have both been viewed by their communities as signs of divine election. This claim to special divine favor is also made by small sects or movements in their struggles against the larger community. The extremist Jewish movement Gush Immunim, fundamentalist Christian groups, and extremist *salafī* Muslim movements are typical examples.

There are texts in the Qur'ān and Prophetic tradition, as in the Hebrew Bible and Oral Torah and in the New Testament and the tradition of the Church, that can readily be adduced to support exclusivist and supersessionist beliefs. Generally speaking, such beliefs are stressed during the early history or zenith of the community's power. But in times of weakness and insecurity they are dramatized and adopted as a present or future eschatological goal. This has invariably led to serious clashes between traditionalism and modernity, both within the faith-community and between it and other communities and nations.

This exclusivist trend, with its consequent internal conflicts, has characterized Muslim reform movements since the early decades of the nineteenth century. These movements, as we have seen, arose in answer to the increasingly aggressive colonial encroachments by European powers upon the sovereignty and territories of a weak Ottoman state. The same fate befell the Mughal state in India, which was replaced by

British rule in the late eighteenth century, and the Persian state, which was nearly dismembered in its war with Russia in the early decades of the nineteenth century. Many Muslim intellectuals and religious leaders, who were awed by the West, called on fellow Muslims to unite in one pan-Islamic modern state, combining Western scientific ideas and administrative practices with Islamic faith and morality. To do this, two things were necessary: a rationalist approach to Islam and a return to the Islam of the pious forebears (*al-salaf al-ṣāliḥ*). This call for Islamic reform was nurtured by persistent dreams of restoring for the *ummah* "the majesty that was Islam."[73]

The twentieth century, with its two devastating world wars, the demise of the Ottoman state and with it the hope of ever reviving the caliphate, as well as the protracted Cold War, caused many revivalist *salafī* Muslims to adopt increasingly anti-Western attitudes. In contrast with their nineteenth-century predecessors, who called for emulation of the West as the only way to achieve progress and modernity, they called for repudiation of everything Western, including Western democracy, capitalism, socialism, and even Western science and technology. One of the primary reasons for such anti-Western sentiments is a perceived Western, particularly American, political and economic domination of the rich natural and human resources of the Arab and Muslim world, through corrupt and despotic regimes. Ironically, many of these Muslim activists are well-educated women and men, trained in the West, or in Western institutions of higher learning in their own countries; many even reside in Europe and North America.

So long as the Muslim *ummah* was peacefully engaged in its efforts to face the political, social, intellectual, and economic challenges of the modern West through constructive and creative dialogue, its hope for realizing its destiny as a faith-community was kept alive and healthy. But the second half of the twentieth century, following the age of direct colonialism, brought new and far more intractable and dangerous problems for both the Western world and the world of Islam. Chief among these were the creation of the state of Israel, the establishment of American military bases in a number of Arab and Muslim countries, and the exploitation of Arab and Muslim oil.

Most Muslims regard the existence of an alien Jewish state in Palestine as an extension of Western colonialism into the heartland of Islam. For millions of Palestinians, Israel has meant displacement into insecure and often unwelcome refugee camps in neighboring countries. Those who were not so displaced continue to struggle against the creation of Jewish settlements on their land and often over their demolished homes. For the rest of the Arab nation, Israel has meant repeated humiliating defeats in wars against a state that is armed and supported by the West.

I believe that the contemporary resurgence of Islam, with its strong emphasis on a statist ideology, is in large part a reaction to the creation by the West of a non-Islamic and foreign state in a land that has special religious and historic significance for Muslims.[74] To many Arabs and Muslims, American patronage of Israel evokes memories of medieval European crusader states. This strong religio-political reaction, which links what it calls modern crusadism and modern Zionism to the old crusades, is based on the conviction that only a united Muslim *ummah*, preferably in one universal Islamic state, can have the political, economic, and military power to face Western hegemony and restore for Muslims their rightful place on the stage of world history.

After the Franco-British-Israeli invasion of Egypt in 1956 and the direct American intervention to end that conflict, America inadvertently stepped into the British imperial shoes and thus ushered in a new era of Middle East history. Growing American economic and strategic interests in the Middle East have led to the establishment of important American military bases in most of the Gulf states, notably Saudi Arabia. To many Muslims, this means American domination over Makkah and Madīnah, the two holiest cities of Islam. Particularly after the 1991 Gulf war, Muslim hostility to Western and especially American presence in the Arabian Peninsula has been expressed in the call to expel America from the land of Muḥammad; a call that people like Usama bin Laden have made their battle cry.[75]

The problems just discussed are symptomatic of deeper feelings of frustration and insecurity that have plagued the Muslim *ummah* for centuries. But frustration, which is often the cause of irrational violence, arises from weakness and insecurity, which are in turn born out of a lack of real direction and leadership. The issue for the generality of Muslims is not freedom and democracy. Rather, it is a question of justice and the preservation of human life and dignity under just rulers, capable of guiding the states that make up the Muslim *ummah* in their struggle to find their place among the nations of the modern world. Muslims wish to accomplish this without losing their faith identity. It is not the *jihād* of violence that is needed to achieve this goal, but the moral, social, and political *jihād* that would allow the *ummah* to shape its own destiny in accordance with its own social, political, economic, and moral and spiritual tradition and worldview.

By tradition here I mean not any particular sect, school, or ideology, but the entire Islamic heritage with all its dimensions and cumulative development from the beginning of Muslim history to the present. This rich heritage must be seen to encompass not only the ideals but also the realities of political history, including the shift from the early caliphate to the dynastic rule of the sultans and kings of pre-modern Islamic states and finally to the modern nation-state. Such a realistic assessment will clearly show Islam to have been a dynamic religious tradition that has always stood up to the challenges and vicissitudes of history.

With the exception of a few cases, such as the Kingdom of Saudi Arabia, some Gulf sheikdoms, and the sultanate of Brunei, all Muslim countries have chosen the nation-state model with its parliamentary system. This means that the vast majority of Muslims have opted for Western parliamentary democracy instead of the absolutist rule of classical Muslim states.

This conscious choice has largely reflected the anxiety of Muslim intellectuals and politicians to safeguard their traditional Islamic identity without appearing to repudiate the universal values of the modern world. Such intellectuals, politicians, and religious thinkers have sought to equate Islam with democracy. Others have rejected modernity altogether and called for a return to traditional Islamic values, the Islam of the "pious forebears," the Islam of the Prophet and his Companions and their successors.

So long as Muslims are willing to debate these and other issues of Islam and modernity rationally and calmly, the possibility of arriving at a dynamic synthesis of traditional Islamic and modern values remains a promising hope. But when ideological movements such as *al-Takfīr wal-hijrah*, *al-Qāʿidah*, and other jihadist organizations[76] resort to open violence not only against the West, but more often against other Muslims, both Muslims and their faith and dignity suffer. Muslims have become the object of an international war on terrorism and Islam has suffered distortion and misrepresentation by both Muslims and non-Muslims alike. Thus ordinary Muslims have generally become victims of opposing interpretations of Islam and its *ummah*: the interpretations of the Islamists calling for universal *jihād* and the interpretations of the West calling for the faith of Islam to be a private affair between the individual and his or her God.

This once more brings us back to the question of private versus public religion. The foregoing discussion has, I hope, demonstrated that Islam cannot live and prosper in the solitude of the home alone; rather it needs the mosque, the market-place, the city, and the world. Like the faith-communities of other world religions, the Muslim *ummah* lived for most of its history both in and against the world. In times of strength and security, the Muslim *ummah* lived in the world and created with the peoples of other faiths in its domains a truly unique world civilization. Building on its rich religious and intellectual heritage, the Muslim *ummah* can also live in the modern world and make notable contributions to the human spiritual quest for meaning and fulfillment. This challenging role, however, requires radical internal changes that the *ummah* must bravely embark upon.

To begin with, Muslims must deal with the modern world, not through confrontation and conflict, but through diplomacy and patient dialogue. This requires the *'ulamā'*, or religious scholars, to strive for a radical change of discourse. Starting from the principles of universal justice and defense of the weak and downtrodden, which together are the goal of Islamic sacred law and true "*jihād* in the way of God," they must construct a new jurisprudence and a new theology of *jihād*. Although good efforts towards this goal have been and are now being made by many notable religious scholars, the current religio-political discourse remains generally medieval and defensive. Hence, it remains out of touch with the harsh realities of the present world order.

Concurrently, the *ummah* must strengthen itself politically, economically, and militarily. While the *'ulamā'* can and must play a guiding role in this sorely needed reform, it should be the task of politicians, intellectuals, educators, and technocrats to devise and execute creative, but realistic programs that can help Muslim nations to cope with the social and political demands and implications of modern economics, science, and technology. The European Union, NATO, and ASEAN would be good models for them to learn from.

For the Muslim community to move towards the realization of the important goal of truly living in the modern world, it needs a common and uniting platform, an Islamic international organization that can serve as a means of consolidation and orientation of Muslim energies and efforts. It would also serve as a medium of communication between the Muslim *ummah* and the rest of the world. The Organization of the Islamic Conference (O.I.C.) can, I believe, be that instrument and platform. It should therefore be strengthened and empowered to be able to play its role effectively and to make the call for reform and integration heard by the world, including all the nations of the Muslim *ummah*. It should also serve as the institution through which the efforts of individual religious authorities can be communicated, critiqued, and appreciated by both Muslims and non-Muslims.

Islam is not a religion of violence, but a religion of power. This includes military, political, economic, and social power. The Qur'ān called on a weak but self-confident community of first generation Muslims to "prepare whatever power and ready what horses you can, in order to instill fear in the hearts of your enemies" (Q. 8:60). It also commanded Muḥammad, "If they [the enemy] incline towards peace, you too incline towards it" (Q. 8:61). That the Prophet effectively applied this Qur'anic principle of balance between military and diplomatic power is clear from the peaceful conquest of Makkah, which would have been inconceivable without the diplomatic truce of Ḥudaybiyah. It may be further argued that throughout Muslim history diplomacy and dialogue produced far better results in resolving conflicts and achieving peace than did military power and conquest.

This Qur'anic view of power is embodied in the Islamic doctrine of *jihād*. Essentially, *jihād* is not violence but the will and effort to change both the individual and the *ummah* for the better. It is to command the good and to dissuade from evil. It is also to defend the weak and downtrodden, as well as the life, faith, and dignity not only of Muslims, but of all of humanity. *Jihād* may at times require armed struggle, but armed struggle must always be a means and not an end in itself. A sincere and dynamic will to change remains the greatest challenge facing the Muslim *ummah* today, for "God will not change what is in a people until they change what is in themselves" (Q. 13:11).

Notes

PROLOGUE

1. Bernard Lewis, "The Roots of Muslim Rage," *Atlantic Monthly* 266, 3 (September 1990): 49.
2. Samuel P. Huntington, "The Clash of Civilizations?" *Foreign Affairs* 72, 3 (Summer 1993): 22–49. His main idea and thesis have been further expanded in his *The Clash of Civilizations and the Making of the New World Order* (New York: Simon & Schuster, 1996).
3. The greater pilgrimage, or *ḥajj*, always begins on the eighth day of Dhū al-Ḥijjah, the twelfth month of the Muslim calendar. It is to be distinguished from the lesser pilgrimage, or *'umrah*, which can be performed at any time.
4. Matt. 25:42–43.
5. Aḥmad ibn Hanbal, *Musnad Aḥmad*, k. *bāqī musnad al-mukthirīn*, h. 8874; Muslim ibn al-Hajjāj al-Naysabūrī, *Ṣaḥīḥ Muslim*, k. *al-birr wa al-ṣilah wa al-ādāb*, h. 4661. (Unless otherwise noted, all *ḥadīth* references are based on the Harf Ḥadīth Encyclopedia CD-ROM, *mawsū'at al-ḥadīth al-sharīf*, version 2.1, Cairo: Harf Information Technology, 2000.) Translations of all Arabic sources (including the Qur'ān) are my own unless otherwise indicated. When translating from Islamic sources I have used the convention of capitalizing personal pronouns that refer to God; elsewhere such pronouns are in the lower-case.

6. ʻAbd Raḥmān ibn Abī Bakr Jalāl al-Dīn al-Suyūṭī, *Jāmī ʻal-aḥādīth wa al-marāsil*, h. 11939, 11970; ʻAlī ibn Abī Bakr al-Haythamī, *Majma ʻal-zawāʼid*, h. 60731, 70731; Abū Yaʻlā Aḥmad ibn ʻAlī al-Mawṣilī, *Musnad Abī Yaʻlā*, h. 3318, 3373, 3481. These references are cited from the Maktabat al-ḥadīth al-sharīf CD-ROM, *al-ḥadīth al-sharīf*, 4 CDs, version 6.0 (Beirut: Shirkat al-ʻArīs, 2002), CD-1.
7. God declares in the Qur'ān: "We have honored the children of Adam and carried them over land and sea, and provided for them sustenance of good and pure things, and have greatly preferred them over many of Our creatures" (Q. 17:70).

CHAPTER 1

8. Muḥammad b. al-Husayn al-Sharīf al-Raḍī, *Nahj al-balāghah*, 4 vols., ed. Muḥammad ʻAbduh (Beirut: al-Aʻlami, n.d.), vol. 1, pp. 14–16.
9. See Ibn Khaldun, *The Muqaddimah: An Introduction to History*, 3 vols., trans. Franz Rosenthall (Princeton: Princeton University Press, 1967), vol. 1, p. lxxviii ff., for a discussion of this social phenomenon and its effect on Arab society.
10. Muḥammad ibn Ishāq, *The Life of Muḥammad*, trans. Alfred Guillaume (Karachi: Oxford University Press, 1995), pp. 79–81.
11. These two verses have been variously interpreted. According to one interpretation, the subject of "then he drew near" is Gabriel, who came down toward the Prophet until he hovered at a distance of "two bows or closer." According to another popular interpretation the verses are linked to the Prophet's heavenly journey, when he came so close to the throne of God that he was within "two bows or closer."
12. Throughout the present text I generally supply the common era (C.E.) dates. When both dating systems are used the *hijrah* date precedes the common era date: 1/622.
13. From ʻAbd al-Malik ibn Hishām, *al-Sīrah al-nabawiyyah*, 4 vols., ed. ʻUmar Tadmurī (Beirut: Dar al-Kitāb al-ʻArabi, n.d.), vol. 4, pp. 198 and 248–249.

CHAPTER 2

14. For the story of Adam in the Qur'ān, see *sūrah*s 7:11–27, 17:61–65, 20:115–127. For major differences between the Qur'ān and Genesis accounts of Adam's creation and fall, see *sūrah* 2:30–39.
15. See the story of Jonah in the Hebrew Bible, the book bearing his name, and in the Qur'ān, 10:98 and 37:139–148.
16. For the man of faith, see Q. 40:28. Since the Qur'ān speaks favorably of Pharaoh's wife (Q. 66:11), she is numbered among the great women of

faith in the Prophetic *ḥadīth* tradition. See, for example, Muḥammad b. Ismā'īl al-Bukhārī, *Ṣaḥīḥ al-Bukhārī,* k. *ahādīth al-anbiyā'*, h. 3159 and 3179, k. *al-manāqib*, h. 3485; Muslim, *Ṣaḥīḥ*, k. *faḍā'il al-ṣahābah*, h. 4459; Muḥammad b. 'Isā al-Tirmidhī, *Sunan al-Tirmidhī*, k. *al-aṭ'imah*, h. 1757, k. *al-manāqib*, h. 3813; etc.

17. See Q. 19:16–33, quoted below.
18. For the story of Jesus, see, for example, the *Qiṣāṣ al-anbiyā'* of Muḥammad ibn 'Abd Allāh al-Kisā'i, translated into English as *Tales of the Prophets* by Wheeler M. Thackston Jr. (Chicago: Kazi Publications, 1997).
19. Aḥmad, *Musnad*, k. *bāqī musnad al-anṣār*, h. 24092; al-Bukhārī, *Ṣaḥīḥ*, k. *bad' al-waḥy*, h. 2; Muslim, *Ṣaḥīḥ*, k. *al-faḍā'il*, h. 4304; Aḥmad b. Shu'ayb al-Nasā'ī, *Sunan al-Nasā'ī*, k. *al-iftitāḥ*, h. 924; Mālik ibn Anas, *al-Muwaṭṭa'*, k. *al-nidā' lil-ṣalāh*, h. 425; etc.
20. The *jinn* are, according to the Qur'ān, an order of creation much like humankind, but whereas they are made of fire, God "created humankind of dry and hollow substance like that of a potter's clay" (Q. 55:14–15). As with humans, the *jinn* received the Qur'ān and some accepted while others rejected it. Hence, on the Day of Resurrection they too will be rewarded for good deeds and faith and punished for wickedness and rejection of faith. See Q. 72:1–17.
21. For this idea and a vivid picture of the terrible portents and catastrophic signs of the Day of Resurrection, see Q. 81:1–14 (quoted above, chapter 1).
22. This definition is found in *sūrah* 2:177: "It is not righteousness that you turn your face toward the east and west. True righteousness is this: to have faith in God and the last day, the angels, the scriptures and the prophets; to give of one's wealth, though it may be cherished, to the next of kin and the orphans, the destitute and the wayfarer, to the needy and for the redemption of slaves; to observe regular worship and to give the obligatory alms. Those who fulfill their covenant having bound themselves by it and those who are patient in misfortune and adversity and in times of strife: these are true in their faith; these are the God-fearing."

CHAPTER 3

23. This important observation was made over a century ago by the noted Hungarian Islamicist, Ignaz Goldziher. See his *Muslim Studies*, 2 vols. (Albany: State University of New York Press, 1977), vol. 1, 201–208.
24. For the full text of this tradition, see Aḥmad, *Musnad*, k. *musnad al-'asharah al-mubashsharīn*, h. 186; al-Bukhārī, *Ṣaḥīḥ*, k. *al-īmān*, h. 48; Muslim, *Ṣaḥīḥ*, k. *al-īmān*, h. 9–11; al-Tirmidhī, *Sunan*, k. *al-īmān*, h. 2535; Muḥammad b. Yazīd ibn Mājah, *Sunan Ibn Mājah*, k. *al-muqaddimah*, h. 62; etc.
25. Aḥmad, *Musnad*, k. *bāqī musnad al-mukthirīn*, h. 8993; Muslim, *Ṣaḥīḥ*,

k. *al-īmān*, h. 51; Abū Dāwud Sulaymān b. al-Ash'ath al-Sijistānī, *Sunan Abī Dāwud*, k. *al-sunnah*, h. 4056; al-Nasā'ī, *Sunan*, k. *al-īmān*, h. 4919; etc.

26. The full text of this tradition is cited at the end of this chapter.
27. See Aḥmad, *Musnad*, k. *musnad al-mukthirīn*, h. 4567; al-Bukhārī, *Ṣaḥīḥ*, k. *al-īmān*, h. 7; Muslim, *Ṣaḥīḥ*, k. *al-īmān*, h. 19–21; al-Tirmidhī, *Sunan*, k. *al-īmān*, h. 2534; al-Nasā'ī, *Sunan*, k. *al-īmān*, h. 4915; etc.
28. Aḥmad, *Musnad*, k. *bāqī musnad al-mukthirīn*, h. 6884, 7387; al-Bukhārī, *Ṣaḥīḥ*, k. *al-janā'iz*, h. 1270–1271, 1296; Muslim, *Ṣaḥīḥ*, k. *al-qadar*, h. 4803, 4805; Mālik b. Anas, *al-Muwaṭṭa'*, k. *al-janā'iz*, h. 507; etc.
29. Aḥmad, *Musnad*, k. *musnad al-'asharah al-mubashsharīn*, h. 64; al-Bukhārī, *Ṣaḥīḥ*, k. *al-zakāt*, h. 1312, k. *al-jihād wa al-sīr*, h. 2727; Muslim, *Ṣaḥīḥ*, k. *al-īmān*, h. 29–31; al-Tirmidhī, *Sunan*, k. *al-īmān*, h. 2531–2532; etc.
30. Aḥmad, *Musnad*, k. *musnad al-'asharah al-mubashsharīn*, h. 179; al-Tirmidhī, *Sunan*, k. *al-īmān*, h. 2535; Ibn Mājah, *Sunan*, k. *al-muqaddimah*, h. 62.

CHAPTER 4

31. See Patricia Crone and Martin Hinds, *God's Caliph: Religion and Authority in the First Century of Islam* (London; New York: Cambridge University Press, 1986).

CHAPTER 6

32. This remarkable jurist traveled throughout the Muslim world and left us a truly informative and entertaining travellog. See his *Travels of Ibn Baṭṭūṭa, A.D. 1325–1354*, translated with revision and notes by H.A.R. Gibb from the Arabic text edited by C. Defrémery and B. R. Sanguinetti (Cambridge: Cambridge University Press, for Hakluyt Society, 1958–2000).

CHAPTER 7

33. See al-Bukhārī, *Ṣaḥīḥ*, k. *al-ṣalāh*, h. 378; al-Nasā'ī, *Sunan*, k. *al-īmān*, h. 4911.
34. Aḥmad, *Musnad*, k. *bāqī musnad al-mukthirīn*, h. 7187; al-Bukhārī, *Ṣaḥīḥ*, k. *bad' al-khalq*, h. 2955, k. *al-tawḥīd*, h. 6855, 6872, etc.; Muslim, *Ṣaḥīḥ*, k. *al-tawbah*, h. 4939, 4941; al-Tirmidhī, *Sunan*, k. *al-da'awāt*, h. 3466; etc.
35. Aḥmad, *Musnad*, k. *bāqī musnad al-mukthirīn*, h. 7928; Muslim, *Ṣaḥīḥ*, k. *al-imārah*, h. 3527; al-Nasā'ī, *Sunan*, k. *al-jihād*, h. 3086.
36. Aḥmad, *Musnad*, k. *bāqī musnad al-mukthirīn*, h. 7115, 8983, 9834, etc.;

al-Bukhārī, *Ṣaḥīḥ*, k. *al-tawhīd*, h. 6856; Muslim, *Ṣaḥīḥ*, k. *al-dhikr wa al-du'ā' wa al-tawbah*, h. 4832,4851; al-Tirmidhī, *Sunan*, k. *al-da'awāt*, h. 3527; etc.

37. Aḥmad, *Musnad*, k. *musnad al-anṣār*, h. 21000, 21049, 21084; al-Tirmidhī, *Sunan*, k. *al-aḥkām*, h. 1249; Abū Dāwud, *Sunan*, k. *al-aqḍiyah*, h. 3119; etc.
38. Aḥmad, *Musnad*, k. *musnad al-mukthirīn*, h. 3959, etc.; al-Bukhārī, *Ṣaḥīḥ*, k. *al-shahādāt*, h. 2457, k. *al-manāqib*, h. 3377, etc.; Muslim, *Ṣaḥīḥ*, k. *faḍā'il al-ṣahābah*, h. 4603; al-Nasā'ī, *Sunan*, k. *al-īmān wa al-nudhūr*, h. 3749; etc. The negative purport of this tradition was mitigated by another Prophetic prediction that God would send, at the start of every century, one who would renew for the community its faith. See *Abu Dāwud, Sunan*, k. *al-malāḥim*, h. 3740 (al-'Arīs CD-ROM, CD-1 referenced in note 6, above). See also the *sharḥ* to this in *'Awn al-ma'būd* by Abū al-Ṭīb Muḥammad Shams al-Haqq (Maktabat Qurṭubah, 1968).
39. The title "*imām*" is used by both Sunnis and Shi'ites. When used by Sunnis, it simply signifies a position of leadership in the community, is non-specific, and can be held by any number of men at the same time; it is rendered in English in the lower case, "imām." When used by Shi'ites, the title refers to a singular individual who is recognized as the one appointed by God to be the rightful leader of the Muslim *ummah*; in English, this is signaled by the use of the upper-case, "Imām."
40. This event and the tradition regarding it have been the subject of a vast Shī'ī literature. See for example the eleven-volume encyclopedic work entitled, *al-Ghadīr fī al-kitāb wa al-sunnah wa al-adab*, 4th edn. (Beirut: Dār al-Kitāb al-'Arabī, 1967) of 'Abd al-Ḥusayn Aḥmad al-Amīnī al-Najafī.
41. For a good discussion of this and other traditions regarding the crucial role of the *mahdī*, or expected messiah, in Shī'ī piety, political and legal theory, and eschatology, see A.A. Sachedina, *Islamic Messianism: The Idea of Mahdi in Twelver Shi'ism* (Albany: SUNY Press, 1981).
42. See Muhammad ibn Ya'qub ibn Ishaq al-Kulayni, *al-Uṣūl min al-kāfī*, 2 vols., ed. 'Alī Akbār al-Ghaffārī (Tehran: Maktabat al-Ṣadūq, 1381/1961), vol. 1, parts 1–3. See also M. Ayoub, *Redemptive Suffering in Islam: A Study of the Devotional Aspects of 'Āshūrā' in Twelver Shi'ism* (The Hague; New York: Mouton Publishers, 1978), 53–68; and Mohammad 'Ali Amīr Moezzi, *The Divine Guide in Early Shi'ism: The Sources of Esotericism in Islam* (Albany: SUNY Press, 1994), translated by David Streight from the French, *Guide Divin dans le Shî'isme Originel.*

CHAPTER 8

43. al-Tirmidhī, *Sunan*, h. 1642; Abū Ya'lā, *Musnad*, h. 4349; Muḥammad ibn Sallāmah al-Shihāb al-Qaḍā'ī, *Musnad Shihāb*, h. 320, 321 (al-'Arīs CD-ROM, CD-1, referenced in note 6, above).
44. R.A. Nicholson, *The Mystics of Islam* (London: Routledge and Kegan Paul Ltd., 1966), p. 115. Cf. Farīd al-Dīn 'Aṭṭar, *Tadhkirat al-awliyā'*, ed. R.A. Nicholson (London, 1905), p. 73, quoted in Margaret Smith, *Muslim Women Mystics: The Life and Work of Rābi'a and Other Woman Mystics in Islam* (Oxford: Oneworld Publications, 1994), p. 50.
45. Al-Husayn b. Mansūr al-Hallāj, *Kitab al-ṭawāsīn*, quoted in Annemarie Schimmel, *Mystical Dimensions of Islam* (Chapel Hill: University of North Carolina Press, 2000), p. 66. See also 'Alī ibn Anjab al-Sā'ī al-Baghdādī, *Kitab akhbār al-Hallāj*, 2nd edn., ed. Muwaffaq Fawzī al-Jabar (Dimashq: Dār al-ṭalī'ah al-jadīdah, 1997), pp. 41–43; Louis Massignon, *The Passion of al-Hallāj: Mystic and Martyr of Islam*, vol. 1, translated from the French by Herbert Mason (Princeton: Princeton University Press, 1982), pp. 126–134; and also Nicholson, *Mystics*, p. 150ff. for a similar quote and the discourse surrounding this famous utterance of al-Hallāj.
46. al-Sā'ī, *Akhbār*, p. 41.
47. al-Sā'ī, *Akhbār*, p. 41. Massignon, *Passion of al-Hallāj*, p. 600.
48. Ibn 'Arabī's theosophy is presented in works of prose and poetry. Chief among them are *al-Futūḥāt al-makkiyyah* ("The Makkan Divine Openings"), his *magnum opus*; *Fuṣūṣ al-ḥikam* ("The Besels of Wisdom"), a distillation of the *Futūḥāt*; and *Tarjumān al-ashwāq*, from which this poem comes (Beirut: Dar Sader, 1381/1961), pp. 43–44.
49. 'Aṭṭār employs an ingenious play on the two Persian words, *simurgh*, meaning phoenix, and *sī murgh*, meaning thirty birds.
50. al-Bukhārī, *Ṣaḥīḥ*, k. *al-riqāq*, h. 6021.
51. The term *ribāṭ* means "keeping watch for the enemy in times of war." The concept is based on Q. 3:200.

CHAPTER 9

52. Aḥmad, *Musnad*, k. *musnad al-shāmiyīn*, h. 16271; Muḥammad ibn Hibbān, *Ṣaḥīḥ ibn Hibbān*, h. 4483; Abū Dāwud Sulayman b. Dāwud al-Ṭayālisī, *Musnad*, h. 1914; Abū Ya'lā, *Musnad*, h. 7376; etc. (al-'Arīs CD-ROM, except for Aḥmad).
53. Shams al-Dīn Aḥmad b. Muḥammad b. Abī Bakr ibn Khallikān, *Wafayāt al-a'yān wa-anbā' abnā' al-zamān*, 8 vols., ed. Ihsan Abbas (Beirut: Dār al-Thaqāfah, n.d.), vol. 4, 267–268.

54. al-Nasā'ī, *Sunan*, k. *ṣalāt al-ʿīdayn*, h. 1560; Ibn Mājah, *Sunan*, k. *al-muqaddimah*, h. 45.
55. In the Qur'ān the Mandaeans are called Sabeans (see Q. 2:62 and 5:69). They represent an ancient religion of star worship, with an eclectic overlay of Jewish, Christian, and gnostic ideas.

CHAPTER 10

56. The Prophet was sent as a child by his mother for fosterage in the desert. See Guillaume, *Life of Muhammad*, pp. 69–73.
57. For a discussion of these and other types of marriage in pre-Islamic Arabia, see W. Robertson Smith, *Kinship and Marriage in Early Arabia* (1903; Oosterhout N.B., The Netherlands: Anthropological Publications, 1966) pp. 93 ff.
58. See Q. 37:125; 4:128; 11:72; 2:228. The Qur'anic usage, however, implies no inherent superiority of the husband over the wife.
59. See Bukhāri, *K. al-nikāḥ*, and Leila Ahmed, *Women and Gender in Early Islam: Historical Roots of a Modern Debate* (New Haven: Yale University Press, 1992) p. 44.
60. Abū Dāwūd, *Sunan*, book 12: *Ṭalāq* 2172.
61. For a concise and clear discussion of marriage and divorce in Islamic family law, see John Esposito, *Women in Muslim Family Law* (Syracuse: Syracuse University Press, 1982), pp. 13 ff.
62. See L. Clarke, "Hijab According to Hadith: Text and Interpretation" in Sajida Alvi, et al., eds., *The Muslim Veil in North America: Issues and Debates.* (Toronto: Women's Press, 2003).
63. Abū ʿAlī al-Faḍl b. al Ḥasan al-Ṭabarsi, *Majma' al-bayān fī tafsīr al-Qur'ān*, commentary on Q. 2:227, the phrase: "and men are a degree over them." For an interesting critical analysis of such *ḥadīth* traditions, see Khaled Abou El Fadl, *Speaking in God's Name* (Oxford: Oneworld Publications, 2001) pp. 210–218.

CHAPTER 11

64. See note 38, above.
65. Aḥmad, *Musnad*, k. *bāqī musnad al-mukthirīn*, h. 10651; Muslim, *Ṣaḥīḥ*, k. *al-īmān*, h. 70; al-Tirmidhī, *Sunan*, k. *al-fitan*, h. 2098; al-Nasā'ī, *Sunan*, k. *al-īmān wa sharāʿi'īh*, 4922–4923; etc.

EPILOGUE

66. The Qur'ān states, "You will come before Us singly, as We created you singly" (Q. 6:94).

67. See Q. 6:38 and text preceding note 21, above.
68. A well-attested *ḥadīth* states: "Surely all Muslims are like one body. If anyone of its members suffers an ailment, the entire body suffers sleeplessness and fever." See al-Bukhārī, *Ṣaḥīḥ*, k. *al-ṣalāh*, h. 459, k. *al-maẓālim*, h. 2266, etc.; Muslim, *Ṣaḥīḥ*, k. *al-birr wa al-ṣilah*, h. 4684; al-Tirmidhī, *Sunan*, k. *al-birr wa al-ṣilah*, h. 1851; etc.
69. This injunction is repeated twice in the Qur'ān for emphasis. In the other verse: "I am your Lord, therefore fear Me"; see Q. 21:92 and 23:52.
70. See M. Ayoub, "Islam and the Challenge of Religious Pluralism," *Global Dialogue* 2, 1 (Winter 2000): pp. 53–64.
71. This call to righteousness and social harmony is a recurring theme in the Qur'ān; see also 6:105; 29:8; and 31:15.
72. For example, primordial wisdom (*dharma*) was employed in the Laws (*Dharmashastra*) of Manu to justify the caste system and the supremacy of the Brahmins, or priestly class. Similarly both benevolent and tyrannical Chinese and Japanese emperors were often surrounded by an aura of divinity and thus ruled by the mandate of heaven.
73. *The Majesty that was Islam* is the title of a book on early Islamic civilization by W. M. Watt (London: Macmillan, 1976).
74. Religiously, Muslims regard Palestine as the land of prophets and Jerusalem as the "blessed place of worship" to which the Prophet Muḥammad was miraculously transported (Q. 17:1), and from which he ascended to the throne of God. Historically, the victories of Ṣalāḥ al-Dīn (Saladin) against the crusaders in Palestine and his rebuilding of the pulpit of the al-Aqsa Mosque in 1187 are still remembered as special events in Muslim history.
75. See Bin Laden's 1998 *fatwā*, or legal opinion, which was signed by a number of Pakistani and Arab religious scholars (*'ulamā'*). This *fatwā* argues that America occupied the Arabian Peninsula following the 1991 Gulf war and calls on all Muslims to wage a universal *jihād* against the occupation. The original text of the *fatwā* was published in *al-Quds al-'arabī*, February 23, 1998.
76. The term "*takfīr*" means declaring other Muslims to be *kāfirs* (rejecters of faith). The term "*hijrah*" means "migration," that is deserting the company of *kāfirs* and their country, if necessary, and moving into a truly Muslim society. This movement began in Egypt in the last quarter of the last century. After the Iranian Islamic revolution of 1979 a number of jihadist organizations and groups appeared throughout the Muslim world. The latest and most familiar international organization is *al-Qā'idah* ("the base" or "foundation"), or more correctly *qā'idat al-jihad* ("the base of *jihad*"), headed by Usama bin Laden.

Further Reading

This list of books for further reading was carefully chosen to supplement each of the chapters of the book. Although the books are arranged in alphabetical order, which I thought would make them more accessible, the titles clearly suggest which book(s) relate to which chapter. It is my hope that this very partial list will help readers who want to pursue any of the topics covered in the book further to make a good beginning.

Ahmed, Akbar. 1994. *Islam, Globalization, and Postmodernity.* London: New York: Routledge.

Ahmed, Leila. 1992. *Women and Gender in Islam: Historical Roots of a Modern Debate.* New Haven: Yale University Press.

Arberry, A. J. 1956. *Sufism, An Account of the Mystics of Islam.* London: Allen & Unwin.

Attar, Farid al-Din. 1973. *Muslim Saints and Mystics; Episodes from the Tadhkirat al-Auliya' ("Memorial of the Saints"),* trans. A. J. Arberry. Boston: Routledge & Kegan Paul.

Ayoub, Mahmoud M. 2003. *The Crisis of Muslim History: Religion and Politics in Early Islam.* Oxford: Oneworld.

Azami, Muhammad Mustafa. 1992 [1977]. *Studies in Hadith Methodology and Literature.* Indianapolis: American Trust Publications.

Coulson, N. G. 1964. *A History of Islamic Law*. Edinburgh: Edinburgh University Press.

Esposito, John L. 1991. *Islam and Politics*. Syracuse: Syracuse University Press.

——ed. 1999. *The Oxford History of Islam*. Oxford: Oxford University Press.

Fernea, Elizabeth W., and Basima Q. Bazirgan, eds. 1977. *Middle Eastern Muslim Women Speak*. Austin: University of Texas Press.

Goldziher, Ignac. 1967–71. *Muslim Studies, Vol. II*. London: Allen & Unwin.

Haddad, Yvonne Y. and Jane I. Smith, eds. 1994. *Muslim Communities in North America*. Albany: State University of New York Press.

Hasan, Ahmad. 1982. *The Early Development of Islamic Jurisprudence*. Islamabad: Islamic Research Institute.

Izutsu, Toshihiko. 1980. *God and Man in the Koran*. New York: Books for Libraries.

Keddie, Nikki R., ed. 1972. *Scholars, Saints and Sufis: Muslim Religious Institutions in the Middle East Since 1500*. Berkeley: University of California Press.

Lewis, Bernard. 2003. *The Crisis of Islam: Holy War and Unholy Terror*. New York: Modern Library.

Momen, Moojan. 1987. *An Introduction to Shi'i Islam*. New Haven: Yale University Press.

Padwick, Constance. 1996. *Muslim Devotions: A Study of Prayer-Manuals in Common Use*. Oxford: Oneworld.

Rahman, Fazlur. 1966. *Islam*. London: Weidenfeld & Nicolson; New York: Holt, Rinehart & Winston.

——1980. *Major Themes of the Qur'an*. Minneapolis, MN: Bibliotheca Islamica.

Schimmel, Annemarie. 1975. *Mystical Dimensions of Islam*. Chapel Hill: University of North Carolina Press.

Trimingham, J. Spencer. 1968. *The Influence of Islam upon Africa*. London: Longmans; New York: Praeger.

von Denffer, Ahmad. 1983–2000. *'Ulum al-Qur'an: An Introduction to the Sciences of the Qur'an*. United Kingdom: The Islamic Foundation.

Watt, W. Montgomery. 1962. *Islamic Philosophy and Theology*. Edinburgh: Edinburgh University Press.

Index